1,000,000 Books

are available to read at

Forgotten Books

www.ForgottenBooks.com

Read online
Download PDF
Purchase in print

ISBN 978-1-5280-3494-4
PIBN 10973967

This book is a reproduction of an important historical work. Forgotten Books uses state-of-the-art technology to digitally reconstruct the work, preserving the original format whilst repairing imperfections present in the aged copy. In rare cases, an imperfection in the original, such as a blemish or missing page, may be replicated in our edition. We do, however, repair the vast majority of imperfections successfully; any imperfections that remain are intentionally left to preserve the state of such historical works.

Forgotten Books is a registered trademark of FB &c Ltd.
Copyright © 2018 FB &c Ltd.
FB &c Ltd, Dalton House, 60 Windsor Avenue, London, SW19 2RR.
Company number 08720141. Registered in England and Wales.

For support please visit www.forgottenbooks.com

1 MONTH OF FREE READING

at

www.ForgottenBooks.com

By purchasing this book you are eligible for one month membership to ForgottenBooks.com, giving you unlimited access to our entire collection of over 1,000,000 titles via our web site and mobile apps.

To claim your free month visit:
www.forgottenbooks.com/free973967

* Offer is valid for 45 days from date of purchase. Terms and conditions apply.

English
Français
Deutsche
Italiano
Español
Português

www.forgottenbooks.com

Mythology Photography **Fiction** Fishing Christianity **Art** Cooking Essays Buddhism Freemasonry Medicine **Biology** Music **Ancient Egypt** Evolution Carpentry Physics Dance Geology **Mathematics** Fitness Shakespeare **Folklore** Yoga Marketing **Confidence** Immortality Biographies Poetry **Psychology** Witchcraft Electronics Chemistry History **Law** Accounting **Philosophy** Anthropology Alchemy Drama Quantum Mechanics Atheism Sexual Health **Ancient History Entrepreneurship** Languages Sport Paleontology Needlework Islam **Metaphysics** Investment Archaeology Parenting Statistics Criminology **Motivational**

LETTERS

WRITTEN BY

THE LATE RIGHT HONOURABLE

LADY LUXBOROUGH,

TO

WILLIAM SHENSTONE, Esq.

LONDON:
Printed for J. DODSLEY, in Pall-Mall.

M.DCC.LXXV.

ADVERTISEMENT.

THE following LETTERS are undoubtedly genuine; and are now firſt publiſhed from the Originals, by Mr. JOHN HODGETTS, of Hagley, in Worceſterſhire, Executor to the late WILLIAM SHENSTONE, Eſquire. The Writer of them was ſo well known, that to ſay any thing concerning her on this occaſion, would be as ſuperfluous as it would be to attempt to give a character of the Letters. They muſt ſpeak for themſelves, Yet it may not be improper to inform the Reader, that in the original Manuſcript Volume of theſe Letters,

Letters, which had been bound together by Mr. Shenstone, in the first leaf he had written with his own hand, as follows:

"Letters from the Right Ho-
"nourable Lady Luxborough;
"written with abundant Ease, Po-
"liteness, and Vivacity; in which
"she was scarce equalled by any
"woman of her time. They com-
"menced in the year 1739, and
"were continued to the year of
"her death (1756), with some few
"intermissions.

"WILL. SHENSTONE,"

LADY LUXBOROUGH's LETTERS.

LETTER I.

SIR, Barrells, November 27th, 1739.

WITHOUT the affiftance of your pen, it will be impoffible for me to return Mr. Shenftone fufficient thanks for the honour he does me, and my humble habitation; and for the agreeable entertainment his verfes afford me: to you, Sir, I owe the pleafure of having enjoyed that gentleman's converfation a few moments; to you I owe the advantage of being reprefented to him in the moft flattering light; and to you I defire to owe the favour of fpeaking my gratitude for his genteel compliment, and my admiration of all he writes:

writes: his offended Muse will I fear repent her ready aid, if he bestows such fine thoughts and flowing lines on such trifling and unworthy subjects, as in his copy of verses inscribed to a person who has no other pretence to merit, or to taste, but that of distinguishing his. As you, Sir, have the art to describe the most simple things with the nicest elegance (as appears by your Pastoral) I must once more intreat you to make known to your friend, the sincerity of my heart in the approbation it gives to his works; to which it pays just praise, though my words could no more express it (without doing wrong to my sentiments) than they could utter the real esteem, and friendly regard, with which I am, Sir,

Your obliged humble servant,

H. KNIGHT.

To the Revd. Mr. Jago, jun.
    at Henley.

LETTER II.

SIR,   Barrells, April 27, 1748.

MR. John Reynalds has this moment brought me your poem, for which I would not defer returning thanks; as I think

myself

myself greatly obliged to you for sending me what has already given me much pleasure, and will do so as often as I read it: that mark of your remembrance, and the honour you do me in counting my approbation as any thing, gives a real satisfaction to, Sir,

Your obliged humble servant,
H. KNIGHT.

To William Shenstone, Esq;
  at Mr. Wintle's, Perfumer,
  near Temple-Bar, London.

LETTER III.

SIR,   Barrells, May 29th, 1742.

NOTHING but an uncommon hurry of business and company, ever since the moment I received your poem, could have prevented my returning thanks for the favour you do me in thinking me worthy to judge of the beauties of it: it was with pleasure I read it, and I admired it on more accounts than merely the novelty of the subject.

The piping Faunus having his pipe in his hands when he came to me, I suppose Rackstrow had followed your advice (which was right) before he finished the figure; which I think a genteel one, but too small to set out of doors.

If you do me justice, you will believe that I am glad of every opportunity of assuring you, that I am, Sir,

   Your most obliged humble servant,

        H. KNIGHT.

LETTER IV.

DEAR SIR,   Barrells, July 28th, 1747.

I AM glad of an opportunity to let you know, that if it should happen to be convenient to you, (as you was so kind to give Lady Luxborough an invitation to your Hermitage) that her Ladyship will do herself the pleasure to take a prospect of the Leasowes before the leaf falls; and will take that opportunity on Tuesday next, August the 4th, to breakfast with you, and dine with you; and return at night with the two scribes, who all join in compliments.

    CROSSE OUTING, his mark Γ.
    J. REYNALDS.

P. S. My secretaries being somewhat idle after dinner, have wrote in such an odd manner, that
          I think

I think myself obliged to subscribe to the truth of what they say:—and at the same time I assure you I am, Sir,
With great esteem,
Your obliged humble servant,
H. LUXBOROUGH.

LETTER V.

SIR, Barrells, August 11th, 1747.

IF my doing barely justice, in commending the beauty of your situation, and the elegance of your taste, can make you vain, you must not admit of any company, if you will become a rigid hermit; nor should I have ventured a visit to the Leasowes, where the more one sees, the more one admires, and that admiration leads towards envy, which, as an hermitess, I ought to shun.

I return thanks, not only for the agreeable reception you gave me, but also for your kind enquiry now. I got home safe, but had one downfal, a little beyond Birmingham, which however did no hurt to Mr. Outing nor me; nor was it any dishonour to my postillion, as the night was very dark, and the moon down, or at least clouded over: but we met with very unhofpitable treatment at Shirley-ftreet, where they refufed to receive us at the Saracen's Head, though it was but eleven o'clock, and we faw a good fire in the kitchen; and a maid, who was fitting by it, took her candle and went to bed, whilft we were at the door intreating, knocking, and at laft threatening, but all in vain: the ftars took pity of us, and appeared juft as our hoftefs difappeared, and guided us in a friendly manner to Barrells, where we arrived at paft one o'clock, and the next day regaled ourfelves with the beft pine-apple I ever eat; fince which time, I have talked of nothing but the beauty of Virgil's grove, and the meannefs of my own; which ufed to give me fome pleafure, but is fo much leffened in my efteem, by comparing it with yours, that I could almoft wifh I had not feen the latter. The only amends you can make me for the pleafure you have deprived me of, is to give me your company foon at Barrells; which will always be acceptable to, Sir,

Your obliged humble fervant,

H. LUXBOROUGH.

I beg my beft compliments to Mifs Dolman, and Mr. Outing defires his to you.

LETTER

LETTER VI.

SIR,   Barrells, February 2d, 1747-8.

MR. Outing, who left this place on Saturday last, desired the inclosed might be conveyed to you; and I take the same opportunity of conveying my excuses for the incivility you must think me guilty of, in not rising the day you left Barrells, to wish you a good journey, and to thank you for the favour of your company. The not doing so, carried an appearance even of ingratitude, as your visit had given me so much pleasure; nor can your own good nature have been my advocate farther, than by lowering my crime, in calling it laziness; to which I would plead guilty, but that, in fact, my intention was to get up when the servant came in to light my fire, but was prevented, by her telling me you was in bed, and, she believed, was not to go away that day: this good news indulged me; and I, with the tranquillity satisfaction gives, took another nap; but waking, found it only an agreeable dream; for you was gone. Mr. Outing, the instant I came down stairs, presented me with a song, which he said he found upon your table; and I read it eagerly, soon finding it to be your stile. It is not necessary to add, that I thought it extremely pretty, and very poetical; but if it had been in prose, I should have been tempted to ask who was that ASTERIA that could make her *hearths* cheerful to you in the rigid season, when I, who had so lately been favoured with your company, was too sensible 'twas not in my power to make mine so, though nobody could wish it more; but want of sun and want of genius is ill supplied by a coal-fire, which was all I had to give; and my ill health unluckily at that time added to my stupidity, when I most wished for spirits to entertain my agreeable company: and now that I have entirely recovered my health, I have lost my company. Such are the chequered chances of this life! so that my *hermitess* and I have entire possession of my little wood, without either fear or hope of being interrupted in our contemplations. I contentedly subscribe to what she has wrote upon her old tree;

" The world forgetting, by the world forgot:"

but would not include in that world the friends I esteem, and whose conversation I admire: nor can ever any of the disagreeable events in LIFE make me wish it to become unsociable whilst it lasts; but cities (no more than forests) do not
afford

afford fociety; it is the *converfation* of a chofen few that fmooths the rugged road of life: fuch as *yours* ftrews it with *flowers*; but as *they* foon fade, fo did *you* vanifh, and all the company that furrounded my *hearth*; which, though abandoned, will afford me fuch converfation as the pen can fupply, whilft I have the pleafure of reading your thoughts; which pleafure I hope you will not deny me, but rather fend me any thing they may happen to add to the collection I have; than which nothing can be more efteemed by, Sir,

Your moft obliged humble fervant,
H. LUXBOROUGH.

P. S. If I miftake not, I heard you fay, you wanted a receipt to make fealing wax; I transcribe one that was given me, but fear you cannot read that, nor this letter, as I write in hafte. —Lady Hertford writes me word, fhe is charmed with your retreat: as fhe has only had the defcription of it from me, judge what fhe'd be if fhe faw it, at leaft if Mr. Thompfon defcribed it to her.

LETTER VII.

SIR, Barrells, March 22d, 1747-8.

THE apprehension that the farmer who carried Inigo Jones's designs, and a letter in the book from me to you, may have delivered them to a wrong person at Birmingham, is the occasion of my troubling you with this, to let you know that I did not fail to send it the very first market day after I received the favour of yours; and he says he delivered it to a man at the post-house, but the post-mistress (who, they tell me, is not the mildest nor most obliging dame) assured Parson Holyoak, she received no such thing; and upon his asking her, if she happened to have any letter since, directed for me, she said, No! neither did she know me, or would trouble herself about it. Which I mention, that in case you write, you will be pleased to send your's to Master Franky Holyoak, at Mr. Bolton's, wholesale Toymaker, upon Snow-Hill, in Birmingham. This (if you did not receive the book) will serve, I hope, to convince you, Sir, that I did my part, being incapable of neglecting to do what my friends desire.

I ac-

I acquainted you in my last that I was lame; but I am now much better, and always

Your obliged humble servant,

H. LUXBOROUGH.

LETTER VIII.

SIR, Barrells, Easter Sunday, 1748.

IT is rather to oblige the ambulatory old gentlewoman who delivers you your letters with so much alacrity, than it is to oblige her *best master*, that I write again so soon; for I am too sensible *my* letters will but ill repay the pleasure I receive from *his*; so that I ought to make a longer pause, and not interrupt my friends in *better company, better thoughts*, and *better diversions*, as Swift expresses it. If that consideration was just, which made him *pause a few weeks* betwixt his letters, I ought to pause years, or rather never write at all; that would be more polite; but it would make me fancy myself ungrateful, and consequently make me hate myself. It is therefore *self-love* which urges me to take this early opportunity of returning thanks for your last

last letter, wrote on Lady-Day. However depressed your *spirits* might be when you wrote it, it revived mine; for it is not in the power even of the north-east wind to depress your *genius*; and to *that* we owe thoughts which must please, however negligently they may be dressed:—the stiffen-bodied gown would not add charms, I believe, to a beautiful woman, no more than Voiture's laboured turns of expression add to his stile: and friendship undoubtedly shews itself in the best light, when least adorned by art. Therefore I hope you will never deprive me of the pleasure your letters give me, nor defer it, because your spirits may not just then allow you to send them out in their best apparel; it is sufficient you *can* do so; and they'll always be as welcome to me in their common garb, which is yet richer than you seem to imagine. I follow the rule I give, and write what comes uppermost; but it is in *me* a fault, as I am not privileged to do so by any of the gifts of nature, except artless sincerity be one.

I read your four sonnets with much pleasure; and am obliged to you for the trouble of transcribing them: they are truly poetical, yet have an ease as well as delicacy in the turn of thought and expression, which must, I believe, be agreeable to all, whether good judges by their

skill

skill and learning; or only judges of good sense and nature. If Dodsley gives a second edition of his well-chosen collection, I hope you will not let your School-mistress be unaccompanied by all her parent's offspring. Now that the boisterous baneful month of March is over, and that the sun resumes his power, I hope, and shall expect to see the productions of your imagination, as much as I shall expect to see those of my parterre, my shrubbery, or grove; and if joined to that satisfaction I have your company here, I shall give double praises to the returning spring. Mr. Whistler, or any friend of yours, will be perfectly welcome; but remember, that though I shall be a great gainer by *his* conversation, I shall also be a loser by his hearing *mine*, and his seeing this poor hermitage; of both which he may perchance have formed an advantageous idea, by your partial account of them; and *that* idea will instantly be destroyed, unless you have been as silent as Mr. Outing was about the Leasowes, before I had seen it: his caution was well judged, but wrong placed. But to shew you that I do not prefer fame (especially unmerited fame) to pleasure and improvement, I desire you to bring him, though at the expence of his being undeceived. I have read over his Shuttlecock several times, and each time

time with redoubled pleasure. 'Tis certainly a beautiful poem: I own myself a very indifferent judge, but it pleases me. It is an uncommon performance, and what many older and more famed poets would be proud of, whatever *juvenile* faults there may be in it; but, I think, the author's youth may rather be remarked by the great spirit and vivacity of his thoughts, than by any errors in his judgment; but if any such there be, you are his friend, and will have a very easy task in your criticism, if you should object to a few words, in order to let it appear perfect to the world, if our present world is elegant enough to be worthy of it. - Its name, and part of its character, had reached my ears before I saw it, but not from you. I think his similies exceeding apt, and his digressions just and lively: if so flight a subject, at so early an age, could be worked up so well, he certainly is capable of raising the intrinsic value of any more weighty, or more lofty subject he undertakes.

Your remark upon Fitzosborne's Letters is most just; for letters that are, or even seem to be, wrote *for the press*, never please like others: yet they are, I think, wrote in good language, and shew, I believe, polite learning and judgment; and the stile would be unexceptionable, I fancy, in *Essays*; but familiar letters require a more familiar addrefs. I find feveral more are promifed, if thefe fucceed. I wifh fome laborious pen may not be writing in the name of that author, and overwhelm us with his *fuppofed* letters: thefe, however, are genuine, as I fuppofe, though I never heard of that gentleman; and am obliged to you for your explanation of the character of Mezentius; that, in particular, might prevent the real names being publifhed: they would have made the book infinitely more interefting; but if that could not be, I don't know whether feigned but common modern names, might not have pleafed better, as they would have feemed real.

You are welcome to Inigo Jones's defigns, as long as they can be of fervice to you; and in return, I beg the favour of you to fend me the height and thicknefs of your wall that has arches funk in it, and the depth, breadth, and height of thofe arches; and let me know whether they are plaiftered on the infide, and if any ornament is on the top, or only a coping: it is to build in fummer a bit of wall (as you advifed) to fkreen me from the cottage that is contiguous to my garden, in lieu of the garden-feat which you and we all thought did not anfwer the hopes I had of it. If I do build that feat, it fhall be to terminate fome walk or view.

The

The chimney in my study was not exactly in the middle of the room; which has occasioned my moving it twelve inches, and consequently moving Pope's bust to be in the center. The lines wrote over it are put up again, (which, you know, are out of Virgil) but the stucco at the back of it must be new done, and the flat pieces of wainscot that make the margins of it, were never ornamented. Perhaps you would invent some more elegant ornament, if you would bestow a thought upon it; or the stucco might be just as before, only some foliage or other carving, to drop down the sides. Miss Merediths write word, that the present fashion at London, is all lead carving, which ladies do themselves, by cutting India, or other thin lead with scissors, and shaping it into flowers, knots, &c. and fixing it to a wire, which is afterwards nailed on in the form designed; and the carving is either gilt, or else painted the colour of the stucco or wainscot, according as suits the place.

I send this to the Birmingham post-office, (as you ordered) by a chance person. If you write an answer soon, pray direct it to Mr. Iron-monger, Master of the Castle-Inn, to be forwarded to me, (for Franky Holyoak is at home) and there is no post nor certain conveyance

ance from Birmingham to Henley where you will direct it to be left for me.

Sir,

I have left myself no room, and the person who carries this, leaves me no time, but just to assure you in the cover of my letter, that I am, (though not ceremoniously, yet very sincerely)

Sir,

Your obliged humble servant,

H. LUXBOROUGH.

P. S. I have writ a line to Mr. Ironmonger, to desire he'll send your letter, if any comes, to the Henley Post-house for me, by some safe conveyance.

LETTER IX.

SIR, Barrells, April 28th, 1748.

TWO of your letters lie before me; of which I am not a little proud: I am also well pleased with myself for having refrained from troubling you with an answer to the first, till I had received the second; which was not till last night. You will allow this to be some merit; at least, you would allow it, if you knew how great is my propensity to write to you; it being always with the selfish view of procuring in return some composition of yours. My self-denial this time has been great, but it is well rewarded by the favour of your last letter, and Mr. Whistler's Flower-Piece; the moral of which is perfectly just, and the thought very genteel and elegant. In this, as well as in his other Poem which you sent me, I think one may observe a great delicacy of imagination: the words altered with a pencil seem to be much for the better, especially the first line. As for his sentiment on enjoying things by reflection, I am not yet a convert to it, but am rather of your mind, that " an absent pleasure is equi-" valent to a present pain." For instance, if I was fond of London and its amusements, or had a taste for public places, I feel that it would give me pain to see St. James's, Vauxhall, Ranelagh, &c. &c. represented in so lively a manner as I see them through an optical glass which I have lately purchased, now that I am absent from them: but as I never was fond of a crowd, I enjoy those places as much as I desire in this reflected way, without wishing myself at them;

and

and I can look on the buildings and gardens of Stowe in the same manner, and with pleasure, because I never was there. But were you to present me with the Views of the Leasowes, I own I should not put them into my show-box without pain, nor see them well represented without regret; as it would remind me of the agreeable day I spent there, and my lost pleasure.

Your friend Mr. Graves's Lamentation is very pretty and pathetic, and seems to come from the heart: he must, I think, be very sincerely and very strongly in love; and yet I cannot but think *that* very inconsistent with his parting voluntarily from his Lucy, and with his sending her to London, without any jealousy: and I confess I also think it inconsistent that a man, who may be supposed to despise the opinion of the world, (since he marries so much below himself, and what the world would recommend) should part from *her* he so dearly loves, only to give her an education proper to please that world which he seems to despise; for it is plain, she pleases *him* without that education. How does he know, but that by losing her rural innocent air, however she may improve in her dancing-master's opinion, she may lessen in *his*, and her acquired charms may not please him as her native charms did the town? Perhaps I judge wrong, and yet I think it seems to be a natural way of judging. However, as he is your friend, I wish him happy, and hope she will not have the fate you threaten your rose-bud, and I threaten my bull-finch with; which last (since I have happened to mention it) I must tell you, is a little foolish *impromptu* I wrote in a letter to our friend Outing, whose answer was, that notwithstanding the moral of my song, he went the night he received it to the Oratorio of Judas Maccabæus, where he was highly entertained; and he speaks with such ecstasy of the music, as I confess I cannot conceive any one can feel who understands no more of music than myself; which I take to be his case. But I suppose he sets his judgment true to that of the multitude; for if his ear is not nice enough to distinguish the harmony, it serves to hear what the multitude say of it. He *would* be offended, if he should know that I think his singing much upon a par with my poetry; and you *ought* to be offended that I send you such foolish lines: but he might have happened to mention them to you, and as they are not worth the trouble of asking for, I prevent you, by sending them, and hope you will throw them in the fire when you

have

have read them: for they are not worth shewing to any, but one who, like you, is capable of excusing all faults in a friend, and who will not account it one in me, that I am no *Poetess*; which reproachful name I would avoid, even if I were capable of acquiring it; for which reason I hope you will throw the Epistle the Bostangy has sent you into the flames, with the Song, and forget I ever wrote in *verse* my real opinion in prose of the Leasowes' beauties.

I am impatient for your Essay, especially as you tell me there is in it a resemblance of yourself. I hope you will give me rules for œconomy; nobody wants them more: but I suspect you will not give me such as I might learn between Temple-Bar and the Stones End. In short, I have no great opinion of your rudiments in this science, though perhaps you may know the theory better than the practice of it: and you may be a good speculative œconomist for what I know; but I never met with a practical one in a soul where generosity and benevolence had a place, or to which a bright genius was joined.

I lament with you the loss of Lady Lyttelton, though I had not the honour of being personally acquainted with her; but her character was known, and all society must mourn so good a member of it, and all the poor so good a benefactress.

Your advice about my chimney pleased me greatly; but forced œconomy forbids my following it: besides that good carving is too fine for my humble roof. The room, consider, is only hung with sixpenny paper, and is so low that I have but five inches between Pope's Head and the Motto over it: so that I can neither have a compartment for that, nor an architrave, as is at Houghton. The contrast between that place and Barrells is so great, that it is ludicrous to name them together: and yet I allow with you, that the chimney in the dining-room there, might give one a hint for my little one; but I have not height enough for it. Upon the whole, as your thought was too good to reject, I have employed my friend Williams (in New-street, Birmingham) to paint the ornaments you would have had carved, in stone-colours, pretty strongly shaded to appear to rise like carving; and I sent him one of the two sketches you sent me, that he might the better comprehend what ornaments he was to introduce. When my brother Bolingbroke built Dawley, which he chose to call a Farm, he had his hall painted in stone-colours, with all the implements of husbandry placed in the manner

one

one sees or might see arms and trophies in some General's hall; and it had an effect that pleased every body. I believe Pope mentions it in one of his letters to Swift.—Mr. Williams is going to paint two ceilings for Mr. Anson (elder brother to my Lord Anson) in Staffordshire; one of them is for the Chinese room: I believe he has sketched them out at Birmingham, but is to go to paint them as soon as the Parliament rises. —Mr. Outing writes that he has sent you a bust of Pope done to look like marble, and that Rackstrow is doing four in that manner for my brother Sir John.—I should like to see your standish.

Nothing can be more just than the criticism upon the Play in the Magazine.—If you read French, I could send you a play just acted at Paris; Lady Bolingbroke sent it me: the chief character is a man who makes it his sole business and his sole pleasure to make mischief, even where he can get nothing by it: it is very well drawn, and I wish one did not see so many people like it.

If ever I have the pleasure of seeing your compositions all together, I could wish to have them ornamented in the manner of Pine's Horace, by yourself; where you would shew your taste in a double capacity, as poet and painter.

But you will say I am too unreasonable, and so I am; for I beg of you to continue to send me gold for glass, which I think is our usual traffick, and consequently you are too generous to, Sir,

   Your faithful and obliged servant,

       H. LUXBOROUGH.

LETTER X.

SIR,   Barrells, May 28th, 1748.

THIS is the first opportunity I have had of sending you the French Comedy you desire, and of answering your query about your standish. My advice is not worth asking in such matters; but since you do me the favour to ask it, it is this:

You have forty ounces of old plate, which, at five shillings and sixpence per ounce, amounts to eleven pounds. You have an inclination to indulge your fancy without much expence: you may then make your standish to weigh only thirty ounces, which, at eight shillings, (which is, I find, the price demanded) will come to

          twelve

twelve pounds: so that it will cost your pocket but twenty shillings, and I am persuaded will weigh enough for a standish, if the dimensions you intended to make it of are so large that thirty ounces will make the silver too thin. I suppose there will be no hurt in making it less in size, as the taste will be equally shewn; and I imagine the use will be much the same: but of this I cannot judge, because I never saw your draught.

The inclosed I received from Lady Hertford, to whom I had sent your Ballad of Queen Elizabeth, knowing it would suit her taste, and believing you would pardon me, as I sent it upon the footing of a trifle; but I will not send more of your compositions without your permission: I therefore beg you will send me back her letter by the very first opportunity, (as I wait for *that* to answer it) and say which of the things I have of yours you permit me or forbid me to send; for I shall religiously observe your directions about that, as well as about *Dawson's Ditty*, which I shall like to see in print, and to keep silence. I have heard *that* sung which he made just before his execution, and which was not made for him. Your *Kid* moves compassion; but it is comfort to think (as you observe) how many evils it would have done, if it had lived to

be

be old; and many it also might have received. Do not imagine what you write can be *middling*; if ever you should cease to write *well*, you will certainly write *ill*; for I am sure you never *compromised* with Apollo, whatever your friend Greaves may do with the *world*.

The Duke of Newcastle *Pantin* charms me, and I don't doubt but it made the peace. I am in doubt, when I hear of this polite fashion, whether it is a mark that the world is returned to its infancy, (as old people grow childish) or whether it be not some coquettish invention, that Mr. Pantin may say in dumb show what the Lady who wears him cannot say for herself. If this supposition should be thought severe upon their reputations, at least it saves them from the imputation of folly and childishness.

Had Shakespeare been used to gather rents, he would not have said

"For who so firm, that cannot be seduc'd?"

since your half day in endeavouring to *seduce* your tenant into paying you for half a year was *ineffectual*, and as my labours that way are as vain. My success in *receiving* money is very similar to yours; and if what you say about the *butter-dish* and the *sluice* is true as to you, it is no less so as to me. The parallel between us may be be carried yet farther; for I am as backward as you at *wringing from the hard hands of peasants their vile trash*; nor could I ever be forced, even by experience, into a proper *veneration for six-pence*, or have the foresight to nurse Fortune; but however, to *eat one's cake* when one is a-*hungered*, is most sweet.—The late King George was fond of peaches stewed in brandy in a particular manner, which he had tasted at my father's; and ever after, till his death, my mamma furnished him with a sufficient quantity to last the year round (*he* eating two every night). This little present he took kindly: but one season proved fatal to fruit-trees, and she could present his Majesty but with half the usual quantity, desiring him to use œconomy, for they would barely serve him the year at *one* each night. Being thus forced by necessity to retrench, he said he would then eat *two* every other night; and valued himself upon having mortified himself less, than if he had yielded to their regulation of one each night; which, I suppose, may be called a compromise between œconomy and epicurism; but I leave it to your decision.

As little as I love money, and as well as I love Lady Hertford and admire her judgment, I grudge six shillings for Hervey's Meditations, because you say they are *sometimes affected*, and ject might have depreſſed my lowered ſpirits, and have made nervous cordials of no effect. My hand ſtill trembles a little, as perhaps you will perceive, which will make me ſhorten this letter; and Parſon Hall's converſation whilſt I write, is another motive to my ſhortening it; ſo I haſten, Sir, to tell you that I am very happy in the thought of ſeeing you ſoon at Barrells, and much obliged to Miſs Dolman for her intended viſit. Every friend of yours is welcome here; therefore ſhe would be ſo, had I never ſeen her: but having had the pleaſure of enjoying her company at your houſe, I ſhould have a very bad taſte not to be deſirous of enjoying more of it. Here I naturally ſhould ſay, the ſooner you come the better; but I will tell you ſincerely, that I am at preſent aſhamed of my ſlovenly garden, which cannot be weeded, nor in the leaſt ſpruced up, till my hay is all in; which employs all my ſervants, and all the hands I can get this buſy time. Mr. Outing writes me word, that in a fortnight he ſhall be at Somerviles-Afton, and that a few days after he will come to Barrells; by which time I reckon my hay-making will be at an end, and my garden put into ſomewhat better order: and as I know he will be greatly pleaſed to meet you here, I hope about that time to ſee you, and

that

that you will not make so short a stay here as you mention.

Your pen gives me a very clear idea of Mr. Lyttelton's castle, and I believe I know the spot on which it is situated; but the proposal you make of my seeing it in so agreeable a manner as by going to Mr. Dolman's, makes me unwilling to content myself with viewing it only in your letter.

I shall be ready to contribute to any encouragement you shall think fit to give to Mr. Smith's Designs; and am glad Virgil's Grove will have a place among them.

I return thanks for your compliment about my Son, who is as *dear* to me as he is *dutiful*, and, I flatter myself, *deserving:* he is returned from Italy to Spa, and is going to pay his duty to the King at Hanover. My Daughter is lately married.—I hope your Brother is perfectly recovered, and that you will pardon this stupid letter, which I am sure is not fraught with the least spirit; but in its lowly way is very sincere, particularly when it assures you of the perfect esteem, with which I am,

Sir,

Your much obliged
  and very humble servant,

H. LUXBOROUGH.

Your letter, though dated the 16th, did not reach me till last night.

At last I am in the fashion, and have got a Pantin. Miss Patty Meredith writes me word, that she sends me a Pantin of the newest sort, and that the woman who sold it assured her it was just arrived in England, and is reckoned to make as genteel a curtsy as any Monsieur Pantin in Europe. She adds, that though this invention must be owned to be a great improvement to the diversion of the town, there is another of later date that is worthy of admiration; for there is a party of gentlemen and ladies of fashion who entertain the company at Vauxhall with the most charming harmony: the ladies crow like cocks, and if any gentlemen of the party are within hearing, they answer them by braying like an ass: That one Mrs. Woolaston has arrived to the greatest perfection, and has the honour of being called the head of the party for her excellence in this art.

LETTER XII.

SIR, Barrells, Wednesday, July 20th, 1748.

AS my laſt letter might poſſibly prevent my having the pleaſure of your company ſo ſoon as you intended to give it me, I take the firſt opportunity of acquainting you, that the obſtacles are removed; for my hay-making is over, and my health is better. As to Mr. Outing's meeting you, indeed I cannot abſolutely anſwer; but I know he left London laſt Monday was ſevennight, with his couſin Walſh, and they were to come to Oxford in the ſtage-coach, ſtay there a day, and proceed to Jacky Reynalds's on horſeback; from whence I underſtood Mr. Walſh would go to drink Cheltenham waters, and Mr. Outing would, in a very ſhort time after his arrival in Glouceſterſhire, make me a viſit at Barrells; and was much concerned he could not meet you and Miſs Dolman here; for I ſuppoſe he comprehended you were coming immediately, and his letter was writ the 5th inſtant. I expect every day to hear from him, and I imagine he will be here next week; but whether he is or no, no, I shall hope to see you, Sir, with Miss Dolman, her brother, or any friend you choose to bring. If you write to me on Saturday, and direct it to be left with Mr. Williams, Painter, in New-street, Birmingham, I have desired him to forward it; and as his brothers live in Henley, he has more frequent opportunities of sending thither than Mr. Ironmonger. He has finished my chimney-piece; which he hopes will not be disapproved by you, Sir, to whom I owe the idea of it.

I am ashamed to own that I have not yet answered Lady Hertford's letter, nor read the books she recommended: in short, I might as well have been a mole and lived under ground, or a dormouse and slept incessantly, as the insignificant animal I have been for some time. Two or three days indeed I was kept awake by a visit from Mr. Meredith, who entertained me with the many gay entertainments he had been a partaker of at London last Spring; but when he was gone, I was left alone with Monsieur Pantin, whom, I confess, I have not wit enough to amuse myself with; so that I seldom let him make his appearance, but when Parson Hall comes; for they shew each other to great advantage:

I have not seen Mrs. Pilkington's Memoirs, (except the specimen in the Magazine) nor

Con.

Con. Philipps's Apology. I will set about getting some of these modern books, to enable me to bear a share in the conversation of, and correspondence with, my friends; which I am sensible I am incapable of at present: and as I should least choose to write to you of any of them, whilst in my state of stupidity and ignorance, I abridge my letter all I can, and hasten to assure you that I am, with great esteem,

Sir,

Your most obliged humble servant,

H. LUXBOROUGH.

I shall hope to hear the beginning of next week, which day I may expect you, if you write on Saturday.—I write to-day to Mr. Outing, by the Evesham gardeners, to say I hope to see him by the end of next week, if not before. I do not know whether they will find him out. —I think you promised me the Poem upon Sickness to read, and I hope for something upon *œconomy*; which will be very wholesome for me; and yet I am persuaded a very agreeable medicine, as it will be made up by such good and skilful hands.

LETTER XIII.

SIR,

I Always respected your man Tom for his honesty and fidelity to his master; but at present I respect him for the good *tidings* he *bringeth*, which make my heart full glad. It is plain your thoughts and mine correspond; for I have been all the last week considering which day I should fix for going to the Leasowes, or whether I should not first desire your company at Barrells.—Mr. Meredith came hither last Tuesday, and went for London on Thursday. We talked of your charming situation; but more of your agreeable company: both which he wishes to be acquainted with; and I offered to carry him to wait on you, as on Monday next, and said he might go on from thence to Cheshire; which he hearkened to with pleasure, but told me he was obliged to get there by Saturday, and that he intended coming here again next Friday, in his way thither; so would not let me write you word, for fear of disappointing you. I sent however to Mr. Hall (as I don't love to jumble in a post-chaise alone) to ask him to go with me on Monday or Tuesday next; but he was posting away to preach the assize sermon yesterday at Warwick, and from thence to go to Rugby the latter end of this week; where he expects to receive his final answer about the Living of Harborough; and in case he succeeds, will be obliged to ride about the country still farther; but if not, will return to Henley next Saturday, and wait upon you with me, as he writes me word. In this uncertain state, confused by all these half engagements, your trusty 'Squire found me, and seemed come to my relief, by bringing me word you was ready to make me happy in your company, and Mr. and Miss Dolman's and your brother's, at my cell. Now the best way I can think of to decide of this affair is, that I should go, at all events, to the Leasowes on Monday to dinner; and that ye all return with me, or immediately after me, to Barrells, as best suits you; by which means I shall have more of your company, and I may attend Mr. Meredith to a place he is so desirous to see if he can put off his journey to that day; which I am apt to think he may easily do, as Birmingham is in his way home: so he will only dine at the Leasowes, where I propose, with your leave, to take a night's lodging; as you was so kind to desire: By which means I' shall

shall have more of your company, and shall see your improvements more at leisure; and your woods will afford a different scenery, when they are embrowned by the shade of the evening, or when the moon glimmers through their leaves: whereas I have never yet seen them but in full sun-shine, and when walking (had it been in any other place) had been a toil. If you do not write me a line to the contrary, by Thursday's post, you will see me next Monday, the 7th instant, at your *Ferme ornée*: and I hope to bring you on the 8th, to my *Ferme negligée*; for that you will find it. Having had so much company in my house, and the hay-harvest having employed my servants, the gardens were neglected just when they ought to have been put in order; and the dry time has prevented the new-laid turf from joining; and my pavillion, when almost finished, was pulled down again in part, to add to it a shrine for Venus: so that it is still uncovered; and the roses, &c. are all faded, and give an ugly aspect to my shrubbery; which waits your directions to be new modelled: But in this imperfect condition, if it affords ever so little pleasure to Mr. Dolman, it will have done part of what I wish it to do: and though I cannot treat him so elegantly as I treated you with truffles and Cassadi-bread, he

will

will be heartily welcome to the beans and bacon my Farm produces, and to the cheese of my own dairy.—I do not wonder your neighbours visit you frequently; but I wish they do not envy you, and endeavour to spy some fault. I am persuaded I shall like your small Gothic building better than their huge one.—I am proud of having mentioned the carpet pavement. I believe the Duchess of Somerset's is not famous enough to have given occasion to the words spoken by the ladies that visited yours. I am also proud of having shewn my approbation of your place, and of the manner of your improving it, even in its infancy; since it is now universally admired by all who have any just pretensions to taste.

I should have begun my letter with condolence upon your late illness, and congratulations upon your recovery; but as it would have done you no good, you will excuse my neglect, and be so just as to believe, that, though it is mentioned last in my letter, my good wishes for your health and happiness are ever uppermost in my mind, however *derangé* the manner of expressing them in my letters may be: for what they want in form, they have in sincerity; which

I am apt to think you esteem better than form. So I shall only call myself

Sincerely yours,
H. Luxborough.

The clergyman, who has troubled the press with his Lamentations over Polyanthos's, and has prefixed my name to his performance, is one Mr. Perks, of Coughton, whom I never saw but twice; and he had never seen Barrells when he wrote it, but came to see it, in order to make his Dedication in praise of it. But I think he forms his supposition of my taking delight in flowers (not from my Shrubbery, but) from the art, with which he says I have adorned my apartments. Parson Allen, who does not pretend to be a poet, has made a Dedication in imitation of the other; but, I think, better.

SECOND POSTSCRIPT; or, *More Last Words.*

My Daughter owes me a grudge for not carrying her to the Leasowes, and I reproach myself for it: but the day we were at Birmingham, it never ceased raining.

A DEDICATION OF A PASTORAL ELEGY HUMBLY IMITATED.

(Mr. PERKS's Dedication to Lady LUXBOROUGH, corrected by Parson ALLEN.)

Here fragrant flow'rs refresh the musing fair,
   Whilst zephyrs waft their odours thro' the air.
Luxuriant shoots, with one united blow,
Rival the colours of the various bow.
The warbling songsters on the blossom'd thorn
Stretch their melodious throats, and wake the morn.
The bee laborious hums around the bower,
And sips the balmy sweets of ev'ry flower.

'Tis thus the varied scene treats every sense;
Displays the charms of youth and innocence.
　　Within, new objects strike the wond'ring eye,
And strokes of sculpture with the pencil vye.
Here breathing shadows each apartment grace,
And meagre bustos shew their marble face.
The robed Peer, full drawn, majestic stands,
And mimic miniature in motley bands.
There Nature's sports, from India's distant shore,
Or dress'd in lighter moss, or clad in ore!
See heaps of shells, old Ocean's glossy store,
Have left their briny cells, and weep no more;
Beneath the rolling wave no longer sleep,
Swept from the rocks and caverns of the deep:
Some skilful hand the pleasing task pursue,
And add new lustre to their native hue,
The grotto's pride, when gayly interchang'd,
They shine, in regular confusion rang'd.
But O! the loveliest sight is yet conceal'd,
By human art never to be excell'd.
Here ev'ry flow'r, that decks th' enamell'd meads,
Or thro' the grove its vernal beauty spreads,
In lively tints so natural, so true,
A piece more perfect Titian never drew.
Thus Taste polite, and Judgment more refin'd,
Feast the admiring eye, and cultivate the mind.

LETTER XIV.

SIR, Barrells, Wednesday, July 27,

I HAVE just time to tell you, that I received your most agreeable and obliging letter yesterday; and shall be glad of your company and your Brother's, &c. next Wednesday, being to dine at Mrs. Chester's on Tuesday.—Outing writes word that if his cousin returns to London, as he intends, next Monday, he will come for two or three days to Barrells; and hopes to meet you and Miss Dolman.—A report prevails at Henley which would give me great concern, but that your letter being dated last Sunday makes me think it almost impossible to be true: yet it shocked me a good deal to hear the many circumstances repeated belonging to this supposed fatal accident; which is, that Mr. Dolman was drowned last Thursday, being a fishing in Grove Field, near Warwick; and that his corpse was brought to Litchfield on Friday, and on Saturday two gentlemen set out separate roads for Oxford to get his scholarship; one of which brought this news to the Swan, and told it to Mr. Hall and Mr. Holyoak, and

another

another Oxford scholar whom Mr. Hall is acquainted with, came the next day to Henley and confirmed the same, expressing great concern. They added, that Mr. Welch's son, of Grove Park, was fishing with Mr. Dolman, but could not save him; and that his estate comes to his sister. How to reconcile all this with your sending me his compliments in your letter on Sunday, some Œdipus must determine. I will hope it is as *false* as *it* is *true* that I am, Sir,

  Your most obliged humble servant,

      H. LUXBOROUGH.

LETTER XV.

 SIR,   Barrells, Tuesday night, August 23d, 1748.

IT is well I am an *invalid*; but even *that* I fear will not be an excuse sufficient for my delaying thanks, so greatly due to you, Sir, to Miss Dolman, and to your Brother, for the friendly visit you made me at Barrells; which I sincerely assure you gave me both health and pleasure: for I look upon *these* two as inseparable

rable companions: and I am certain the *rugged walk* to Ulenhall Chapel (however conducive to *health*, according to the Phyſician, or to *happineſs*, according to the Divine) would never have inclined me to undertake it, had not the company I was with ſmoothed the road, and levelled the ruts; for ſuch was the effect it had at leaſt upon my imagination. But the roads are as *rough* as ever, and I as *lazy*; which ſhews that *we hermits* are to blame, droning away our time in our cells. For my part, I had a fever, and kept my bed yeſterday: I am not very ſtrong to-day; but to reſtore my ſtrength and health, (at leaſt to give me pleaſure) I propoſe to wait on Miſs Dolman at Brome next Monday (the 29th) to breakfaſt and dinner; and to return to Barrells after viewing the *Giants* Caſtle at Hagley. I will then deliver to you the books you lent me, as alſo the *green* manuſcript which I ſo much valued myſelf upon having ſtole from your pocket. Nothing could make me releaſe it but your promiſe in your laſt letter of giving it me with Additions. *Theſe* I ſhall always covet; and amendments I ſhall never require.

I have not yet been well enough to anſwer Lady Hertford's letter; ſo have not ſent her any thing more of yours. Queen Elizabeth

you

you know she has.; and as *she* pleased her as well as myself in her first dress, I have not sent her in the other.

Mr. Outing (*notwithstanding* the syllabubs) arrived here about two days after you left Warwickshire. He tells me nothing about maids or widows; but does not seem very ready to make new syllabubs, nor to forget old friends: but I confess that his neglecting the opportunity of telling them so, does not set his friendship off to the best advantage. Perhaps he leaves those marks of it in the dark, to let them appear in the more resplendent manner when he has held out the lantern of truth to enlighten them, as to his late seemingly remiss conduct. And upon this affair he is now I believe employed, having asked for ink and paper.

I think I saw a locust on Sunday last: Mr. Bradley found it in his corn singly. If it is one, one might call it a *flying grashopper*; for it is exactly like the grashopper, only two inches and a half long, and has a brown complexion, and six feet and four wings; and eats leaves.

Smith's Designs would undoubtedly (if well coloured) be delightful objects, as I suppose them all drawn in perspective: and for the colouring, you need be in no fear of either error or or expence, as you can do them so well yourself.

My niches are as hollow as when you left them. The mason I have not seen; and the intended alteration I had almost forgot, for want of seeing the place. Such indolence is inexcusable; yet it does not make me in the smallest degree forgetful of what regards my friends, nor of their advice; which I am ever grateful for, and wish only I had spirits good enough to hasten the execution of the workmen.

My paper allows me only to say, that I am,

Your faithful servant,

H. LUXBOROUGH.

LETTER XVI.

Barrells, Monday night, Sept. 5th, 1748.

SIR,

IT is with great pleasure I learn within these few hours, that Barrells is eight miles nearer to the Leasowes than I have hitherto thought it; and that the deep ruts I had formed an idea of, are levelled down to bowling-greens. *Such is* is the account my friend Johnson gives; who serves me with coals; lives at Northfield, is acquainted with *Hales Owen*, the *Grange*, and with the *Leafowes*, where he says lives one Mr. Shenstone. He, by my desire, puts my postillion into that lucky road to-morrow to carry you this letter; by which I acquaint you of the pleasure I propose from it: for in case it proves as *he* says; and that you are not otherwise engaged, you will see me at the Leasowes any day you please to name, either of this week or the next after Wednesday. Mr. Outing and Mr. Hall will accompany me: and we propose going early in the morning and returning at night to Barrells.—You see, Sir, what an agreeable place, adorned with taste, and more agreeable conversation, subjects you to: yet you might for this season have escaped the trouble of our company, had it not been for your neighbour Johnson's *good report*; who, had he been a divine, might perhaps have conducted more pilgrims to heaven by this favourable account, than others have done by the merit they propose to them, in reward for labouring through thorns, and struggling with dangers; and might by the same rule have freed you from the interruption our visit may give to eremitical retirement; if, like other more pious divines, he

had

had left your roads as rugged and perilous as they appeared to us before he traced them out.

I write a line to Miſs Dolman, (whom I hope to meet at your houſe) and return her Pilkington's Memoirs, which entertained me agreeably. I find, upon reading them over, that the perſon ſo often mentioned and diſtinguiſhed by the letters J. W——le, is Mr. Worſdale the Painter.

I ſuppoſe Saturday or Monday next will not be diſagreeable to you for our viſit: but leave it to your choice.

Pardon this ſcrawl, wrote after midnight; and be ſo kind as either to ſend my ſervant to Broom with my meſſage to Miſs Dolman, and the book; or elſe to take charge of them for her.

My compliments to Mr. Joſeph Shenſtone.

LETTER XVII.

Barrells, Sept. 11th, 1748.

YOUR benevolence, Sir, to your friends does not leave them at your gate, but accompanies them home; and, left it should not remain in their memory, is refreshed by new marks of it. As such I look upon your message and letter to-day; and have the pleasure to assure you, in answer to your kind enquiry, that I am so far from bodily suffering, that I am better in health than I have been for some time past; and my mind is greatly regaled by the ideas your charming situation and more charming improvements have indulged it with. I must in particular commend your last alteration; for I never saw a more advantageous one than the clew you have given to lead to your wood, &c.

Your apologies in point of lodging, suppose me to have neglected your invitation, for fear of not meeting with so good a one at the Leasowes as in the ruts of the Port-way, or some dirty lane nearer home; which might have been our lot, as it was dark. But I hope you will do

me

me more juſtice than to ſuppoſe I would have been ſo unkind to myſelf as to have quitted a place where I was ſo preſſingly invited, and ſo agreeably entertained, had I not been obliged to return home that night. But leſt you ſhould think this a compliment, I promiſe faithfully (and as it is for my own ſake, you may believe me) to ſtay, next time I go to the Leaſowes, all that night, and as far of the next day as you ſhall think reaſonable and ſafe for travelling. This promiſe, or rather threat, you may depend upon: ſo beware.

I was glad of the *honour* of meeting Lord Dudley and his Siſter at your houſe; and hope for *that* of ſeeing them at mine. The reſt of the company which happened to come to you were extremely agreeable; and I regretted nothing but want of day-light which deprived me of ſo many pleaſures at once.

As to Parſon Hall, I never thought there was any offence given him: if there was, *I* gave it firſt; but being unconſcious of it, I never made him an excuſe; but, on the contrary, reproached him for leaving my chaiſe a quarter of a mile from home; where, when I came, I found him very good-humoured, and he lay here. However, when I received your letter this afternoon, I ſent it to him to Henley to read: he returned it immediately, with the inclofed anfwer; and I believe him fo fincere, that he never once imagined any perfon could take any thing that was faid but as a joke: and I confefs myfelf not only fo *fincere*, but alfo fo *ftupid*, that I did not conceive it could be fuppofed otherwife; or that what was faid was capable of admitting of any other interpretation, till your letter reminded me, that perhaps before ftrangers it might not be proper: but if fuch is the cafe, before ftrangers one muft few up one's mouth, and be exceeding bad company, left they fhould imagine one wants common humanity to one's own friend; which would here be the cafe, as I look upon Mr. Hall as mine.

In the hurry yefterday of pleafure and fatigue, I forgot to return thanks for a fine greyhound I received from the Leafowes by my fervant the laft time I fent. He has catched me a hare; and feems of a race to catch many.—I beg my beft compliments to Mr. Jofeph Shenftone, whofe obliging temper is to be liked by all, and is much regarded by me.

I fuppofe Mifs Dolman is returned to Broom; but hope you will make my compliments to her and her Brother in the moft friendly manner; and wifh fo many miles and rugged ways did not part us. I begin to envy the ants, who are

hid

hid from the world, and the world from them, till the fummer fun returns to enliven it. *This* you will fay is a fad profpect I have propofed to my view; perhaps more really ferious than Mr. Hervey's of the Tombs! But *true* however it is, that winter in the country is too folemn to give pleafure, though it may give awe; and I love it as much as a child does a rigid parent. But to put off the evil day, I hope you will affift by lengthening out the autumn as long as poffible, by your company here and your Brother's, and by your agreeable letters when I do not fee you.—I dare not name the Green Book now, though *precious* to me; for you have paid great intereft for the loan of it, by the fix lines you fent me to-day, which are delightfully pretty; and which Lord Dudley and myfelf ought to think ourfelves honoured by: but yet, the *intereft* paid, the *principal* is ftill due, and the *Green Book* is ftill my object. Whatever you write, or defign, is fo; therefore it is faying no more than you have heard me fay before; and which I am hopeful you will believe, knowing that I deferve by my fincerity to be efteemed

Your moft faithful fervant,

H. Luxborough.

P. S. Mr. Sanders speaking of the dimension of his Optic Glasses yesterday, put me in mind of measuring mine. It is near three inches and a half diameter, convex on one side, and flat on the other; in which latter account it resembles his: but I hope you will have some further instructions from him about it, as he seems to be very ingenious and curious, and I may glean after you.

LETTER XVIII.

SIR,   Barrells, Sunday, October 16th, 1748.

THE impatience with which I waited for the pleasure of hearing from you, in answer to my last, I looked upon as a proof that nothing I could read was so agreeable to me as what you wrote: and had I been doubtful in my opinion, your letter and Autumn verses would have confirmed it. This is no compliment, nor am I guilty of flattery. I speak my mind; so that if I am guilty of an error, it must be in judgment: and I do not believe it possible, even for all your modesty, to pack a jury that would find me so in *this case*: yet *just* as I

am

am to your writings, I am partial to the autumn
feafon:—perhaps you will become fo when
grown fomewhat older; and not exclaim againft
that *penfive* feafon (as you call it) which, if it
does not afford all the gaieties of fpring and
fummer, is however attended with fewer difap-
pointments. Would you in fpring enjoy the
beauty of your parterre, a fudden fhower drives
you home; in fummer you are obliged to fhut
out the delicious profpect of the ripened grain
and the various labours of the peafant, left,
like him, you fhould be fcorched by the fun-
beams, which your fpreading waters reflect the
more ftrongly, or be catched, though under the
fhelter of an oak, by the mercilefs lightning:
whereas in autumn, though more languid, the
fun has ftill power to chear, and its gentle
heat caufes no pain; it ftill ferves to ripen
fruits, which are to be your confolation in winter; and though the days are fhort, every hour
of them may be enjoyed in meads and groves,
where indeed the trees lofe their verdure; but
it is no more than changing their drefs (as fome
lowly nymphs have done of late) from a plain
green gown to a rich brocade mixed with ten
thoufand fhades: and as it is wove by the hand
of Nature, fhould ftill pleafe in its variety,
though not equally as in its bloom; nor fhould

its more solemn and decent appearance anticipate by reflection the rigours of winter. Too soon she will make her shivering naked appearance, and make us wish ourselves buried with the ant, till spring returns, unless some social friends assemble (as at Barrells in 1747) to supply with their conversation the absence of the sun.—I cannot persuade Mr. Outing to allow of my indulgence to autumn; though, to favour my argument, Nature has been so remarkably kind this last October to adorn my Shrubbery with the flowers that usually blow at Whitsuntide, and deck my apple-trees with blossoms, which we saw upon two of the trees three days ago, and have now primroses and polyanthuses growing. Perhaps it is not so at the Leasowes; for though the same sun lights us, it may be clouded over there, and your flowers *withered all when Thomson died.*—Nature indeed should mourn for one who sung so well her praises; but *that* debt paid, and his urn placed in your grove, (so worthy of its reception) she will no longer weep her Poet, but adopt you her favourite to succeed him.—His Castle of Indolence I have read at last, and admire several parts of it. He makes the Wizard's Song most engaging: but, as Lady Hertford observes, it is no wonder; for

" He needs no Muse who dictates from the Heart;"

and

and Thomson's heart was ever devoted to that Archimage. Do not copy him too nearly in that; it would be cruel to your friends, if, like him,

"——————— your ditty sweet
"You loathed much to write, nor cared to repeat."

I shall be glad to see the model of your urn; but more glad to see the urn itself in your grove, and its shadow trembling in your transparent stream. I hope it will be well executed, as it will give you a pensive pleasure, and to all who see and read how you have celebrated the memory of one who so well deserved it. Future urns no doubt will be raised to you, but long may they remain unnecessary! though, according to your proposing to *end your labours* (which is ending your pleasures) as soon as two more things are erected, I should look upon your death as very near, and that you imagine he is to snatch you to his arms just as you are laying the last white brick of the second garden-seat: for no less a monarch than he could stop the course of your elegant improvements. If I guess right, the most rapid current, or (what is yet stronger) the most aspiring ambition might as well be stopped as your inclination cease which forces you to adorn your villa, or ever
your

your taste descend to the vulgar rule of leaving things as you found them. I often wish I had had that same useful vulgar prudence; and yet how ashamed should I have been of it, when friends of taste had seen me enjoy the thistles and nettles that adorned this savage place, as contentedly as the ass that feeds on them!

If your *expostulations* with Mr. Lyttelton were *brusques*, his visit was as much so; and upon such occasions I never love to be behind-hand with *great* people.

The eldest son of Archimage, and the little round fat oily Man of God, talk of making you a visit the week that is now coming in; and for that I waited to write: but unless weather, roads, and all conveniences conspire, I tell the former, I am sure he will not set out. But he says I do not form a right notion of him; so I leave it to him to prove. In the mean time, they desire their compliments to you; I suppose I need not say I mean Mr. Outing and Mr. Hall.—I will send Dodsley's three volumes by them.—As to your thought about improving the Show-box, I do not despise it for believing you took it from the thing called London Cries, which children play with; for the great Handel has told me that the hints of his very best songs have several of them been owing to
the

the founds in his ears of cries in the ftreet: and why may your eyes not take a hint from the manner in which they are exhibited in the fore-mentioned little machine? but I queftion if it can be fo well performed in fo large a thing as thefe machines we have. The paper would rumple if not faftened to pafteboard, and if faftened, would be too ftiff to roll round the rollers; yet I do not know whether, as you obferve, fome fort of canvas might not do. It would be a good amufement in the Wizard's Caftle; for by this means it would give no trouble to bring all the beautiful gardens and palaces of the world to your view, as his chry-ftal globe by turning fhewed him the various turns of man. For my part, I propofe to have at my Caftle of Barrells Æolus's Harp; a mufic which will never ceafe here as long as the winds maintain their power.

I do not complain of your punctuality as to paying intereft for the Green Book; but I am ftill as impatient for the principal, as if you had allowed me nothing to live on. I am alfo jealous of the Red Book, who robs me I fear of your time. Mr. Outing's anxiety is for the Red one; fo I expect no compaffion from him: all I defire is, that, whether green or red, you will let me have *fome* of your *Works* to fubfift

upon

upon this winter: and if I did not fear to make too many demands at once, I would also beg for *some* of your company.

I am, Sir,

Your most obliged humble servant,

H. LUXBOROUGH.

LETTER XIX.

SIR, Barrells, November 2d, 1748.

IN the last letter I wrote you (which I hope you received) I promised to send you Dodsley's Miscellany by Mr. Outing and Mr. Hall the week following; but finding they have not yet fixed a day for their journey, I am resolved to venture sending the books by your faithful postwoman, (to whom Mr. Bradley will deliver them) rather than to wait any longer for messengers who may perhaps never perform their promise: for the beauties of autumn will soon decay, though they are not decayed yet; the roads grow bad, and the days, which are already short, will be shorter; and Mr. Outing's business, which obliges him to be in London
before

before this month is out, may all serve as reasons perhaps for their not going to the Leasowes this year, and may be the cause of my seeming to neglect what you desire of me; which I am incapable of: and therefore, in justice to myself, I send the books another way; but in justice to Mr. Outing, (whom I often accuse of indolence) I must say that his inclination and friendship in this case got the better of his laziness, and of every dragon that might fall in his way to obstruct his journey; but not caring to go alone so far, and Mr. Hall being bent upon the same visit, they agreed to go together; and the latter, after fixing several days, and being prevented by his Father's illness once, and various things at other times, tells Mr. Outing now that he has no horse, and had rather defer going till spring; so that I foresee Mr. Outing will be deprived of the pleasure he proposed for the present, unless you will be so good as to come to Barrells, where you would not only see him, but give me the pleasure of your company, which you did promise me when I saw you last; and which will make me very happy: since I value it greatly in the blooming season of the year, you may judge what a cordial it will be in the frozen solitary season that approaches. I ought not indeed to invite you at such a time,

but

but it is a proof that I am fenfible of your good nature, which takes pleafure in nothing fo much as in *obliging*; and I have for that reafon ventured to point out the way in which you are fure of obliging greatly,

  Sir,

   Your faithful humble fervant;

     H. LUXBOROUGH.

P. S. Could you lend me the *Shuttlecock?* It is for Mr. Allen to read once more.

Mr. Outing begs his compliments to you; and hopes you will be convinced (and I hope the fame) that, notwithftanding my joke about his lazinefs in my former letter, he was ready and defirous to perform this journey; and he now repents waiting for Mr. Hall; fo that you cannot fcruple favouring him with your company here; or if you fhould be fo ceremonious as that, *I* might yet claim a vifit from you.

My beft compliments, pray, at Broom, and to your Brother, whom I hope to fee here.—I am impatient for the Green Book.—Mr. Outing and I are gathering flower-feeds proper for your grove; which I will fend you to fow in fpring, with fome *Star of Bethlehem* and fome Layers of *Paffion Flowers* for your Hermit, and to make your

your Hermitage more proper for the reception of Mr. James Hervey, if he should travel your way.

LETTER XX.

Barrells, Sunday Evening, Nov. 13th, 1748.

SIR,

THE uncertainty of my receiving an answer from you in due time, according to the date, and also my present uncertainty as to which day of this month I am most likely to have the pleasure of your company at Barrells, and, above all, the fear of being by some accident deprived of it, or by my absence seem undeserving of it, are all reasons which oblige me without the least delay to acquaint you, that, before I received your last welcome letter, I had yielded to Mr. and Mrs. Reynalds's strong invitation to Somervile's-Afton; where, had I refused to go, yet Mr. Outing must have gone, having part of his wardrobe there (as his first visit from London was to them); as also, some business which he says he must go to finish, even if I should again be prevented from going where I have been so long expected: and I dare say you would be forry to find him gone from Barrells; and more fo, to have a fecond time reafon to think his friendfhip remifs in its duty. Therefore, Sir, thefe confiderations weighed, I determine to fend a meffenger to the Leafowes to-morrow with this, and my compliments to you and Mr. Jofeph Shenftone; and to acquaint you, that our day of march from Barrells to Afton is fixed for Friday next, the 18th inftant; and that of our return for the Friday following, the 25th: and we fhall depend upon feeing you the firft moment your bufinefs or inclination permits. How readily would my pen and wifhes fix the 26th, that being the earlieft moment; but you obferve in your letter to Mr. Outing, that fixing days is an encroachment upon liberty; therefore I am filent, and fubmit to the time which fuits your conveniency. And as I do not intend to make any more excurfions till fpring returns, and do not expect any company here, I fear no interruptions from this fide the *Lickee*, (how do you fpell it?) and flatter myfelf there will be none on the other: then fhall I fee you arrive perhaps through fnow or rain, which will heighten my gratitude, but moderate my joy. The Green Book will add greatly to my pleafure, and your converfation will make me prefer

winter

winter to my favourite autumn, though I have
refused that preference to spring: but to say
the truth, no season can be disagreeable in company one likes; nor none agreeable with the
insipid or unsociable, the unfriendly, or the unmeaning; the designing, the tale-bearing, the
pedantic, or the ignorant, &c. &c. from all
which may the Divine Powers deliver us; and
may I soon enjoy the reverse company in my
chimney corner! then shall I be agreeably entertained; Mr. Outing be eased from his fears
of not seeing you before he leaves the country;
and Mr. Hall be enabled to make his own excuses to you, and in particular to Mr. Joseph Shenstone for not performing his promise. He seems
penitent, and I galled him a little, though with
your gentle and kind reproaches, which he felt,
notwithstanding at that instant he was wrapt in
ecstacies of joy and admiration; for he had purchased an incomparable horse the day before.
The beauty of novelty is great with him; but it
will be decayed before this month is out, and he
will then have the more time to give you marks
of his friendship; which I dare say is always sincere, and not transient, as his passion for his
horse may be.—Now I have answered for him,

permit me to say for myself, that I am most steadily,　　　Sir,

　　　　Your sincere and obliged
　　　　　　　humble servant,
　　　　　　　　　H. LUXBOROUGH.

If it suited you to go with us to Somerviles-Afton, I can answer for your welcome there, as well as for the additional pleasure it will be to me and to Mr. Outing; who would tell you so himself, but the messenger who is to carry the letter cannot wait; and he expects to see you so soon, that my pen only speaks for him now.

Lord Dudley gave me hopes of coming to Barrells, which would do me honour and pleasure.

LETTER XXI.

Wooton, Sunday Evening, Nov. 20th, 1748.

SIR,

THE inclosed, of ancient date, will inform you of the dilemma I have been in.—Having a kind of hospital of sick servants was no
agreeable

agreeable circumstance; and the fear of disobliging my friends at Somerviles-Aston, or of missing of the pleasure of your company at Barrells, had you come whilst I was there, were reasons that diminished the happiness I proposed by both those visits; mine to them, and yours to me. To prevent these misfortunes, I was sending a messenger to the Leasowes with the inclosed, when my housekeeper was taken dangerously ill, and obliged me to send my messenger to Aston, instead of the Leasowes, to acquaint them I could not go thither according to my promise: but he met Mr. Reynalds on the road coming to fetch me. He stayed with me from Tuesday till Thursday, every moment expecting you; and the more so, as he found by me, that your design was to come whilst Mr. Outing's business permitted him to stay in Warwickshire, which was not to exceed this month. In short, Mr. Reynalds left me on Thursday, but insisted upon my promising to go to Aston on Wednesday next, and you with me (for he concluded you would be at Barrells now, because it wants but ten days of the end of the month).—My servant is got pretty well.—Mr. Outing is still here, though he expects every day or hour to receive a summons to go to London; and Mr. Reynalds

nalds has sent his servant purposely to-day with a letter to desire us not to fail to go on Wednesday, and that he will come again to fetch me; and also an invitation to you to go with us: already he has contrived to keep room for you, therefore you will not stay away upon a supposition of any inconvenience to him. I shall return home on Wednesday, the 30th inst. and shall hope you will return with me, and enliven this melancholy season by your agreeable company.—Mr. Outing despairs of seeing you, unless you come to Afton with

    Your faithful humble servant,
      H. LUXBOROUGH.

LETTER XXII.

SIR,   Barrells, December 12th, 1748.

METHINKS I see you by your chimney-side, your pen in your hand, and the Red or Green Book before you, just going to express with poetical elegance some refined or sublime thought, which might have afforded pleasure and improvement to present and future ages; when you are interrupted by your old postwoman, who presents you my insipid letter; *you* frown a just dislike to the interruption, *re-*
          venge

venge yourself with your heel on the innocent plaister of your room, and then you begin to consider seriously what can have drawn upon you the plague of an epistolary correspondence, to which you had endeavoured to put a stop by not answering my two last letters: and you will not guess at the reason, unless I tell you that I write now chiefly for other people's business. In the first place, Lady Hertford, at my recommendation, (thinking it would be agreeable to you) consents to subscribe to Mr. Smith's Drawings; which you will be pleased to acquaint him of: and I was willing to let you see the success of my recommendation as soon as I could. You seemed to espouse the man's interest, and to approve of the Views he is going to publish; and I could have wished to serve more essentially any person recommended by you.—I am next, Sir, to return Mr. Allen's thanks and his compliments to you, with Mr. Whistler's Poem. Mr. Reynalds's devoirs I am also desired to pay you, and those of Mr. Outing; who were both sorry you did not accept of the invitation to Someviles-Afton.— Here ends my embassy.

Before I conclude, I must tell you, that I went to Afton on the day I wrote you word I should go, and returned hither on Thursday, the first of this month: which was only one day later than I intended, and that was becaufe of the death and burial of one of the invalid fervants, which (as I wrote you word) made an hofpital of my houfe at that time.—Mr. Outing returned with me, hoping to find you here, and did not leave me till laft Thurfday. I am now alone, and the feafon not inviting to travellers; but the weather and roads are good; and as you find fewer horrors in Winter than in Autumn, I will hope that you will once more enliven it with your company: my hearths will blaze the brighter, and Eolus will fet his harp to fofter mufic, or feem to do fo, if you are here; and focial Winter will vie not only with fruitful Autumn, but alfo with flowery Spring, and be fure of fuccefs, if you favour my Hermitage with your company.

I fend you Lady Hertford's (or rather the Duchefs of Somerfet's) Letter to perufe, and defire you will return it as foon as poffible, for I have not anfwered it.—If you have the Peruvian Letters, I fhall be glad to fee them.

Mr. Hall ftays for this fcrawl, and only allows me time to fay that

I am, Sir,
Your moft humble fervant, and
Conftant Correfpondent;
I wifh

I wish I could say, in the style of the weekly News-papers,

"*Your constant Reader*,"

H. LUXBOROUGH.

My compliments at Broom; and I hope to see Mr. Joseph Shenstone here.

LETTER XXIII.

SIR, Barrells, Sunday, December 18th, 1748.

THOUGH there were not in the reproofs I took the liberty to give you, the same delicacy as in those the Duchess of Somerset gave me, I may venture to say they arose from the same motive; which I am proud of, and will, I hope, produce the same effect; which will give me great pleasure. Her's have already obliged me to be more than punctual; for I have wrote to her Grace twice in eight days, to atone for having wrote but once in eight months: and you, Sir, have already atoned for all the remissness I accused you of, by the very obliging letter I have received this evening; and by reviving my hopes of seeing you soon at Barrells. It is sufficient, that your not coming or writing sooner, was no way owing to your want of friendship: *that* ensures your pardon; and I find myself now become the penitent sinner, but expect the same pardon; for I am sensible I was too severe (though meant in raillery) when I reprimanded you for not coming or writing into Warwickshire; whereas I ought to have considered I was in another county nine or ten days, and that you could not guess I had left orders to be sent for if you came, or to have your letters brought me if you wrote.—After my return, indeed, Mr. Outing's expectations of seeing you were raised by our not hearing from you; which he attributed to your design of coming here before his return to London; and his expectations raised my hopes; so that the last six days (which was the full time he could allow himself to sojourn here) seemed so many years to him, and made me think the time the longer, though I had not equal reason to grieve at the disappointment, being sustained by hope, whilst he has cause to despair perhaps for many months to come. But really, as he was the aggressor last year, the affair seems to me to be already compromised between you, without

out the least occasion of reference to a third person.

Mr. Allen was here last week, but is gone; so that I cannot make your compliments to him now, but I can answer that he will be glad to make his to you in person, as he has a great esteem for you. He thinks so well of Mr. Whistler's Poem, and is so pleased with most of the thoughts, that he wishes them new dressed, or rather the whole thing revised by some good poet of age more mature than that gentleman's then was, and imagines it worthy of their care.

Permit me to interrupt what I am saying with a curse against crow-pens. If I was to add to the curses in the Service for Ashwednesday, the crows would be loaded with them; or rather, the men who invented putting their quills to this use, which at present gives me intolerable fatigue, and will prevent my saying half of what I would say to you:—How much more friendly are the geese! Mine were all retired to rest before I returned from my devotions at Henley; and I never once thought or imagined that turkies could produce a quill capable of writing so good a hand as your letter is wrote in. Surely the bird you killed for Lord Dudley, and with whose quill you wrote

to me, muſt have been a phœnix in diſguiſe!
How could we have been both ſo elegantly
feaſted by any common bird! If my turkies
carried ſo much wit in their quills, they ſhould
not live till morning, but ſhould be ſacrificed
to you. But if, on the contrary, they can only
convey *my wit*, let *them* live, and let *me* be
ſilent for *your* ſake.—Your want of gilt paper
was no more to be regarded than your want of
a coronet or crown. My want of a pen and
ink is really want of common neceſſaries,
bread or water: yet the fact is ſo, that I can
come at neither that will make what I write
intelligible. All I can do for you is, to make
my letter the ſhorter. But I muſt firſt commend
your intended alterations in your houſe, though
they prolong the time of your abſence. The
room you deſcribe, is of a good dimenſion, as
well as elegant: the library will be the ſame,
and will be a laſting pleaſure to you. It is now
only in embrío: the improving it to the perfection you propoſe, will be a daily amuſement. Your fine proſpects and waters will aſſiſt
you in making every thing round it enchant-
ing: but if you ſhould be as ſenſible of the
beauties of the Leaſowes as your friends are,
they would never be able to get you from it;
and as I ſhould be one of the greateſt ſufferers,

I will

I will not encourage you to like it too much. Yet I may venture to say, that I think the building you send me the sketch of, will be a fine ornament to one of your woods, and your urn a very proper and friendly addition to the other. You say nothing of either of the Sketches, so that I do not know which you have fixed upon: I think those I have marked with 2 and 3, are too common a shape, and would do better in a church than a grove; *that* you have wrote the inscription upon, is a better shape in my eye; but I think the top-ornament not very pretty, though better than the flame in the second. The garland of flowers mends the shape of the third: but I imagine you have fixed on the first, and think it will be very handsome. I do not think the pipe, &c. on the fourth would be ugly if hung by a ribband to the knot which joins the foliage; but I do not so well like the base of the urn: but I speak with great ignorance, and consequently with great submission, which you will say is not always a consequence of ignorance; but it ought to be so, and is so where the ignorant are not by nature fools: *à propos* to which, permit me to say, that I must be a great one, if I think myself capable of criticising upon your writings of any sort.—The elegies you have the goodness to

intrust

intrust to me, shall be as secure as if they were a treasure locked up in an iron chest, and screwed to the floor. I will indulge *myself* whilst they are in my possession, with looking them over; but am incapable of assisting *you*, by giving my judgment upon them: without appearing too humble, I may say this, even without censuring Nature; for there must be some learning as well as common sense, to be able to correct works of that kind: however, if you will do as I have heard some great poet did, (I think, Moliere) who read his Works to his ignorant footman before he published them; judging that what appeared wrong to him was wrong, because it must be unnatural; I may be of about as much use and no more.

Mr. and Mrs. Reynalds wished your company at Aston, when I was there, for a double reason:—their own pleasure, and the pleasure they take in entertaining all their guests with what is most agreeable to their several *tastes*; and they knew your company would be agreeable to *mine*. They do not talk of coming to Barrells at Christmas, nor before the winter is over; but I am persuaded Mr. Reynalds himself would come with speed, if I could let him know when you would be here. It is a journey of only three hours on horseback.—I return thanks

thanks for the Flower Piece, and will read it with pleasure, as you recommend it.

My head-servants are recovered. She who died was a young housemaid. I am obliged to you, Sir, for enquiring.—My five cows continue well, though every body's cows die round them. I look upon it as a peculiar blessing to me, who am indebted to them for perfect health. I eat heartily, grow too fat, and have not tasted wine, beer, nor cyder, these two months or more.—I am now busy in planting the lane that joins the coppice, and have chosen my trees according to my years. The abele is what I plant; which in four years time will produce multitudes of setts, and grow to be a good shade. Sir Robert Cocks has sent me an hundred or two of them as a present.

My compliments attend Mr. Shenstone and the family at Broome: Mr. Hall's attend you, —and I am inviolably

Your sincere friend and servant,

H. L.

LETTER XXIV.

Barrells, January 4th, 1748-9, Nine at Night.

SIR,

I RECEIVED your letter of the 30th ult. this evening, in my bed; to which I was confined by a nervous fever. I could not even read it; for I had not seen day-light since the sun set, the evening before; which tedious time was not once indulged with sweet repose. I am now up, and think it should be morning; but as yet, there appears to me as much irregularity in time as there is in my pulse, and as you are sure to find in my letter; especially as it is wrote under these circumstances. I imagined I could not hold a pen, and I find it only possible by intervals. I have however remembered the late rough notes of my croaking crow enough to reject the assistance of his quill, and have recourse to the goose to return the compliments you make me, imagining the quill of that bird would favour me as it did you: but I am disappointed; she is still stupid; and her sister, who served you so well, must have been bred at Paris, if one judges by her politeness: and if you have ever employed her in the Poetical Pieces you have sent me, I shall think she has studied at Parnassus.—Why must the silly look of the goose entitle her to be the emblem of nothing but stupidity, when the more silly gravity of the owl allows him to be the emblem of wisdom? Henceforward I shall prefer geese to all other of the feathered kind: at least, the geese of the Leasowes.

I am glad your parlour wants no more to finish it than stucco. Mr. Wright of Worcester stucco'd my Summer-house; which is well done, as to workmanship. Where more elegance is required, he employs an Italian under him. They did the new work at Warwick Castle, at the Priory, and the inside of the Temple at Lord Archer's.

Mr. Smith's letter to you, Sir, is exceeding polite; and I rejoice that he looks upon the Leasowes in the light that place appears to me: my vanity is indulged by it, as is my constant desire to perform what is agreeable to you, since he seems so well pleased that the Duchess of Somerset's name should be added to his list, and that I have had the good fortune to procure it. Her Grace has been very ill, and is far from being recovered, though she did me the

honour

honour to write me a compliment of condolence upon the death of Lord St. John, my Brother (at Naples) which she says she did, *knowing that I ever write benefits on a rock, but injuries on sand.* I have, indeed, in this very instance, felt that she does me justice; for the news of his death, which my Brother Bolingbroke wrote last Monday sevennight, was the first cause of my disorder.—I have been disabled from reading over your Elegies with the attention *I* could wish and *they* do merit; but I am well persuaded, they will please better judges, as they do me; and that they want but little of the assistance of those judges to make them as perfect as yourself and your friends can desire. I confess, the length of the Preface gave me some pain, lest the impatience of many readers might make them lay down the book before they got to what *that* is meant to introduce them to: and in some persons it may raise scruples as to the propriety of the Elegies; which they would not ever have thought of objecting to, as it is a kind of dissertation upon that species of poetry; and might perhaps (if necessary at all) be better printed as such after the Elegies. The many tedious and bad prefaces that have fatigued the world, may have perhaps caused a dislike to such introductions,

however

however perfect they may be, and made them be condemned by numbering the pages, rather than by reading them; and whether they are right or wrong in doing so, I believe all writers are under a sort of necessity of submitting to the fashion of the times, or of renouncing applause, even when they best deserve it: and that *that* should be your case, who deserve so much, would be a concern to all your friends, and to none more than to me. I confess, I was doubtful if I ought to object to this preface to yourself, though I thought as I now write about it; but was diffident of my judgment, till you mentioned an intention of curtailing it at least. The seventh Elegy I like as well as any I have had time to look over, and was the more inclined to read it, as you had Lord Beauchamp in view in the latter part; but I am apt to think the Duchess would rather be *hurt* than *pleased* at the application of it, because the late Duke was so barbarous as to say that she sent her *son* over to kill him.—Might not the intention and the sense of the Elegy end as properly at the fourteenth stanza " the beauties " of Britannia's mind?" Perhaps I talk very foolishly; for my small genius (if ever I had any) is grown rusty for want of opportunities of using, and of brightening it, by conversation:

G and

and my imagination has been robbed of every fpark of fire by the fever, to kindle a flame in my blood and fcorch my body, whilft my thoughts freeze: yet it has left in my heart enough warmth to keep friendfhip alive as long as I exift. And as long as that is, you will be fure, Sir, of having

A moft fincere friend
and humble fervant in
H. LUXBOROUGH.

I depend upon your promife of coming foon to Barrells; for the fymptoms of my illnefs are not fuch as threaten its duration, or my death.

Saturday.

P. S. Mr. John Reynalds has lain here one night fince you wrote to me; and fays he will fly from Afton to Barrells at your call. Mr. Hall will have equal pleafure in feeing you, and lefs way to come. Mr. Allen has been immured in minced pies, (as I fuppofe) and has devoutly paid his homage to *his* god *Whift* fo long, that his devotion (like that of other bigots) has made him forget his friends, and every worldly duty, beyond the limits of his parifh: fo that I have not feen him, but am perfuaded he is not yet fo *hardened* in his *ido-*
latry

fairy, but he will be recalled the moment you come to convert him; which I the more readily answer for, as the twelve days are now over.

You are to remark, that though my letter was wrote on the 4th instant, my Postscript is not wrote till the 7th at night: and I have the pleasure to tell you, I am recovered from my indisposition, and wait impatiently for your company, and will keep the Elegies safe till then.

You had no need to make an excuse for *grouping* many subjects in the last short page of your letter; for a good master knows how to put every object in its most advantageous light, though they were ever so numerous, and to place them so, that the more closely connected, the more pleasing the groupe, and the more is the judgment of the artist admired, who with his pencil cannot exceed your quill.

LETTER XXV.

Barrells, Ash-Wednesday.

IT is true, Sir, *life is chequered*, and with great exactness too. I have often thought it, and now experience it: for your letter was delivered to me last Friday at noon, and gave me exquisite pleasure; and that same evening I was seized with exquisite pain in my right foot, which for three days continued raging, and would make me rave, if I did not think it Justice Divine: for to me to be denied the power to *walk*, is as great a punishment as it is to some (Outing for instance) to be obliged to *ride*. Many perhaps in my case would vainly *blame the Powers above*; but I allow their *dispensation* to be just: for a more moderate pain would not have been adequate to the pleasure your letter, and the Verses inclosed, afforded me. Do not think this a poetical fancy; for if such in *prose*, it would deserve the name of impertinent affectation,—the thing I most despise: but seriously, I am quite lame; and though the pain is gone off, the swelling remains so as to oblige me to wear a man's shoe,

shoe, and consequently the confinement remains, which is less supportable to me than the pain; for I am so unknowing in the science of amusing myself without walking about, that I can scarcely write a line when my standish is brought me, because I did not fetch it myself:—Such is habit! but such also is the order of Providence; and I submit without repining.—Hope assists me greatly upon this occasion; for as you promise to send me soon some more of your poetical performances, I already fancy my pain turned into pleasure.—Had I been a lover of money rather than an admirer of wit, I should have founded my hopes upon the notion some of my neighbours have, that my lameness is the gout, that distemper being as it is said generally accompanied with riches; but I neither believe nor wish them to be in the right. I am sure I am not rich, nor should I be if Peru was mine; and I am as sure, I would not willingly suffer an hour of pain to become so; yet I would suffer many such without murmuring, to hear the conversation or read the sentiments of those I esteem, and who express their thoughts with elegance.

Now I leave my gout and my morals, to hobble into my study for Ware's Book of Inigo Jones's

Jones's Defigns; and fhall be glad to fee what you will execute from the ideas they may give you. And when every body admires it, I fhall perhaps boaft that I helped you (though at the third or fourth hand) to that idea, by lending you the book; as you might boaft of helping me to a found foot if you fhould fend me a crutch. May I never want crutches till you want bright ideas, is the felf-interefted wifh of,

Sir,

Your obliged

and moft humble fervant,

H. LUXBOROUGH.

All I can fay in excufe for Parfon Hall, is, that, notwithftanding his garb, he is rather forgetful than revengeful.—I fent the letter you wrote him about your bufts inclofed to Mr. Outing.

Have you feen what Dodfley has lately publifhed? viz. Bolingbroke's Tracts, Fitzofborne's Letters, and three volumes of Poetical Mifcellanies: I think he calls it a Collection of Poems; fome are old, fome middle-aged, and none I believe quite new; but are

all

all such as deserve to be distinguished and preserved. Your School-mistress is among them. The Tracts you have read often in single pamphlets of flying sheets. Fitzosborne's Letters I never saw before, nor ever heard of the gentleman; but they are exceeding pretty, in my mind.

LETTER XXVI.

SIR, Barrells, March 23d, 1748-9.

YOUR great punctuality in returning the books has prevented my sending a servant to thank you for your visit; which I may do with infinitely more justice than you can thank me for my *reception*, which was far from deserving to have the word *elegant* joined to it: the word *hearty* is the utmost it could claim, and *that* I may venture to insure for as long as my life lasts; for till *that* ceases, my sincerity will not cease; and my esteem for you, Sir, in particular, I am certain never will. But I always wish to enliven that *heavy* idea which the word *hearty* conveys, by some entertainment agreeable to your taste, whenever

ever you favour me with a visit: but, alas!. I have had as many disappointments in my wishes as any person ever had, during several years of my life, I also find one in this last desire; for the weather, or my spirits, or both, are generally depressed when I wish them gayest; and my solitude is commonly more strict when I wish it to be varied, by the arrival of some merry companion or other to entertain me and my friends: yet I might live at least five hundred years in this place before one quarter of the incidents happened which are related in any one of the six volumes of Tom Jones. I have not yet read the two last; but I think as you do, that no one character yet is near so striking as Adams's in the author's other composition, and the plan seems far-fetched; but in the adventures that happen, I think he produces personages but too like those one meets with in the world; and even among those people to whom he gives good characters, he shews them as in a concave glass, which discovers blemishes that would not have appeared to the common eye, and may make every modest reader fear to look in such a glass, as some do who have been beauties, and would choose to fancy themselves so still. The Beauty herself might shun it equally; for

that

that fort of glafs would not flatter, and defects would appear, as there is no perfection in us mortals.—If Mr. Fielding and Mr. Hogarth could abate the vanity of the world by fhewing its faults fo plainly, they would do more than the greateft divines have yet been capable of: But human nature will ftill be the fame, and would, I am afraid, furnifh them, if they lived till the world ended, with fuch imperfect objects to reprefent.

I thank you, Sir, for Irene, and as much for giving me your opinion, which I look upon as a fure guide with which I may travel through it with fafety and profit. I hear it is not much liked at London; but though the Public are far from being in general unjuft judges, they are apt to condemn or commend too fuddenly; and, if one thing difpleafes, to be difpleafed with the whole; and the fame, when one thing happens to pleafe; their praife and their condemnation being in extremes: and they often damn a play for one fingle fault, or extol it for a fingle beauty.

I fend you a book for your bookbinder's pattern: but as to your wax, you are (for the firft time in your life) a little *ungenerous* in challenging me to match its colour; you might as well bid me match the *vermeille of the rofe*,

or

or the *vermeille* of one of the French *Chanoine's* cheeks, such as Boileau was so well acquainted with. Is not the wax of your creating?

There wants no novelty to make the Leasowes agreeable. If you ceased absolutely to add to it, it would still be new; Nature would furnish it with never-dying charms; but I know you cannot help assisting it, so that I shall discover some unconfessed beauty which you will seem careful to hide, when I next pay my annual visit and acknowledgments to you.—If any thing is done here, it will be owing to the advice you are so kind to give me.—I doubt whether I rightly understand in what manner you would have *the Hermitage become part of the shrubbery, by means of about three yards of shrubbery on the outside of my lime-walk?* I should be glad to make this connection; but will it not lay my garden open to the field through which passes a foot-road to Henley? and yet, according to your advice, might I not plant that straight walk, which is now gravelled, full of shrubs, and not let it lead to the Hermitage, but return in a serpentine manner one of my crooked sand-walks beyond the Ha! Ha! so as to meet the walk which is bordered by servicetrees and fenced with rails, and does lead in a curve to the Hermitage; in which walk might also

also be shrubs and a serpentine sand-passage? This could be done, but I question if it is your meaning. The cause of my doubt is your saying *behind* the Lime-walk; whereas I have no limes but from the Pheasant Yards to the White Gate that leads to the Field; and *behind* those limes is only the lane which is much below the garden, and is lately planted with abeles: the walk in the field which immediately leads to the Shrubbery is planted with *service-trees*. Set me right when I hear from you next.—I cannot venture to put up my pavillion this summer, unless you extend your kindness so far as to come over in the warm season for a few days, to instruct me and my workmen; for I am persuaded they will err, though Mr. Hands the Joiner will perform his part well, in laying out the ground as he has done in the woodwork; but the Masons I shall never manage, nor be able even to instruct; and as to the planting round, I think to defer that till the latter season, but in the mean time make the short Ha! Ha! on the green, and plant the two elms on each side the walk before the house-gate, which I will do.

Mr. Holyoak went last Sunday to preach for Mr. Allen, and found him surprizingly better. I will give him the pleasure of knowing

ing you enquired after him.—I wrote Mr. Hall word that you did him the same favour; and I inclose what he writes me in a postscript.

The north-east wind has prevented my walking out till this day, when a false report of its being changed hurried me out; but I had too much courage to retreat, and I do not perceive any ill effects from it.—The Spring shews at least the beauties of childhood; for there are plenty of snowdrops, primroses, polyanthuses, and even violets, which promise more sweets. I hope you will smell them before the hated Autumn robs them of their perfume.

I am

Your ever faithful servant,

H. LUXBOROUGH.

P. S. As to Mr. Hall's affair, he had a laudable ambition to have you write an inscription to perpetuate his Father's memory. You said you knew him so little, you desired I would give you some hints to guide you; but I knew him not at all, nor ever saw him in my life. The general character I have heard, was that of an honest man, a faithful steward, and withal

withal knowing; so that his advice was often asked and followed with success; and he was careful of his family and prudent. More I know not; but once read a letter of his writing upon an accidental affair, which was a little intricate, and observed in it much prudence, judgment, calmness, yet not unfeeling calmness, and much delicacy of sentiment; from which letter I judged the better of his heart and head; yet it was written in the evening of his life, and when a private misfortune had ruffled him and lowered his spirits. Since that, I have only heard that he was lamented by many; and you know how much his son was affected with it; and his zeal and affection for his father makes him wish more should be said of him than barely that he lived and died, and with something more elegance than the common form of what the sexton writes on a gravestone; but he does not desire flattery or flourishes. According to this, and to obey your commands, I have wrote down a kind of specimen, which I beg you to peruse, and reject or alter, or amend, as you shall see proper. As to the first line, I am dubious if I should have it or not to begin, "Here lie," &c. which may be too common and dry; and yet the other may for

what

what I know appear too flourishing. If it was to be set up in Westminster Abbey, I think I should venture it; but to the readers in Tanworth Church-yard, perhaps it will not appear that the Reverence here meant is only as to an honest man.

I can only add my excuses for pretending to put my hints into any method, which I should have left to you; but I considered the Green Book might be at a stand, whilst your thoughts were employed on this Epitaph.—Thus self-love works even on the most *disinterested*, which I thought *I* was; but find myself mistaken when interest points to me a method of obtaining any of your Works; which in this case I do at the expence of my friend Mr. Hall, who will have me, instead of you, to plan his father's monument; and I am quite unequal to the task. Pray burn it or mend it; and for his sake write another, or add a few lines to this.

Pray write an answer for Thursday next.—Pity my hurry, and excuse my scrawl.—Compliments to your Brother.

Pray do not forget the Green Book.

LETTER XXVII.

SIR, May-day, 1749.

I HAVE no more than time to let you know that I had your book first and your letter after, very safe; and to thank you for your little sketch of alterations in my Shrubbery. In order to follow it, I have begun by taking down the styles, that no foot-road may prevent the execution of what we propose; and am ungravelling the lime-walk and laying mold on it; which is the whole that can be done till the planting season. In the mean time, I have finished my lower garden, by turning the seven grass-plats that were in the shape of Lord Mayor's Custards, into one large one; and have widened the gravel-walk round from five feet and a half to twelve feet and a half broad. As to the court, the pallisades are removed, the end-walls built, the turf taken away, the slopes made more gentle, the pillars removed to the extremities of the pallisades, and the sun-dial is set in the middle, and the court levelled, raised, and gravelled; the two gates are making. The upper garden is ungravelled, and
is

is making into a bowling-green; the pavillion will be set up next, and the white pales taken away from the wall-side of the stable-court to enlarge that in autumn: the way to the Coppice will be altered according to your directions; and I hope then you will be so kind as to assist me; for it is impossible for you at a distance to judge so well as on the place.—I do not know if you would have the little gates left or no at each end of the Service Walk, though they are to be hid with shrubs. I propose coming into the Coppice from the Service-Walk at the farther end between the Chairs that overlook the Pit, and the farther corner of the Wood beyond what answers to the top of the Hermitage Pit.

I wish for Mr. Hall's sake you would make a new Epitaph; for mine is scarcely worth your retouching. There is one line in particular I do not like: I think it is,

"As a friendly Counsellor he gain'd Affection."

The word *Esteem* I believe is not used in the whole; though I really forget: but in short, I like none of that line; and very little of any part of the thing.

Mr. Williams has been darkening the ground of his performance in my library, so that I must

must scrawl this over in a strange manner, to give him time to return home. Excuse me therefore, and believe me to be

Your ever obliged, humble servant,

H. LUXBOROUGH.

LETTER XXVIII.

Barrells, Sunday, June 4th, 1749.
SIR, From my Chimney-corner.

YOUR approbation rewards amply the pains I have taken lately in following my workmen, and adds a relish to the pleasure I take in endeavouring to improve the environs of my cottage. My pavilion is finished all to tiling and flooring. I believe I shall be obliged to pen it in with pales to keep off beasts of all kinds; those in human shape chiefly: but the fence will be hid in time with a hedge, and the building shaded behind with trees, and on the sides by shrubs. The Ha! Ha! is digging.——The court has been honoured with Mrs. Kendall's coach and six, which found room sufficient.

The bowling-green begins to look tolerably green since this late rain, which I hope will join the turfs perfectly. The Abele Walk, and that which was gravel, will be filled in the planting season, and the Serpentines altered to lead to the Coppice; but the manner of it I shall leave to your direction, hoping to see you long before that time here, especially as Mr. Dolman does me the favour to propose making me a visit whilst my Shrubbery is in beauty; which ought to be now: but it is still winter here! It is true, there are various shrubs well blown, but it is so cold and wet, one cannot walk to see them; and on the dry days the winds are so high, that it is equally disagreeable, and the flowers droop towards the ground when scarcely full blown.—You seem destined never to see the embroidery Nature bestows upon my Coppice in Spring; where we had even this year great variety of cowslips, primroses, ragged-robins, wild hyacinths both white and blue, violets, &c. &c. In the Shrubbery, I think the finest ornament is the large bushes of Whitsun-roses, which are still in blow, and give one an idea of snow-balls this cold weather. The lilac is already over, and has given place to the syringa; of which I have enough to perfume the place with the help of the sweet-briar;

briar; and several of my roses are in blow. If this and the next week should prove more like summer than the last, I shall wish you and Mr. Dolman would come.—Mrs. Reynalds from Gloucestershire is now with me, and desires her compliments to you, and will be glad to see you here. Her husband is to come on Tuesday to stay here the rest of this week. She will stay here during the next week also; but the week after that, I expect Mrs. Meredith from London; and how many she may bring with her I cannot tell.—Outing will either be at Jacky Reynalds's next week, and come here at your call; or else he will come here with Mrs. Meredith for a few days, and go from hence to Jacky Reynalds's, where he will be all summer, except when he is here.—Parson Allen is well, and will meet you at any time.—Mr. Hall is happy in the hopes you give of touching the Epitaph; and I am proud that you think it worth your attention enough to mend some parts of it.—I am glad your bookseller has improved upon mine. In France, when they gild the edges, (which they do better than us) they marble that gilding with faint colours, which looks very pretty.—Those persons who cannot find pleasure in trifles, are generally wise in their own opinions, and fools in the opinion of the wife, as they neglect the opportunities of amusement, without which the rugged road of life would be insupportably tedious. I think the French are the best philosophers, who make the most they can of the pleasures, and the least they can of the pains of life; and are ever strewing flowers among the thorns all mortals are obliged to walk through; whereas, by much reflection, the English contrive to see and feel the thorns double, and never see the flowers at all, but to despise them; expecting their happiness from things more solid and durable, as they imagine: but how seldom do they find them! One meets indeed with disappointments in trifles; but they are easier borne: yet I confess I was much concerned last week at the disaster which befel my poultry, and found myself punished for my presumption in daring all my neighbours to produce such fine turkies as mine, of which I had thirty-seven, and six of them were fit to eat; whereas a polecat fetched away twenty in one night, and eight at three in the afternoon next day, and sucked the eggs of the turkies, ducks, and chickens, and (what vexed me more upon your account) of the Guinea Hens.

Mr. Hall tells me that Lord Archer asked him at London, ten days ago, (though he was but

but an hour with him) what you and I thought of his obelisk?—My bricklayer promises to alter the Niches this week. My stone-mason mistook the breadth of the two steps up to the pavilion exactly half, so that I have been obliged to have them pieced, which is ugly.—Mr. Williams has darkened the ground of the chimney-piece, but cannot alter the shades without new doing the whole.—I keep Langley's Book till you come to pick out some serpentine-walks. I wish his ideas had been more confined, or my territories less so. Is it not the same Langley who published very pretty Designs for Pavement? Mr. Belson got some executed with a shade of black, white, and brown small pebbles.—The Duchess of Somerset has a floor to a pavilion in all coloured small pebbles, placed so as to look like a Persian carpet.—Somebody in Hampshire has a dead fawn or deer represented in pebbles at the door of a grotto in a park; but Langley's are only regular geometrical figures.

The thunder interrupts me, and it is church-time; so I hasten to release you. I hope you will answer this by word of mouth, and believe me to be, Sir,

Your ever faithful servant,

H. Luxborough.

I send one of your books.—As the prisoners in gaol repeat " Pray remember the poor;" so, I do " Pray remember the Green Book."— Compliments to your Brother, and your friends at Broom.

LETTER XXIX.

Barrells, June 24th, 1749, past Eleven at Night.
SIR,

I OUGHT to have thanked you sooner for yours, of the 3d, which, as I suppose, crossed mine upon the road: but in mine I told you I hoped for your answer, by word of mouth, to view my Shrubbery with Mr. Dolman; after which ensued the most stormy weather I ever knew, which destroyed all my *Summer* schemes, and left me no comfort but the hopes of converting you to my opinion of giving to *Autumn* the preference over Summer. —As to *Spring*, the beauties of it are entirely banished our hemisphere; and you will be obliged to owe to my favourite season every ray of sun unshaded by a cloud, or impending shower, that you have enjoyed this season. That is also a season which gives me one annual

day

day of pleasure at least, as it invites me to the Leasowes, or rather, as I naturally point to it, and you are so kind to receive me, and give the Nereids (your Maids of Honour) orders to do it in the most elegant manner; and no commands were ever better obeyed. I have no such servants as those aquatic nymphs; and even my terrestrial slaves scorn to obey me: nay, I fear I am not even heard by the aërial beings, since they so seldom favour me with a smile. The rains have made my roses droop before their time; but several sorts have made their appearance, and have died in their prime: others are coming on; but I fear my Shrubbery must lose more than it is possible to gain by the ensuing season, however fine the weather may be.

I have been obliged to put off the visit designed me by Mrs. Meredith and two of her daughters next week, and our friend Outing, with them, because I expect my own daughter and Mr. Wymondesold (her husband), and do not know but their attendants may be numerous; and my house is not adapted to receive numbers of people. It is true, one might be supposed to make free with a daughter; but my case is peculiar. She is now nineteen years old, and I never lay under the same roof with her

her since she was only six; and her husband I never saw in my life, and have only heard that he is an exceeding good-natured man, and have seen that he writes very sensible letters to me; but further of his character I do not know. He is used to very fine seats, &c. of his father's, and here he will meet a cottage in comparison. What stay they make I know not; but will acquaint you when I know; hoping then for your company, Mr. Dolman's, and Outing's.—Mrs. Reynalds spent a fortnight with me, and flattered herself you would come at the same time. *Jacky* was part of that time here.

I had a letter last post from the Duchess of Somerset, which being less than usual in the rural style, I should not send you, but that I think you will like the design she mentions of a stove in the Chapel; so I send her letter, which you will return.—Twenty or thirty thousand pounds laid out at Northumberland House, will be a kind of Roman vanity, and contribute to the beauty of that part of the city of London, and to the conveniency of the populace in particular, if the Strand is widened.

I saw to-day in the London Evening Post a letter, which reflects upon my Brother B———ke,
in

in regard to Mr. P——pe's treachery to him; in which the blame seems to be thrown from him upon my Brother. I have not yet seen any one thing more that has been published concerning it, except a Preface in a Magazine in his favour, the truth of which I could attest; and have often wondered he could so long stifle the abominable usage he met with from P——pe in printing his Work, which he had intrusted to him to review, intending that it should not be published till after his own death. The letters between P——pe and the Printer, bargaining for the price, were found by Lord Marchmont, whose business it was, by P——pe's last *Will*, to look over his papers jointly with Lord Bol————ke: but as to the subject of the book, I know nothing of it; nor is that to the purpose, as to P——pe's baseness to the best of friends; without whom he had never shone in the Essay on Man.

I like extremely your Weekly Verses, and should value greatly a collection of them. Pray favour me once a week with the lines of the day.—As to the preservation of your flowers, I fear those you sent me will not keep the people that read them from gathering as many as usual, unless it should make them dread the resentment of Fairies and *Hobgoblins*, which
undoubtedly

undoubtedly they have formed a perfect notion of, though your reasoning and your lines will not be understood by them; but if you once persuade them you can conjure up spirits by your pen, I think you may be secure in your grott from all intruders, and see your Shrubbery prosper unmolested.

Pardon me for differing with you in opinion. You are not the idle man of the creation. You may be busied to the benefit of society without stirring from your seat, as much as the mischievous man with seeming idleness may be busied in the destruction of it. You give innocent pleasure to yourself, and instruction as well as pleasure to others, by the amusements you follow. Your pen, your pencil, your taste, and your sincere unartful conduct in life (which are the things that make you appear idle) give such an example, as it were to be wished might be more generally followed—few have the capacity, fewer have the honesty to spend their time so usefully, as well as unblameably.

Your little Gothic Bench I admire. I hope you will execute it at the low price you mention, with your own timber; and properly placed, it will be a far more perfect thing than

our

our famous restorer of the Gothic style in building (Mr. Miller) has yet given us.

I am to dine at Lord Archer's next Tuesday, when I shall see the Obelisk, and be a better judge how it appears from the saloon it is seen from: Mr. Hall, you know, thinks it appears from thence too taper. Talking of Mr. Hall, I must tell you that he desires his best compliments, best thanks, &c. &c. and acknowledges he ought to have wrote to you, and would do it now, but he has been, and still is, very much out of order. He rode in one fortnight seven or eight hundred miles; to Bath one day; to London two days after; lay there but one night, and away to Rugby; upon several Rosinantes who plunged him in the waters or on the sharp stones: his view was a good living: he was the ninth competitor, and since that has two more that follow him in their hopes or pretences. I do not find it is decided who shall have it; but one thing is certain, that riding so hard, and in bad roads and bad weather, heated his blood, threw him into a high fever, and he is now moving about in a more limited sphere, but clogged with half a fever at least. In this condition he was unable to consider of the lines you were so kind to send; but just read the

three

three Epitaphs over, commended in general, and was thankful for your kind attention, then retired to his physic, &c. hoping to regain more equal spirits than his are at present, and a more *steady* pulse, which I tell him may make his head more *steady*; and he hopes as much, that he may be able to talk over this little affair with you, Sir, and me at Barrells. If his pursuit after *trash* (which he himself despises) should cause him very ill health, how might you hug yourself in your idleness!—But to return to his Father's Epitaph, (though I think it would be our best way to make his first) I am persuaded I have wrote what wants much amendment; and shews your *hesitations* (as you politely call them) to be very just. As to the second line, I believe Mr. John Hall may afford a better cadence; but I rather thought the simple name (as you do) more elegant; and I find my Brother Bolingbroke's Epitaph for Daniel Pulteney is the same in that particular, there being neither *Mr.* nor *Esquire*. In the same Epitaph is also

" The Loss of so much Private Virtue
" Is a Public Calamity."

Your word *Extensive*, substituted in the place of

of *Large*, is certainly better. I believe the jingle of *Large* and *Small* caught me; and I also believe " *renders his death*" would be better: but whether so much exactness in grammar is expected in this kind of writing as in plain prose, you are the best judge. The word *Example*, in the 13th line, was *Experience* in the copy I kept at home, and was a slip of my pen in transcribing. *Nature* and *Judgment* may not be altogether proper to be contra-distinguished; but I do not know how to mend it to please me: *Temper* is not more to be distinguished from Nature; and in short, these three lines puzzle me. *Diffused* may be put to advantage, I think, (as you observe) instead of *Dispersed*, in the fourteenth line. *Skill* and *Prudence*, as you say, may be understood as not enough opposite, though I think they are a good deal so:—might not one say

" Skill equal to his disinterested Fidelity."

In the nineteenth line, *Esteem* instead of *Respect*, we both agree in. I do not well know as to the doubt you make, whether they are peculiar enough to each, but am again at a stand for words to change those for. -As to the twentieth, twenty-first, and twenty-second lines, Mr. Hall desired me, soon after I sent you the copy,

copy; to leave them out entirely. I should choose to leave out, as you observe, "*The Rich Bless'd:*" might it not be

> The Poor blest, the Oppressor fear'd him;
> Nor did those who envy'd presume to censure his Reputation:

or else,

> Nor did Envy's Breath presume to censure his Reputation.

Because if I said, *those who envy'd*, it might imply that somebody did; which I do not know. *Zeal* being placed after *Affection*, is certainly better, for the reason you observe; and must be so, if used at all. But upon the whole, I would have Mr. Hall take one of the three copies entire, as you was so kind to send; and I suppose he will, when he is restored to his health, sense, and judgment; before which, or then at least, I hope we shall talk it over in one of my cells, or under my new pavilion, which he calls *too low*. If it had been higher, it must have been in proportion too broad for the walk, and must have cost me a great deal by a lead covering; and my house would have appeared lower than my pavilion. It is, to be sure, small, but the plan in the book is not above seven inches deeper, and the front is the same length

length as in the book.—I keep your Book of Serpentines; for I long for your contriving the entrance into my grotto. In the mean time, I keep off all the intruders from their old way to Henley, and have given them a better, which shuts their mouths; and none clamber over the hedges but those who are not yet apprized of the alteration. Sir Robert Cocks has as many hundred abeles ready for me as I can wish, against the busy month of October next.

It is just come into my mind, Sir, that you love good writing, good impressions to seals, and all other proper decorations of a letter: I ought therefore to secrete mine, and neither send it, nor ever let you know that I was capable of intending to send such a scrawl: but I consider *this* must go or none; for I never made a copy of a letter in my life, and my hand and pen being upon the gallop, will stumble sometimes. If this excuse will not do, you shall have the next as *prim* as Lord S———d's cravat (so celebrated); but it will not be half a quarter so long. Let me know your taste against the next, and believe that (though I scrawl it over in a slovenly manner) my paper conveys the most friendly sentiments, and those of esteem and value, which I must

have

have whilst I live for you, Sir, who deserve them so well.

H. LUXBOROUGH.

LETTER XXX.

SIR,   Sunday, August 20th, 1749.

AS I believe you sincere in the impatience you express to visit me at Barrells, I hope you will be so just as to believe me equally impatient to receive you here, and doubly disappointed that a continuation of your disorder should occasion our not meeting at the times appointed.—For God's sake, do not venture a journey too soon; yet come as soon as you can. The nature of your illness gives me pain; your frequent relapses increase it; but the strength of your constitution, the opinion of your faithful servant Tom, and the spirit I perceive in your letters, give me pleasure, and encourage me to hope a speedy as well as certain cure; and consequently that the next week will be as favourable to me as I imagined, and was persuaded *this* would have been.

been. Mr. Outing's being here added to my
defire it fhould happen fo. I put nobody off
upon your account; fo be eafy. My houfe,
though fmall, will never deny me a place for
you and your friends, whom I look upon as
mine.—I beg my compliments to Mr. and Mifs
Dolman; and need not add, that their company will be always agreeable to me, as well as
your Brother's.

How pleafed fhould I be if I could help you
to a proper Motto for your Gothic Building,
which even Spenfer has denied you in your
prefent fearch! You could eafily fupply his
deficiency, and I dare fay you would do it to
advantage in his own language. You have
fhewn yourfelf capable of *that* already: fo,
without putting him or me to the blufh, make
an *old* Englifh Motto as you have made a
Gothic Building, and you will be approved
by the moderns, and envied by the ancients.

As to the lines you defire me to write in
my own hand upon one of your fkreens, I
am ready to do it; for I fear not the cenfure
of thofe who may read them, let the multitude
be ever fo great, fince you have read them,
and have not difapproved: but I never yet
was fo puzzled in making my judgment and
yours tally. I conceive them to be *bad*, but

I you

you say they are *good*; therefore I *err*, and perhaps *I err* in saying that the fourth line, filled with monosyllables, is an exceeding bad one. I shall submit the moment you speak; but in the mean time imagine, that

"Preserving still their Parents beauteous Face,"

might be as well as what I wrote before, if not better. All I wish about it is, that you will believe me sincere, even in rhime; and that I long for an opportunity of scrawling over your seat at the Leasowes with my pencil, and of shewing you (as well as Mr. and Miss Dolman, and Mr. Joseph Shenstone) at Barrells, that I am, *sans cérémonie*, but with the greater truth,

Yours sincerely,

H. LUXBOROUGH.

P. S. I should not be grateful for the civilities I received from my Lord Dudley, particularly for his invitation to me to lie at the Grange when you was ill, and his invitation to me to dine there when you was well again; if I neglected sending my compliments to him: and hope you will permit me to do so here.

I saw Mr. Hall and Mr. Allen last night, who

who enquired after you. I heard the former preach to-day, but did not speak to him; so could not make your compliments.

LETTER XXXI.

Barrells, August 29th, 1749.
Tuesday Night.

SIR,

YESTERDAY and To-day have been spent by Mr. Outing and myself in looking out to spy you coming towards us: but we looked in vain; and our flattering hopes begin to give place to unwelcome despair, which is aggravated by the apprehensions of a fresh relapse of your illness, and is the cause of my sending a servant to enquire after your health; of which I hope to hear a good account; but rather wish to see it in your person, and to hear it from your own mouth.

Mr. Hall came yesterday in the evening to kiss your hands, but found Outing and me lamenting your absence; one seated on a turf, the other on a stone at the Hermitess's door, who has acquired a new bed, which may hold not only you, if your colic should oblige you

you to lie down, but also all the agreeable company I hope to see with you. It is the Bed of Ware, the vulgar say: our friend Outing says it is only a sociable bed for two hermits and two hermitesses: but I am not in the humour to joke whilst I suppose you ill. Relieve me pray from my pain, and believe me to be faithfully and inviolably

Your most obliged

H. LUXBOROUGH.

Compliments from us to Mr. Joseph Shenstone, and Mr. and Miss Dolman.

Mr. John Reynolds was coming here from Afton to meet you, but being disabled by a fall from his horse, hopes (as he writes word to Outing) to see you there.

P. S. I send you (as a sick man) six Guineahen's eggs for your supper, out of about as many more which I could have sent you, and would, but that the learned assure me they will come to nothing if set so late in the year; whereas the few remaining in the nest may entice the hen to lay more for your suppers at Barrells.—For want of a proper place for my poultry, or rather for want of a careful
Mrs.

Mrs. Arnold, I have reared but one single Guinea-chick this year.—If I had such a command of corn and of water as you have, I should be apt to fall into the expence of a Ménagerie; and as well as I love pine-apples, would prefer it to a hot-house.

I beg my humble service to Lord Dudley, and Mr. Outing his respects.

LETTER XXXII.

SIR, Battells, September 8th, 1749.

I AM doubtful whether I should write to you now, as I may expect you are upon the road hither; for Litchfield Races have, as I imagine, left Mr. Dolman at liberty ere this; and your disorder has I hope left you free to pursue your inclinations, which Mr. Outing and I are vain enough to believe would lead you hither. If he denied it, he would not gain credit, as all his friends well know he has put off other journies upon that account; and if I denied it, I am sure I should be unjust to you, who shew so much partial favour

vour to me and my habitation. This fact therefore being laid down as certain, joined to your not having wrote on Saturday last, as you promised, creates in me some fears, lest your illness should have returned upon you, or not have left you long enough for you to trust yourself from home. If this should be the case, I shall be doubly disappointed: yet I cannot blame you for choosing to be in your own house, when confined to a house, and on your own bed, when constrained to lay on one at hours when one most wishes and most expects to be able to converse with one's friends, viz. after meals, which are the most sociable hours in life, when one is blest with friends and health to enjoy them. But, Sir, since blankets and white-wine-whey have not cured you under the care of physicians, I ought not to suppose I could perform that wished-for task; and yet I will answer for it, that were you at Barrells, you would not be tempted to transgress the rules prescribed by those physicians, no more than you would be by the Persian Rice and Sherbet you mention; and that might be one step towards a cure. You would find no costly viands here; and as for liberty, which you say you must have to eat what you have *not* a

mind

mind to, you should have it; but as for liberty to eat what you *have* a mind to, you should *not* have it: so pray do not think when you come here, that your steps

"—— to the Huxter's fav'ry Cottage tend;"

for were I the uncontrouled dame that awed you with birchen power, you should not find that I greeted you with such cates, as, by indulging your taste, might pamper your illness; nor should you walk out in unwholesome fogs or dews, nor have I power to walk you round the margin of brooks and fountains if I would: so that, in short, you would be here as insipidly safe as ever Valetudinarian was in the closest retreat.

The lines you sent me I like greatly; but since Mr. Lyttelton objects to the two first lines of the last stanza, and that you do not seem much pleased with them, what if you were to write on your Gothic Seat only the two first stanzas, which are unexceptionable? for though the " *Beechen Bowl,*" &c. is well expressed, and would be vastly pretty in some other place, I question if it is necessary here: and the threat (if I may so call it) in the last stanza, is perhaps less necessary; as any thing like threatening is what the simplicity of a rural swain avoids; which character you seem to assume in the inscription. I had the pleasure to read the other inscription in one of your moss-seats, and have it also by me in a former letter of yours.—I see you have put *Harm betide* instead of *Ill betide*: the difference is of small consequence; yet I am unwilling to give up the first (*Ill betide*). If you have a mind for a little more criticism from such a No-Critic as myself, I think *Sportive* Fawns may supply the place of *Rural* Fawns, as they were jocular Deities. You have put *Fringed* Cell instead of *Mossy* Cell; which Oberon at first called it; but I love *Mossy* still; so attached am I to the first of your Editions.

That many parts of your Farm were extravagantly commended by Mr. Lyttelton, Miller, &c. I do not wonder at, though I cannot properly term it *Extravagantly*, because it was so justly and reasonably: and as to the Scape-Goat, (as you call your Summer-house) it has now some merit, and had all the merit you required of it at the time you built it; but I confess what you have done since must degrade it: yet I would not have it quite disregarded, and rather wish it could be turned to some useful ornament.—Have you a dove-house? The nearness of the water would pleafe please the pigeons; and the fight of them would please you: but let the building become what it will, if it remains there, I would have it change its colour from red to white.—Talking of changing, I must tell you of my changes at this cottage. Mr. Outing has put *O Venus Regina Gnidi* in the new Pavilion over Venus's Shrine, opposite my house, instead of over the Summer-house door, where it was; from which Summer-house I have banished the two motto's on the side-doors, as you advised. The Piping Fawn is retired from the front of the Aviary to his post in the Wood, where he stands in the Double Oak, in lieu of the motto *Huc ades*, &c. which being taken down, *Habitarunt Dii quoque Sylvas* is to supply its place.— I have found a kind of natural arbor in the Coppice, with an oak in it, under which I have a mind to raise a bank of turf and put my Tapping Fawn upon it to dance, with

Gaudet invifam pepuliffe foffor
Ter pede terram

for a motto. Query, (fays Mr. Outing) Whether a Fawn may be supposed to be a Ditcher? —I think to put over my Aviary

"Idle Muficians of the Spring,
"Whose only Care's to love and sing."

Which

Which lines are Lord Roscommon's, and are, I think, more strictly true of my birds incaged, than of the wild ones who have employment enough to seek food for themselves and their young.—Pray let me know how you make your *Moss-Seats*; for I want some such greatly in my Coppice.

I beg my compliments to Lord Dudley and Mr. and Miss Dolman. Mr. Outing desires his to you and them, and to Mr. Joseph Shenstone; who is, I hope, persuaded of my regard for him, and that you are as well assured of my being,

Sir,

With the strictest truth,

Your most obliged humble servant,

H. Luxborough.

Last Friday Sir Edward Boughton sent his steward for Mr. Hall to go and receive his Presentation to the Living of Harborough; which he did, and is now gone for institution to the Bishop of Litchfield and Coventry.

LETTER XXXIII.

SIR,   Barrells, September 11th, 1749.

THIS is Monday; and on Saturday last I wrote you a letter of great length, which I sent to Henley to be conveyed to the Birmingham Post-Office, directed to you, to be left there; but finding your illness continues, and not having heard from you since the letter in which you promised to write to me last Saturday was sevennight, I cannot be easy without a more particular enquiry concerning your health. This is the only subject of my present message and letter. The last letter was a medley, which if you are ill, will tire you to read, and will tire you more to answer; so I leave you free to make yourself easy about that, only beg you will let Mr. Outing and me know how you do. As to myself, I expected to have gone to London this week, but my scheme is altered; nor would I have gone if you had sent me word you would come. As to Mr. Outing, he has waited till now, and last night fixed upon Thursday for his departure, despairing of seeing you; and Mrs. Meredith writes me word she will come with her family next week: but if my servant finds you as well as I wish you, I hope still to see you and Mr. Dolman, &c. this week, and will endeavour to prevail with Mr. Outing to disappoint Mr. Reynalds once more, and defer his journey till the beginning of the next; but he says I answer for more than is possible for him to perform; and adds, that he would have gone to the Leasowes, had he not expected you here daily. Such are the aggravating circumstances of your disorder, which, without such aggravations, would have given more than sufficient pain to your friends; of which number I hope you will believe me none of the least zealous; for I am,

 Sir,

Most sincerely,

  Your obliged and faithful servant,

   H. LUXBOROUGH.

We desire (that is Mr. Outing and I) many compliments to your Brother and your friends at Broom, as well as to Lord Dudley; and Mr. Hall desired I would give his to you when I wrote next.

     Pray

Pray let somebody tell my servant how your little Moss-Seats are made that are in the Grove.

LETTER XXXIV.

Barrells, Wednesday, September 20th, 1749.

SIR,

COULD I suppose that you laid any stress upon ceremonial, which is only the shadow of friendship, where you are secure of its substance, I would make you many apologies for sending this letter by the post, which I ought to have sent to the Leasowes on Monday by a servant, who should also have gone to Broom to enquire how all the agreeable company that left Barrells on Sunday got to their respective houses. The omission of these civilities I confess, and hope to be absolved when you consider that they do not proceed from an ungrateful mind. I could not have performed them without a good deal of inconvenience to myself; and I know they could not be of any consequence to you: but 'you may be assured, that your obliging visit gave me much pleafure, and its fhort duration much regret, however wanting I may be in expreffing it.

Mr. Outing left me yefterday morning, much lamenting that he did not go the day before, when he feemed to grudge every ray of fun that was feen at Barrells, and to dread every drop of rain that might fall the next day on the road to Afton. His fears fhould have made him confult fome fkilful almanack-maker; but trufting to his own obfervations, I believe he met with a little rain, which (however lightly it might fprinkle him) would I dare fay make him curfe the *unjoyous* weather, and call himfelf an *unfortunate* hero more than once.

I fee in the news-paper an advertifement of a Poem, dedicated to the Duchefs of Somerfet, about Family Prayer, by one who feems to be a great admirer of Mr. Hervey. I fhould imagine it to be by the Chaplain fhe talks of in her letter; but do not know.

The firft thing I did on Monday was to order the Ha! Ha! to be lowered two bricks; but found it not neceffary to lower it even one; for the paper you ftuck up is feen from the Hall-Door by lowering the earth a confider-

able

able length of way. So much higher was it than the Ha! Ha! that it was *that* which obstructed the view totally, and not the wall. I also staked out the ground for the sweep of pallisadoes and trees at the hither end of the Long Walk, and I banished the auricula-pots from the Library-Window; and yesterday I wrote to bespeak the pediment for the Pavilion. More I could not do in this short time; but will have regard to your advice about the Shrubbery.

Should you, if you chose to erect in my Coppice an urn to the memory of a friend, place it in one of the corners where the trees seem to form an arbour, or in the Middle-Walk, from whence you now see Claverden? As the latter place is to be filled with trees, it might be perceived through them perhaps to some advantage from the Shrubbery and Summer-house; but if so, it would require to be higher than in the remote parts of the Wood. How high should you like the pedestal? and how high the urn in either place?

I hope to hear your colic is become a stranger to you, and that you will not provoke it by nuts, &c. and I wish all your improvements may prosper, and gratify your own taste,

which

which is so pleasing to others, and which affords particular pleasure to,

Sir,

Your obliged humble servant,

H. LUXBOROUGH.

If Miss Dolman has left the Leasowes, pray be so kind as to convey the inclosed card to Broom.

LETTER XXXV.

SIR,   Tuesday, October 10th.

AS I am at present in as languid (though not in so painful) a condition as you have lately been, I might have been excused by you, had I not wrote till I found myself better; but I should not be excused by myself. My own reproaches would be continual torments to me, did I not take the earliest opportunity of returning thanks for the Ode you sent me, and for the unmerited compliment it makes to me, and to my little retreat. Were strict

strict truth as necessary to poetry as it is to history, you would be guilty of a great fault in placing the scene here, where the Muses never come, except when you bring them. But as poetical licences are allowable, this error may be so too: and I am persuaded no other can be found in your plan; nor do I believe that even *you* can find any thing in the composition to amend, and yet I will not give a copy till you permit me, because I would not willingly disobey any of your commands.—Besides the pleasure your letter and verses afford me in reading, and the pride they indulge in making me the subject of them, they give me a third satisfaction, which exceeds the others, and that is, the looking upon them as proofs of your late disorder having quite left you: which I think I may do; for illness would disable your genius from working with that vigour one may observe in these productions of it. And indeed the very impressions which bodily pain commonly leaves, would be yet too recent in a vulgar mind to allow it the free use of its faculties: but yours is superior to others, even when it is most oppressed.

Monday, 16th.

I was too much out of order to continue my letter till to-day; but am now so much better,

better, that I proceed to tell you that my only architect (who is a joiner at Warwick) happens to be very ill, so that the pediment is not finished: perhaps not begun. I have ordered him to make it low, and agreeable to the Doric order; as the pillars of the Temple are. I mentioned three urns: he talks of three figures. I do not know if three balls would not be as well. Lord Burlington uses them a good deal.—When I have an opportunity, I will enquire of the knowing which are the proper books of Architecture for your use; and in the mean time will send you the only one I have that teaches the rudiments of that science: Worse print or worse paper you never saw! It cost me five shillings at one of Osborne's sales, thirteen years ago. Perhaps you will get a better printed one of the kind, if you like this upon looking it over.—As to the urn for Mr. Somervile, he has wrote me the price of a plain one in wood, and also in Warwick stone; but it is only twenty inches high at that price: which I suppose is not half high enough; and he sends a frightful common pedestal in the inclosed draught.—I have a fancy for an urn on a round altar, and have scrawled out such a thing myself, and sent it to Mr. Williams to put in oil, and to paint green trees round, that I may guess at the effect it will have. The urn I drew from a little pair the Duchess of Somerset turned for me in wood, from an antique urn the Countess of Pomfret brought her from Italy. It has no cover. You will see how it is when Williams sends it back. In the mean time, pray think of a place to set the urn in; for I cannot please myself about it.

Just at this place of my letter I am interrupted by one from Miss Patty Meredith, to desire I will send four of my horses to join two of Mrs. Meredith's to bring them hither from Wolseley-Bridge on Friday next the 20th; so I will not send this epistle till they come, choosing to wait, in order to make it more worth your reading, by sending you Miss Patty's opinion, and Miss Harriot's, about placing the urn.

I will only add here, that I am sorry for the usage you have met with from your Parson: but hope your path goes on, and could wish it had been where you proposed, in defiance of ecclesiastical spite; but since that is impracticable, at least flatter myself that you will disappoint his malicious intent, by making a path on your own land equally pretty, and out of the reach of their powers, who endeavoured to prevent the dictates of your taste. Place it ever so far from them, it is possible their envy may reach it, and trace it to its full extent: but what of that, if they cannot molest it otherwise? And I will fancy you can have one that will even exceed in beauty that which you first thought of.

Wednesday, October 25th.

By various accidents I have waited in vain for Mrs. Meredith till this day, and have not yet had time to write, nor weather to seek for situations in the Coppice.

Friday, 27th.

To-morrow morning a sketch of Miss Patty's will go to the Leasowes, in hopes of saving the town of Birmingham; but it is impossible to find time to write a line with it.

LETTER XXXVI.

SIR, November 1st, 1749.

PRAY read the inclosed letter first.—I hope you received a Sketch on Saturday.—This beginning will seem abrupt: more so than Mr. Whistler's! but my reason for it

is

is the same as his. If he is pardoned after a
silence of six months, perhaps I may receive
the same favour. My silence was not of such
long duration. My crime was not so great,
because it did not deprive you of so much
pleasure; and my contrition is as great as his
can be: and if you will believe me, I blush as
much as he could do; and neither of us can
express *that* upon paper; therefore, I hope
you will believe us both, and restore me as well
as Mr. Whistler to your friendship. My
pleading for him is an act of supererogation,
as he has pleaded so much better for himself:
and yet I have no other way of shewing my
gratitude for his mention of me. How proud
should I be of what he says of me, were I not
at the same time humbled, by knowing my
merit cannot have attracted his applause, since
he never was in my company! The same consideration should make me wish he never might
be in it, lest he should be undeceived to my disad-
vantage. But upon the whole, weighing my losses
and gains by the notion I have conceived of his
conversation by what I have seen of his writings,
I think I would venture to let him discover my
ignorance, rather than be deprived of his company; which you promised last year to give
me, by his accompanying you to Barrells;

where

where (by the way) if you pleafe to come now, I can offer you more than I have yet been able to do; which is the converfation of Mrs. Meredith and four of her daughters.— The Yellow Room which Mifs Dolman lay in, when you was laſt here, is empty.—I fhould rejoice to fee you.—The month of October calls upon you to affift me in planting; and I know you would not choofe to be remifs in acts of friendfhip. I offer you an occafion of fhewing yours; and unlefs you go to London to meet Mr. Whiftler, I think I may expect you will do me this favour before the new moon decays. I would fain endeavour to wipe off the prejudice you have taken againſt Autumn; and if thefe four young ladies do not affift me, I fear I fhall never meet with fuccefs; nor can any thing be more likely to enliven the melancholy afpect you dread when days grow fhort and leaves turn yellow.

We have fearched every corner of the Coppice, and can find no oak-tree favourable to our defign, unlefs it is the great double oak, within which Outing placed the Piping Fawn. The tree is unexceptionable for that ufe; but the fituation you will think, I dare fay, too much expofed, efpecially as the entrance is fo very near from the Abele Walks: if that can

be

be obviated, perhaps thickening that part with trees and ever-greens may render it more proper: if not, Miss Harriot, nor Miss Patty, nor I, can think of no place but the brink of the Pit, a little below which stands an oak, that spreads a good deal over it; against which oak Miss Patty, in the inclosed Sketch, proposes to set the urn and altar, and to shade it round with yews, laurels, &c. and give up the rest of the Pit to the open field, and also to plant the Sand Walk that now leads into the Coppice and up to the Two Chairs, full of trees, and let the way be a narrow serpentine path through it, backward from the Pit, leading into the inward part of the Coppice; on the right side of which is an old stump of oak, which may make a proper back to a root-seat, from whence you will view the urn in a direct line fronting so as to be able to read the inscription.—Let us know if you conceive my meaning and Miss Patty's Drawing; and whether our idea is likely to appear well when put in practice.

I received two days ago, Mr. Williams's *Sketch*, as he calls it, though he has made it a real Picture from my Sketch, and has made the pedestal square instead of round, saying it is most proper as the urn is round: his painting has no regard to situation.—The steps in Miss Patty's Sketch are, if you remember, leading into the Pit from a corner over against the great oak, and terminate by some willows.

Miss Harriot says,—Query. Would it be amiss, instead of planting the Sand-Walk, to throw the earth down so as to make it a turfed slope from the Coppice, instead of a perpendicular side of a Pit as it now is? and would it not help to take off the ugly look of a marle-pit which it now has?

Miss Patty is amusing herself in copying Watts, and I in being a thief, which she complains the more of, as the boy she was drawing is not finished; but I will inclose it in spite of her, because I am

Your faithful friend
and humble servant,
H. LUXBOROUGH.

P. S. I sent your letter to Outing in one of my own, but no answer.

Mr. Hall desires his best compliments, and sets out for Oxford and London next Monday.—As I am in a stealing humour, I have stole the original and only copy of his Assize Sermon to send you, because I heard you say you

you wanted to fee it. Pray fend it back, for he abfolutely forbade my fhewing it, as not deeming it worthy. I do not think my difobedience is a breach of friendfhip, becaufe I like the fermon.

Compliments to your Brother, to Lord Dudley, and to Mr. and Mifs Dolman.—Permit my fervant to ftay till morning.—Mrs. and Mifs Merediths are obliged by your mention of them, and defire compliments to you.

I am forry old *Emma* is deprived of the pleafure of conveying this packet. It is large enough, if its merit was judged by its fize, to fave forty fuch towns as Birmingham.

LETTER XXXVII.

SIR, Wednefday, November 8th, 1749.

I HAVE heard of giving one guinea to a mufician to play, and ten to leave off. Thus are you, I believe, by this time inclinable to reward old *Emma*, and to difmifs her from the office of poftwoman. For her fake I ought to write feldomer, unlefs I could make my letters fuch as could render her

welcome

welcome when she presents you with the large packets she finds at Birmingham from Barrells.—What occasions my troubling you again so soon is, that Mrs. Meredith and her daughters leave me the beginning of next week, and I should be glad to know before that, what size you would choose the urn and pedestal should be of: for as to the lesser ones at Hagley, you do not mention their dimension; and the twenty inches Mr. Hands talked of, was caused by the mistake of a figure in my letter. The little nook which you have forgot, is over against you when you sit under the great double oak, and from it go down winding steps which I had cut a great while ago in the earth to lead to the bottom of the Pit, but are shaded by the trees which grow on the brink of it; and a little before you come to the bottom, there is like a narrow landing-place, where grows a short row of willows, which form a kind of little hedge at the foot of an old oak which grows on the bank, and there is the spot we proposed to set the urn. Miss Patty drew it wrong, when she made it of a line with the tree; and Miss Harriot's proposal is to slope off the bank quite from the trees on the left side the walk which now is, down to the said willows, which

are

are at present four feet and a half below the edge of the bank; and I believe it will have a good effect. Miss Patty has *scrawled* (for she can do nothing well with compasses) three views of an urn, viz. one front, and two end-views.—Query, Whether the harp and the reeds should be carved flat on the urn, or project as in Nº 1, and whether you like the shape; as also if this Ionic pedestal is suitable, and whether with or without the bay-wreath or the square for the inscription?—I never intended four lyres. We did intend to leave the lower part of the Pit, from the Willows downwards, perpendicular.—I am glad you like balls for the pediment. The sweep is formed by the palisades: the elms are all moved from the lawn on the south-side my house, to stop up the opening of the Coppice on the east from hence as you directed, and some limes are among them.

I thank you for sending Gibbs's book; which I will take care of, but never yet could admire his taste in Architecture. The monument for the late Duke of Newcastle gives a specimen of it; and even his genteelest things he disgraces commonly with some awkward ornament. His building at Cambridge I have seen, but never could like.—Pardon me

for

for giving my opinion, which is of no value: it cannot hurt Mr. Gibbs, nor can it be of any improvement to you. So I will leave off here, and haften to affure you, that I am,

 With perfect truth and efteem,

  Your faithful and obliged fervant,

   H. LUXBOROUGH.

 The Ladies defire their compliments, and return thanks for yours, and wifh to fee you here. I have hopes Outing will come too before they go.—Pray write on Saturday.

 Pray give me a few Englifh words expreffive of Mr. Somervile's character; for I had only thought of putting

"Sacred to the Memory of William Somervile, Efquire."

 Your Latin Motto's are, I am perfuaded, very well chofe. Perhaps a Lady fhould not put up any in *an unknown tongue*; but I have already erred that way, fo may as well go on.

LETTER XXXVIII.

SIR;
  Barrells, Wednesday, November 29th, 1749.
  Begun Tuesday Night, 28th.

I DO not know whether I am making reparation for my paſt offence, *Silence*, or committing a worſe, by *Babbling*: for I not only anſwered your letter by your ſervant, but wrote again the very next day; and ſtill upon the ſame ſubject, *Urns*. I hoped for an anſwer laſt Thurſday; but not having one, I now torment you with a third epiſtle, which will probably draw another from you; and, was your politeneſs out of the queſtion, I ſhould expect it to be an order for me to ſtop my pen: I think it would be juſt; and as the French ſtyle (and French every thing) is faſhionable, it might be allowable for you to ſay in that language to me, *Cela ſuffit:* which phraſe I have often heard uſed by thoſe who would be ſhocked to hear in rough Engliſh "*Hold your tongue;*": though I think *ſound* makes the difference, not *ſenſe*. Talking of that, who would have thought a pack of French ſtrollers could ever in any ſhape have influenced the chooſing or rejecting a Member

of

of the British Parliament? and yet the advertisements about the Westminster Election shew them to be *Personages* of Consequence.—It is it seems fact, that a pretty good set of English Actors who made an attempt to set up a stage in a province on the out-skirts of France, (where our language was a little understood) were driven off with the utmost scurrility; and yet our *Noblesse* support their strollers here; for they are, I hear, established in spite of the fracas made by the Gallery; being well supported by our Lords, Ladies, and still more by some of our Officers, who though they ran away from the French in Flanders, are eager to follow them here, and to pay their obsequious devoirs to the outcast of them.—What will not Englishmen now bear!

Were it permitted to find fault with M——ſty, I should be angry Penlez did not receive the Royal Mercy. But on the other hand, I am pleased with the K——g's answer to the D——ke of N——, who went to his closet exulting with joy to inform him of the fortunate event of Sir Watkin's death: "I am sorry for it, (answered his M——ſty.) he was a worthy man, and an open enemy." This fine answer makes one regret that his Min——rs govern instead of him.—But how happens it pray, that

that I talk something tending towards politics
to *you?* I do not conceive what could make
it enter into my head: but when it did do so,
I can easily conceive it would fly away with
my pen; for so negligently as I write, the
first ideas that present themselves go off to my
friends, unpolished and unconnected: but to
others I give only a very little *flummery,* and so
conclude. This word *flummery,* you must
know, Sir, means at London, *flattery* and *compliment* ; and is the present reigning word
among the Beaux and Belles! Pardon my
telling you what your Dictionary would not
have told you; and pardon me also for boast-
ing of knowing something about the fashions
my neighbours do not know, and which, thanks
to Chance, I do know!—I hope this self-exalta-
tion will not draw upon me the guilt of the
arrogant Pharisee. My knowledge does not
extend very far, as learned as I am; and yet
I know that it is the fashion for every body
to write a couplet to the same tune (viz. an old
country-dance) upon whatever subject occurs
to them; I should say upon whatever person,
with their names to it. Lords, Gentlemen,
Ladies, Flirts, Scholars, Soldiers, Divines,
Masters, and Misses, are all authors upon this
occasion, and also the objects of each other's satire: it makes an offensive *medley,* and might be
called

called a *pot-pourri*; which is a potful of all kinds of flowers which are feverally perfumes, and commonly when mixt and rotten, fmell very ill. This coarfe fimile is yet too good for about twenty or thirty couplets I have feen, and they are all perfonal and foolifh fatire, even feverally; fo I will not fend them: but to make amends for my grave politics, I will fend you a good pretty innocent Ballad, wrote by a Mifs Jenny Hamilton, a pretty girl about town, who is going to marry *More*, the author of the Foundling, and writes word of it herfelf in this manner to an intimate friend in the country. It confifts, as you will find, of puns (or as the French properly call it, *Jeu de mots*) upon his name; and though I never was a lover of puns, I do not diflike the natural fprightly turn of thefe; and I hope they will amufe you a few moments, for the reafon you quote from Cibber (himfelf!) "That "fmall matters amufe in the country." The truth of which moft people have felt, or are unfeeling and unhappy.

As to myfelf, I have ftrayed three days of the laft week in the woods; or to be lefs poetical, I have ftood from Eleven to Five each day, in the lower part of my Long Walk, planting and difplanting, opening views, &c. I wifh

I wish it may be for the better. There were sad scrub-trees, if you remember, planted as if it was to represent a shooting-bow; for they formed a curve on one side, and a straight line on the other: this led to the lower gates that part the Lane from the Walk. Twenty-seven good straight elms, instead of them, make the lines parallel; and I have hopes of knocking down ten *ecclesiastical* trees, which obstructed the prospect (as you and Mr. Hall assured me) from the Old Summer-house.—If the whole College of King's in Cambridge should be more favourable to me than one single joint of a foe (I will not say limb) of a College which you had to deal with, I shall triumph: but I must not brag too soon; perhaps my scheme may prove as abortive as yours.

I want to know your answer about the Urns being under the Double Oak.—Pray tell my friend Tom I make my servants collect all the roots and lay them at the door of the Coppice, against he exerts his skill in rearing them up into the form he proposes.

The asking you to come here at this season, is downright Irish assurance: but it is allowable, I hope, to wish it.—Whenever *wishing* is mentioned, the Green Book presents itself to my view: but it is as in a dream that vanishes.

L   —I have

—I have sent a special messenger to Somer-viles-Aston, to Outing; not without reminding him of your just reproof (at least it is *just* as far as concerns *writing*; for as to *riding* you cannot expect it. I am sure he would not reach the Mines of Peru at this season, if they were but thirty miles off, in a fortnight, though he were to bring away as much as he could desire of their riches. He thinks it impracticable to come to Barrells, which is fourteen miles, though he promised, though his cloaths are here, and though the Birmingham-coach could carry him any Monday from Henley to London, by Oxford; which conveniency is newly established, to our great emolument. Would it not be a good scheme (this dirty weather, when riding is no more a pleasure) for you to come some Monday in the said stage-coach from Birmingham, to breakfast at Barrells (for they always breakfast at Henley); and on the Saturday following, it would convey you back to Birmingham, unless you would stay longer, which would be better still, and equally easy? for the stage goes every week the same road; it breakfasts at Henley, and lies at Chipping Norton; goes early next day to Oxford, stays there all day and night; and gets on the third day to London:

London: Which from Birmingham at this season is pretty well, considering how long they are at Oxford; and it is much more agreeable to the country than the Warwick way was.—But why has this coach induced me to begin upon another sheet of paper? It is a shame to torment you so, and with such nonsense.—You once, I remember, Sir, commended my hand-writing and correctness; but this will shew it was all *flummery*.

I asked you what your new *books* were, or *pamphlets*? You did not answer me: perhaps you had not gone through them.—I wish the people in town would give themselves time to write, and amuse us a little: but I believe they neither write nor read. How can they, as their time is taken up with new-fashioned amusements, which, like Eternity, have neither beginning nor end? I imagine *sleep* will be left off, for I do not hear of an hour allotted for it. As to *thought*, it has employment enough in weighing these different amusements, and sorting them so as not to lose any in the twenty-four hours: And booksellers I believe might shut up shop, if it was not for us country-puts. Perhaps when the *Jubilee* is over, there may be a cessation to the present whirl of diversions.

My paper and the clock remind me that it is late; so I employ the rest of the space left, in assuring you that I am, with great esteem, and without one particle of flummery, Sir,

Your faithful and obliged servant,

H. L<small>UXBOROUGH</small>.

From my Bed-Room, Wednesday, 29th.

My writing a Postscript after so long a letter is not according to the † *fitness of things*, I confess it; but I cannot well avoid it, for here enters the messenger whom I sent yesterday to Outing.

Past Five in the Afternoon.

This proved a mistake, and the messenger is not yet returned; and I am obliged to send this letter away now, or it will be too late to give it in charge to those who are to carry it to-morrow.

My compliments to your Brother, and at Broom.

† Be it known, these words thus applied are fashionable.

LETTER

LETTER XXXIX.

SIR, Barrells, December 6th, 1749.

YOUR letter of the 26th ult. and mine of the 29th, croffed each other at Birmingham. The next day yours arrived fafe at Barrells, and gave me more than wonted pleafure, as my fpirits much wanted fuch a cordial, being depreffed by various things, particularly by the death of Mr. Davis, who leaves his Widow, (my friend) whom I love and efteem, in deep affliction, though without tears, or pomp of forrow. He was a gentleman-like man, generous, and capable of being a friend; which many in higher life are not: and to her he was Brother, Father, Friend, as well as tender Hufband. She had not recovered the concern the lofs of her only child had caufed her, when this greater misfortune befel her.—We are all born to fuffer afflictions; and I have had a large fhare: but I fincerely proteft none has ever been felt by me fo feverely as thofe which have befallen my friends. And as if *that* was well known to my evil ftar, it fheds its influence over moft of thofe perfons I have an affection for.—Pray God it may not reach you!

Here I break off to tell you Outing's anfwer to my meffage in his own words; which are thefe, " My motions are at fo great an
" uncertainty, that it makes me uneafy to
" myfelf and rude to my friends. The hopes
" of feeing Mr. Shenftone prevented me from
" writing to him; and now that I am able to
" do it, *Will*'s impatience prevents me from
" telling him fo."—This faid *Will*, you muft know, is the meffenger I fent early one morning, and he did not return till late next evening, becaufe Mr. Outing kept him to have time to anfwer my letter; which he did anfwer about the tenth part of: the diftance is fourteen miles, and the meffenger a fpeedy one. —Jacky Reynalds has been here fince, and tells me he is at prefent at Sir Robert Cocks's, confulting every perfon and every map to find out (not the longitude, but) the neareft way to Portfmouth, whether through London or acrofs the country. His perfon is ftill as I fuppofe in Gloucefterfhire, his beft cloaths are at Barrells, and his thoughts on board the Hazard Sloop (where the lad he has the care of is to be placed) or rather on the road thither, where I do not doubt but he fancies there

are dragons innumerable waiting for him; for an indolent person may form as many difficulties when he is to undertake a journey, as a child frightened by its nurse, or a person who has the *night-mare* sees bugbears.

The hopes you give me of the Green-Book feeds my imagination, and I flatter myself the first swallow will bring it; for I do not imagine you will honour the robin-redbreast with your errand; and he is the only feathered visitant I am likely to have for some time.

If I was not tender of encroaching upon Mrs. Emme Scudamore's rights, I would propose to you to exchange a pair or two of pigeons of the carrier kind (of which I have some) next spring; and by winter they may convey letters to and from the Leasowes and Barrells with great diligence, without her assistance, or her friend William's. Why should it not be done here as well as abroad, as it is especially by our merchants in the eastern countries, who often gain riches by early advice that expeditious way? and why should the fund of fortune be still supplied with care, and that of friendship neglected? It is to the latter I would raise an altar, and wish to have it blaze as bright as that seems to do in the

ingenious

ingenious device you sent me, which is (*sans compliment*) the prettiest of the kind I ever saw for a seal; and hope you will permit me to make use of it by having one cut according to it.

Sunday, December 10th, 1749.

Here I broke off, with an intention of copying my letter, and sending a neater edition of it, this being full of blots; but had not an opportunity of sending it safely to Birmingham; when on Friday I received yours, of the 5th, and this moment your last, of the 7th, by Pedley's son. As he is to return in the morning early, and I am to have Lord Archer and other company at dinner to-morrow, I shall not have time to copy it over; so beg you will excuse it, and receive this incorrect epistle for the sake of its candour, not for its wit or its beauty: for it has no more pretense to either, than a hurdygurdy has to harmony.

I think Mr. Meredith's account of your Grove is a very true one; and as to what relates to the buildings (since he chooses to make a parallel between them and those at Hagley) I dare say you will not dispute giving the preference to the latter; nor set your Gothic Bench in opposition to their Gothic Castle: and yet give me leave to say the former is in the better tafte and proportion. Mr. Meredith never faw Hagley, therefore I wonder how he came to fpeak of it as a judge: That he admires the Leafowes is certain, and is juft.—I hate puns as much as you can do; but they ferve now and then, as fuch difhes which the French call *Hors d'œuvres*, to interfperfe amongft thofe of more fubftance, and are counted as nothing.

I like your fancy of making your parfon Bifhop of Nova Scotia, which would be making him of fome ufe. I have not experienced the good luck you wifh me with ecclefiaftics: fo cannot fay any thing in their favour; though I wifh I could, becaufe of their function, which puts it in their power to do good or hurt: and they generally choofe the latter.

It is time to fpeak to you about the Urn; which I cannot do without returning you a million of thanks for your interefting yourfelf fo much in what gives me pleafure, and for the trouble you have given yourfelf in drawing out the feveral fketches of urns; all which are in exceeding good tafte, if mine may be permitted to judge. I fent one (the fmalleft in the drawings) to Warwick, to afk what it would coft if executed quite plain with the pedestal, and the size of the lesser ones at Hagley, according to what you wrote me about them; and am to have an answer next Tuesday, though I do not propose having it made yet; for the weather will not allow it to be set up with safety, as I imagine, till about April.—I would employ Pedley preferably to any other workman, if I had it worked at home, both from your recommendation and his own skill; as also from compassion for his misfortunes: but I have several reasons which prevent my having it done at home; and amongst others, I have no place to have it worked in, nor any to keep it in when finished, till it is a proper season to set it up. Had Pedley had any dwelling where he could have made it, and from whence I could have sent for it, I would order it immediately, though it were to cost me more; but as it is, I cannot employ him, because I cannot have it done at home; which I am sorry for, especially as you, Sir, recommend him, which weighs not a little with me; nor shall any one else do that or any thing in his way for me but him, if ever I have any stone worked here.

LETTER

LETTER XL.

SIR, Wednesday.

WHEN I answered yours by your servant, I told you I had not time to examine the urns you kindly sketched out for me (Mr. Allen, &c. chattering round me). I have now looked them over, and like them well. I think the proportion of the large one (N°. 5.) seems to be very just; and I believe the lesser size is big enough for my small Coppice. I cannot admire the foliage at the necks of the urns, either at bottom or on the cover. I think those fluted thus are better; and it is full ornamental enough, if they must not be quite plain. As to the placing the Poetical Attributes either on the urn or the pedestal, or on both, you have given variety of agreeable specimens. I confess, what pleases my eye most is the fistula and pipe on the fifth urn, and the oval wreath on the first pedestal. The lyre, erect as it is shewn on the second pedestal, I cannot admire; nor do I like the surrounding festoons,

N°. 1,

N°. 1, 3, 4, so well as the slight festoon in the middle: so that I had fixed upon having the pipe, &c. on the urn, and the wreath on the pedestal, and was considering about what should be on the other side, when I recollected, that if the urn is placed, as I last proposed, under the great Double Oak, there will only be one side seen perfect, viz. that which will front the new entrance at the corner of the Pit; the opposite side will be hid by the tree, and the side towards the Service Walk will be filled up with trees, and the same on the other side: Therefore if you think that something ornamental should be seen through the trees, we must have a surrounding festoon of natural flowers tied with knots, as in N°. 3: But (if you have no objection) I should rather like to have the urn plain all but on one side, as is for example Mrs. Lyttelton's urn in Hagley Church, where she is lying on a couch; and nothing is represented on the other three sides. In this case, I would by all means have the pipe, &c. as you have introduced it (N°. 5.) on the large urn, and the oval wreath on the pedestal, with the English inscription within it, as it is on that you sent, (N°. 1.) and the *His Saltem* on the upper plinth, as in N°. 4. But then, where

where can we write the *Postquam*, &c.? May it not be just above the wreath? All this would enrich the front, and the rest would be plain, and only beautiful by the shape and proportion. I cannot like lyres or even masks on an urn, I mean any thing that projects so much on the sides; it takes off that roundness which is its beauty.—I thought to have the urn and pedestal worked at the Marble-yard at Warwick, and to send my own team for them. I suppose Pedley made my urns which are on the New Summer-house there, and that he still works there. He can guess at the value of such a one as we propose, if you are so good to ask him; and I should be very willing to have it made by him. You may know the price if quite plain, or one side adorned as abovementioned; or else the festoon round, and the wreath on one front of the pedestal; or the slight wreath in the middle on three sides, and the tibia, &c. on the fourth, with the pipe and a lyre obliquely placed with it, instead of the sprig of laurel, as the laurel-wreath will be below it. But after all, this last will be a dearer way, because the pedestal would require something on four sides: so, if you please, we will stick to carving only the front, as I mentioned before; and if that

should

should be quite improper, I must in that case submit to the surrounding festoon; but shall give up the fistula and pipe with very great regret: so hope it is allowable to keep it.

If you was not as anxious as myself to have due honour paid to the memory of our worthy friend, I should not be so rude as to interrupt thus often your amusements, and turn your thoughts from the pleasing decorations you are daily adding at the Leasowes to those humble ones I exhibit here.—What would I give for a little stream to run at the foot of this pedestal! I dare say you would be generous enough to part with a small rivulet, if you could persuade it to run down hither.—I imagine your islands must have a pretty effect. —Is your Summer-house yet transformed; or does it remain a butt for Mr. Lyttelton's and Mr. Miller's censure? They find so much at the Leasowes to raise their envy, and consequently their spleen, that it is happy for them some one object offers that they can vent it upon: when *that* is removed, they will wish it up again; so vexed will they be to find themselves under a necessity of commending. What can be a greater misfortune to a critic? Pope would have died many years ago, had he been obliged to refrain from satire, the
sole

sole delight of his little peevish temper. How happy was he to meet with a Timon at his villa! The world furnishes many: but those who would find one, must not seek him at the Leasowes.

How charitable would it be, Sir, if you would take a trip to this little Retreat at this melancholy season!—The English hang themselves, it is said, in the month of November, and I find the French begin to catch the infection; for they go to *la Trappe*; that and hanging are synonimous. What then, if, to indulge the splenetic humour which the density of the air and the shortness of the days incline you to, you should come and spend them in my chimney-corner? Nothing will put you enough in mind of spring to make you regret it, unless it is the singing of my two Canary-birds; and they shall, if you please, be sent out of the parlour; after which the most profound silence will reign, and dulness be triumphant. This is what I invite you to; but you will be no sooner here than the scene will appear to me quite changed: my proposal is therefore mercenary: I confess it, self-love will have it so.—*A propos*, Where is the Green Book? Why did I ever trust it out of my hands? Will it not, when copied over, honour

nour the picture of the intended urn with a place, and honour me with the irregular Ode? May I hope that you will set about it in earnest, at your leisure hours?—Adieu: I scarce know what I write.—Parson Allen kept me up till Three to hear his stories; and on Sunday I sat up all night, and shall not keep much more regular hours till after next Friday; for I am to dine and sup at Spernal, (the Parson will have it so) and on that day (or rather on Saturday morning) I shall take leave of the present moon: nor shall I have occasion to use the next; for the roads will be impassable by that time for a carriage that quarters, and indeed there will be nobody scarcely left in the country to visit. If you do not come, I shall wish I had the power of transforming myself into a fly that lies sleeping or dead in some obscure corner, till the sunbeams wake him, and warm him into life.

Shall you not hear from Mr. Whistler from London? his letters will entertain you; and you will I dare say let me partake of the pleasure.—When the Duchess of Somerset returns from Bath, I suppose I shall hear from Her Grace.—Miss Patty promises to write; but I much suspect the numerous amusements London affords to one of her age, and who has

never

never spent but the laſt ſprings there, nor ever seen it before, will often prevent her sitting down to write.—Amongſt other diverſions, I find they act plays ſometimes at home, to which all Mrs. Meredith's acquaintance are invited. Mr. Meredith and ſome other young gentlemen do the mens parts, and Miſs Patty the top part of the women—They have ſcenes from the Play-houſe, and make proper ſtage-dreſſes—Her acting is much admired. I made her do a ſcene or two, to give me a notion of it, and it ſtruck me.—Monimia was what ſhe acted at home: but I think ſhe does ſome of the mad parts (which Mrs. Cibber is fa-mous for) very finely.—Next ſummer they propoſe a much longer ſtay at Barrells, where I hope you will meet them; and they may ſhew you ſome of theſe kind of amuſements, ſo uncommon in theſe unfrequented ſhades; if we can muſter up performers.

I juſt now perceive the word *Adieu*, two pages back. Am I mad to write ſuch an *Addenda?* But I let my pen gallop on, and you never will permit me to ſtop it; ſo you muſt not complain of its impertinence.—Emme will, I dare ſay, be thankful that the pacquet is ſo large; as ſhe will judge of its merit by

its

its weight. You will, I hope, excuse its faults, because it conveys one inviolable truth; which is, that I am

Your most faithful
H. LUXBOROUGH.

LETTER XLI.

SIR,   Tuesday.

YESTERDAY must be marked with the blackest ink in the kalendar of my life. My friends and neighbours seemed to combine, and leave me at once to solitude and regret. Mrs. Meredith and her four daughters set out from hence, at eight o'clock, in their coach with my horses, for Oxford; and Mr. Hall set out at the same time from Henley in the stage: he will not be at London before ten or fourteen days: they will be there on Thursday.—Mrs. Meredith and I sat up all night on Sunday, by choice; the rest went to bed; by which contrivance I secured to myself some rest last night: whereas if Sleepiness had not forced me to it, Thought would have deprived me of it.—Nothing is so terrible as parting from friends: and to have

taken

taken leave and then have gone to bed, had been such an image of death, that I avoided it as much as possible, and endeavoured to banish them all from my mind.—Luckily a man came to fell some trees, just as they were setting out: and immediately looking upon him as upon a tutelar angel sent to my assistance, I never returned to the house, but walked, under his protection, all over my grounds, and particularly to the farther end of the Long Avenue; where I ordered a crooked row of scrub trees to be fallen, and a strait row of elms to be planted, and other views to be opened, by felling and transplanting about the Old Summer-house; as also near the Grove-Pool, to shew the winding of the walk from the Coppice and other points; and several roots to be stocked up for future root-houses.—*A propos:* I have taken the liberty this moment to send your trusty Tom to reconnoitre a place in the Coppice for a root-seat; as also some roots I have stocked, to see if there are enough. You will permit him some time to assist me in making one. This I have thoughts of placing in a corner near where the two chairs now stand; from which one shall just discover a bit of a Gloucestershire hill over the Pit; but it will be through a very

very narrow winding-path, the reſt of that Open being to be full planted.—Since I am ſpeaking of that part of my environs, I will tell you of a new ſcheme I have formed for placing the urn. I thought, before I received yours, that the area round the bottom of the pedeſtal would be too narrow in the place we had once fixed upon for the urn; and I alſo think the tree, which would be its canopy there, is too inconſiderable: ſo that my preſent deſign is to place it under the Great Double Oak, whoſe venerable trunk will ſupport and branches ſhade it more properly than the other oak could have done. It will be like raiſing a throne, as well as a monument, for Mr. Somervile; and could he ſee it, he would, I believe, think himſelf more honourably placed than if he was *kicked* down below one's feet, which might offend his elevated ſpirit.—What think you then of filling the end of the Service Walk, where the entrance now is, with trees, reſerving glades for the proſpects, but hiding the houſe and gardens, and of placing the urn there, as much ſurrounded with ever-greens as poſſible, and having a ſmall entrance from the field, in the nook near the corner of the Pit, which will front the fore-part of the urn, but which is not to be the common entrance

entrance to the Coppice? Perhaps a little root-feat may be there, under the shade of the hedge, instead of where the Chairs are; from whence one may contemplate the urn one way, and have a prospect through one of the openings of the Walk the other:—But this last thing of the seat comes into my head only now as I write; the rest I thought of before, and scrawled it on a bit of rumpled paper, only to make myself comprehend my own meaning; and when I had done, was going to throw it in the fire, when I received yours; by which I conceived that you had doubts about the propriety of the lower situation. This makes me venture to send this same rumpled scrawl, which may perhaps give you an idea of my last intention, which I shall execute, unless you disapprove it.— Miss Harriot's thought is undoubtedly right, and shall be pursued. The Serpentine shall not be on the brink of the Pit, as described in the paper, but shall go through the midst of the trees, and the Pit be all given to the field from the willows. The slope shall be turfed as far as the willows: below that shall be perpendicular. Some white pales I have, may go where the steps now are, to reach the willows, and fence out the cattle. If they or the sheep come into the front of the Pit, so much the prettier; and they can do no harm.

Two o'clock.

Mr. Allen is now making his entrance, and comes to eat some of Lord Archer's venison; so I shall not have time to look over the urns.

Five o'clock.

I have looked at the urns with Mr. Allen. He approves extremely of "*His Saltem*" on the plinth, and "*Postquam,*" &c. and of the bay-wreath on the pedestal.—We all like the simplicity of No. 5. and the tibia and fistula in the middle. I am for having no other ornament than *that* to the urn, and no other than the bay-wreath to the pedestal.—What if a lyre was added obliquely to the tibia and fistula, or else hung upon the other side of the urn, and the bay-branch left out, as the pedestal will have bay enough upon it?— The Coat of Arms would be greatly absurd, for the reasons you give; but I could wish I had a medallion of him carved within the wreath: but that is not to be had.—I shall leave the proportions to your judgment, but think the lesser one at Hagley
will

will do well.—I do not like the foliage that forms the foot of the fifth urn. Why might not the foot be fluted as the cover? Upon the whole, I would have it very plain: the wreath on the pedestal, and the fistula and wreath on the urn are sufficient. Masks or lyres, or any thing as handles, spoil the look, and the proportion, in my opinion.—Could you not complete your favours, by asking Pedley what he would do it for in Warwick-stone?—I return Gibbs; and cannot like Mr. Coulston's dress and full-bottomed wig on a tomb.—You are welcome to keep my old book as long as you please; and I will enquire about modern ones.

Methinks I smell the *sans pareille* hither. How could you tantalize me? and how could you treat it as a *moderate* matter? Stinking tobacco is no *moderate* matter to those who love it.—Let me know where your perfumer lives, and Mr. Hall shall be wrote to, to buy me some.

Lord Dudley's call up to Town is not singular. All who are supposed to vote for the Court have received a letter to the same purpose; but all have not agreed to obey.—The more haste is made, as the K— goes early to Hanover.

What are your new books and pamphlets? Let me see some; or rather, let me have your company. You are generous, and I am become an object of compassion in this solitude and these short days.—Outing treats me as he does you. Gloucestershire monopolizes all his courteousness.

They talk round me, and oblige me to write mere nonsense, or to conclude in haste. The latter is best for your sake.—So adieu.

Yours with esteem and sincerity,
H. LUXBOROUGH.

I could wish you had a busto-seal like what you were about inventing; and that you sealed with dark-coloured wax, and could gild the busto as you have done the Viola's Head, with which you sealed the roll to-day.

I send a Blind Boy Miss Patty drew at candle-light, to hide the dirty scrawled paper with the Oak and Urn.—Mr. Allen and Mr. and Mrs. Holyoak's compliments.

One word more about Urns.—I send you, Sir, the inclosed; being an answer from Mr. Hands, who was desired by me to enquire at the Marble-yard the expence of an urn and pedestal, according to the dimensions of the lesser

lesser ones at Hagley that you sent; because (as I wrote you word by young Pedley) I had not conveniency to have one worked at home.—I sent the N°. 6, of your last drawings, because I liked the form. As to ornaments, I never named them; and could wish it could be executed quite plain; and yet something expressive of him as a poet should be too.—Would not the laurel-wreath encircling the inscription be sufficient? The shape and proportion of the urn is all I should wish perfect; and had rather it had no ornament, or next to none. I know you will be so good to oblige me with one more draught according to this plain scheme, with the inscription and motto's, and I will have it executed. A thing much ornamented would be no proper expression of friendship from me, nor would it become the place: which is exposed a good deal to the licentiousness of our mob, which is not near so decent as yours. I am sure you will say *sufficit* to this: So I have done; but have not ceased to be

Your much obliged, humble servant,

H. LUXBOROUGH.

P. S.

Tuesday Night, Dec. 12th, 1749.

P. S. For once I thought to have spared you the trouble of reading a Postscript; but I must tell you that Lord Archer dined here yesterday, and I shall dine there to-morrow. He asked me how far off you lived? and added, that a gentleman had told him lately that yours was the prettiest and most elegant place in all these parts; and that he imagined by the description, it must be like Mr. Southcote's.—I depreciated it in one sense, imagining he had conceived a grand idea of it; and told him it was what I had taken the liberty to call a *Ferme ornée.* " And what " (said he) " is more agreeable ? It is the very " thing one should choose; and what I have " heard Lord Bolingbroke made Dawley." But I told him, as to that, my Brother's calling it a Farm was only meant as it was really one; for he then kept 700 *l.* per annum in hand: but that the house was much too fine and large to be called a Farm. But on the other side, its environs were not ornamented, nor its prospects good,

LETTER XLII.

SIR,   Barrells, December 28th, 1749.

THE hopes you give me of seeing you here these holidays, are more welcome than any New-year's-gift I could have received: and as the frost is over, I depend upon their not being frustrated.—Your compassion for Mrs. Davis shews a good heart; and I think she deserves the opinion you have conceived of her; of which I acquainted her, being glad to contribute towards every pleasure she is capable of feeling in her present melancholy circumstances. The remarks they suggest to you, are perfectly just and philosophical: but the difficulty is, how to put in practice what you would advise; for I know by my own experience, that the things which amuse when the heart and mind are at ease, cease to do so when they are strongly affected, and when amusements are most wanted to divert thought from the subject that causes grief: And yet I am still so far of your opinion, that I cannot be sorry (though she is so) that it is her lot to have a multiplicity of business to go through (being sole
executrix

executrix to her husband); nor that she has already quitted the house she lived in, having let it; for the hurry this has caused, joined to the examining various books of accounts, &c. must, I think, sometimes have obliged her, notwithstanding delicacy of imagination, to turn her thoughts from the dead to the living. It is true, she looks upon these affairs as irksome: but as she is now incapable of relishing those diversions which are calculated for pleasure, I think it is well these others present themselves; without which, I am persuaded she would give herself up to unavailing regret, though not with that pomp of sorrow, which I never can forbear supposing to be more affectation than it is reality.—I have invited her to Barrells; but when, or whether her affairs will permit her to come, I am ignorant.

Mr. Allen desired his compliments to you, when he left Barrells last Saturday; as did Mr. Hall, by a letter I received the post after (viz. Christmas-day); expressing his great hurry, perplexities, and uncertainty of the time of his return; all occasioned by the sudden death of the Bishop of Litchfield and Coventry; by whose order he went to his house at ten o'clock on Friday morning to be examined

(which

(which he had already been at Lambeth); but "Lo! (he says) the Bishop himself was "called upon at Five the same morning, to "be examined at a great and just Tribunal:" so that he must go for the third time to Lambeth to get a new fiat; and, in short, be at much more trouble and expence by this unexpected accident. He adds, that he had secured a dispensation before the Bishop's death; but I suppose the holidays are also obstructions to the proceedings in the Courts.

I humbly beg Mrs. Emme's pardon for having once presumed to substitute carrier pigeons in her place. She ought not, I confess, to have them set up as rivals against her, since she is as true to her trust as the doves can be, and as expeditious as Nature will allow her to be.

I cannot imagine how I could suppose Mr. M—— to mean Mr. Meredith; and I can less suppose how Mr. Miller could make so absurd a comparison about the Leasowes and Hagley. Would it not have been sufficient for him to have spoke the truth, by saying the Leasowes had more beauties than Hagley; and better use was made of the gifts of Nature, such as water-views, &c. and have left structures out of the question, which

are

are owing to the purse more than to the taste; and with which you never pretended to vye? As to myself, I am not ashamed to own that I like even a root-seat at the Leasowes better than I do his *modern ruin* of an *ancient castle*; nor is it extraordinary. How many are there, besides myself, whose eyes oblige them (without knowing why) to be more delighted with the Banquetting-house at Whitehall than with Blenheim Castle, and with the front of Covent-Garden Church than with St. Paul's Cathedral!—Such is the force of truth, exemplified by that of proportion.

Lord Archer, &c. dined here; and I dined and supped at Umberslade last week; and I believe they go for London next week: As they come into Warwickshire but every other year, I fear I shall not have an opportunity of introducing you to his Lordship, nor him to you at the Leasowes, before the year 1751: but if the weather proves favourable when you are here, I will carry you to see the house and gardens any morning you please.

Now for the inexhaustible topic of Urns. I approve greatly of your last urn, N°. 5; which answers to the shape and simplicity of what I wished for, and will execute: and I agree with you in preferring two plinths to one.

one. It remains then only to difcuſs the one point, *Decoration*; in which point the placing the motto's are included. The *His Saltem* upon the upper plinth muſt be undoubtedly; and I am much pleaſed, as is Mr. Allen, (a better judge than myſelf) with the *Poſtquam te Fata*, &c. But we propoſe to you two things: his is, That, below where Mr. Somervile's name, &c. is placed, ſhould be added

"Multis ille bonis flebilis occidit."

But this he entirely ſubmits to you: only I think with him, that as the other motto regards him chiefly as a poet, this laſt will record him as a man who deſerved the eſteem of every good man; and was regretted accordingly. As to my own propoſal, I fear you will not like it: but you and I may both be in the right, in agreeing to the inſcription's being in Engliſh—

"Sacred to the Memory
of
WILLIAM SOMERVILE, Eſq."

It may be uncuſtomary; but a woman may be privileged to ſwerve from ſuch rules as ſhe may be ſuppoſed not to underſtand: and it will better pleaſe the generality of his and my common acquaintance, as well as the mob,

whom

whom you call your friends. There will be less affectation in it, and will more become me. As also, to have the whole seem plain, and not costly. And also, the reason of my erecting it, to be as plainly understood to mean no more than my esteem for him as a worthy Man and a good Poet, who had honoured me with his friendship: but I would ward against the *foolish* and the *censorious*, who might be capable of forging several such ridiculous reasons (notwithstanding his age and every other circumstance) that might draw on a reproach upon me for paying this tribute to his memory; and although I am in no sort afraid of unjust censure, yet I have suffered too much by it not to be cautious.—As I have taken the liberty to give you this hint in a friendly way, I am almost sure you will willingly agree with me to leave out garlands of flowers, &c. and (exclusive of the reason above-mentioned) I am charmed with your thought of alluding to the Chace; which you very justly say *would be the most proper ornament*, a *Wreath* and *French-Horn*: but then you say, *you give it up, because you cannot manage it well.* I know you could; and I see some rough sketches on the back of your paper, which

do

do not displease me. Permit me to ask, Would it be amiss (though draw it I cannot) to have a French-Horn suspended from the bottom of the mouldings of the upper part of the pedestal by a riband, and two branches of laurel to be crossed through it, turned upwards, so as to form three parts of a wreath? Nobody but yourself could ever be supposed to comprehend such a scrawl as this; and yet I dare say, you will comprehend my meaning, and then throw it into the fire, as I request. If after these hints you will allow the motto's, as well as the inscription, to be all in the front (the urn being plain) I think the whole will be fixed: but here you will have the trouble to draw the wreath and horn afresh. But I do not ask pardon for giving it you, as it is not meant to assist me in adorning my farm, but in paying due honours to our deceased friend; who is as much lamented by you as by myself.

 You will receive this on New-year's-day I suppose: may it be propitious to you! and so may every succeeding year! This wish is unlimited; so is my esteem and friendship for you. Need I add that I am

  Your obliged humble servant,
    H. LUXBOROUGH.

 Pray either come and surprize me, or else let me know when you will come, by the first opportunity.—I forgot to mention that our intended situation for the urn will not shew any ornament or inscription, except such as are in front; so that they will be needless: and as we have agreed the urn shall be plain, the fewer ornaments upon the pedestal, the better. But I cannot forbear thinking, as there are two plinths to support the urn besides the pedestal, the whole proposed scheme might be executed on the one side; that is, on the front of the pedestal.—Where do you get your thick gilt paper? Mine is transparent.

 N°. 1. I think the fistula suspended has a good effect *hanging to the wreath*. N°. 2, 3, are very proper, (especially that without the lyre) in case a circular wreath is admitted. N°. 4. The proportion to my eye is agreeable; as I dare say it is to the justness of the composite order. N°. 5. The proportion of the Corinthian pedestal does not please me equal-
          ly;

ly; but I am (perhaps for want of skill) prejudiced against that order. The medallion I like much, and think it an ornament greatly in taste; but it will be difficult to get such a thing executed, and more so to preserve it from moss, which would disguise the features. Yet, had a bust been made of him, as was proposed by Richardson, I would have had the medallion done from it, and have liked it better than any thing else. N°. 6. (This is sent to Warwick) I think this the prettiest shape for the urn; and it most resembles those little ones the Duchess of Somerset turned in wood for me; which she copied from an antique urn brought her by the Countess of Pomfret from Italy. I send one of them for you to look at. N°. 7. This is undoubtedly the front view I prefer as to ornament; but do not like the shape of the urn for the reason you give. N°. 8. This mantling is very well, (especially that with flowerets) in case it is necessary to have any thing on those sides of the urn that are not in front.—Query, Whether the wreath left entirely out of the laurel-pedestal, and the laurel-sprig added to the fistula and tibia (as in N°. 5, of the *first drawings*) might not be as well; but placed something higher on the urn, and not sus-pended;

pended; as there will be in this cafe (of a plain urn) no wreath to hang it to?—I fhould like the whole to be as plain as poffible: that is to fay, as far as is confiftent with expreffing my friendfhip for Mr. Somervile, and his poetical genius; trophies of which muft undoubtedly be on one fide the urn: but all the reft would be as mere ornament to the work and to the place, which is in no fort my intention. Neither would I have it expenfive (for more reafons than barely that of faving money); but I would exprefs with as much fimplicity as poffible my refpect for his memory, without flattery or pomp; and that it was my friendfhip only which made me raife this memorandum of him: fo that my firft thought of all was only to have had an altar, without any urn, and fomething wrote upon it equivalent to what you have put round the blazing altar you drew out in your letter, viz. *Sacred to Friendfhip*; or to that effect. But as an urn will undoubtedly be handfome, I am, upon the whole, for having an exceeding plain one, in as juft fymmetry as poffible; and on one fide, only fome proper trophy to him, fuch as the tibia and fiftula only; and the laurel on the pedeftal to inclofe his name, &c.—The places you propofe pose for the other motto's on the plinths, are very proper; and nothing can be more proper than the *His Saltem* and the *Postquam*, &c. unless one could have found one in his own Works, which was suitable, and good at the same time; which I confess I do not find in those I have seen of his. Outing's memory (which is a good one) had not recorded any: for which reason, when the thing was spoken of, he said there must be a Latin one; and desired me to advise with you; and mentioned none himself, but *His saltem accumulem donis*, &c. and was for having an altar ornamented with flowers, &c. besides the urn: but of all this he spoke to you before, without my knowledge.—So, as to my present plain scheme, agreeable to the form and method you seem to approve, and to the motto's you chose, I beg the favour you will draw one more, and it shall be executed, provided you will further promise to come and direct where it shall be placed; that is, on which spot,

"Under the Oak's protecting Shade:"

(as himself expresses it): for the double oak shall be his canopy; unless you change your opinion and mine.

I forgot to say that I have a strange dislike

to *strawberries, acorns, artichokes*, or any vegetable that I have hitherto seen, for the handle of any vase or urn; and had rather have none, or at most a small round nob on the top of the cover, such as you have given to N°. 6; which, as I mentioned before, is sent to Warwick.

LETTER XLIII.

SIR,   Barrells, January 31st, 1749-50.

IF either of us regarded ceremony, I should wait till I had the pleasure of hearing from you, before I troubled you with renewing our correspondence; and then I should endeavour to express how much joy your company here had given me, and how much regret your absence had caused me. But as I always suppose, when the rays of friendship appear, ceremony vanishes, I take it for granted, you will use none of it with me, nor expect any from me: It is but a vapour.——This point settled, I must tell you that I have been more than nine days (the common period) confined with a cold; and, very happily for you,

you, have been unable to set pen to paper. My first act and deed, which is writing to you now, shews how many such you have escaped: and still greater would you think your escape, if you knew how very stupid my illness made me.

Not the self-flattery of J—— G—— C——, junior, Esq. in his Preface to the Life of Socrates, nor his smart scourges of great men in his Notes, have awakened me enough to read all his book; but I will do it soon, as your very just remarks in the margin carry me agreeably through the road which this young Biographer seems to have, sown with nettles: but as he raises himself upon that bank, I wish they do not sting him when they come to maturity.

I send you a letter of the Duchess of Somerset's; which I desire you will return as soon as you have read it: for till then I cannot answer it.—That she should agree in liking all you write, I do not wonder; but am not a little proud of having chose out a poem of yours to send her, which pleases both Her Grace and her chaplain. For though it would stand the test of all the Duchesses and their chaplains in England, yet that *my* Duchess judges as myself, raises my vanity, and increases my pleasure.

You left yourself in safe hands, when you intrusted me with several things of your writing: for all those you called incorrect, or did not commission me to shew, I never did; though, according to my own opinion, I might have done it without offence to your Muse: but it would have been an offence to you; and friendship is with me sacred.

This is wrote on the paper you was so kind to give me; but with the worst of pens. Take pity of me; and let Aris at Birmingham know that you desire, if I send to him for any thing in his way, you would have him serve me as he does you. I shall reap the benefit of this, and you will have some of the gleanings.

I had almost forgot to tell you, that my strict obedience to your commands has nearly incurred displeasure from Mr. Outing; to whom I wrote upon business (and was obliged to send to Somerviles-Afton on purpose); and in my letter said you would have gone there from hence, but that myself and my servants had told you they believed the house was filled with friends of Mr. Reynalds's from Montgomery; and that hearing he was gone to Sir Robert Cocks's, you judged it might be to make room: To which he anfwers, "He is " forry you was hindered from going. That " under that *hofpitable roof* there would have " been room for you: and that it was not " want of room there which fent him to " Sir Robert Cocks's."—I repeat, as near as I can remember, his words; and am forry if any perfon here faid any thing to determine you contrary to your intentions. I fhould add, that he fays he hopes to make all up with you by letter, as I hope he will; and tells me he will be in London at his old lodging in Charles-court, the end of this week.

It is more than time to releafe you; and it will be, I hope, unneceffary to add, that I am

Your faithful and obliged

H. LUXBOROUGH.

I fcratched out the compliments I improperly placed on the other fide the paper to your Brother, and Mr. and Mrs. Dolman; but mean them very fincerely, not as compliments barely, but ftedfaft wifhes.

Have you not a relation who is printing a book concerning Prayer (his name I think is Pearfall)?

Pearfall)? I have fubfcribed to it by Mr. Hall's defire.

LETTER XLIV.

SIR,   Barrells, Valentine's-day, 1749-50.

EVERY day brings us ftrong and frefh proofs of the folly of being folicitous after grandeur, riches, power, or indeed after any other earthly bleffing; which is fnatched from us as foon as poffeffed.—You guefs that the death of the Duke of Somerfet caufes my prefent reflection; which millions of things might daily oblige one to make, and ftill give greater caufe for. The death of a man of fixty-fix, who has been tormented many years with the gout, cannot be deemed an uncommon or unexpected event: and yet I confefs it furprized me when I received the news, near as much as when I received that of the death of his Son, Lord Beauchamp. The efteem I had for His Grace, and the friendfhip I have, and have long had, for his Duchefs, could not let me hear of his death without fhedding tears of regret: and the account

count she gives me of the establishment of his health in her letter of the 21st ult. causes my being so much surprized at its happening thus suddenly. And as every trifling circumstance increases the perturbation of thought upon such occasions; so did my happening to be sealing up a letter of congratulation and directing it to Lady Betty Smithson upon the birth of a son, just as the post-letters and news-papers were brought in, which I chanced to cast my eye upon, and immediately saw the article, which rather demanded condolence than congratulation from me; and would have made my letter very unwelcome, and the more improper as she lies-in, and that possibly Sir Hugh (now Earl of Northumberland) might not have chose she should receive any, lest they might move her passions in her present circumstances. This *faux-pas* however I escaped, and threw my letter in the fire, with one I had intended for the Duchess; wherein I promised to send her the Ode you honoured me with after your illness; and introduced your intention of getting acquainted with Mr. Lindsey the Duke's chaplain; which I expressed in such a manner, as to make her understand that you meant it as a step towards an introduction to Her Grace: But what avails

it

it now? "*L'homme propose et Dieu dispose,*" as the French Proverb says.

Outing got to Town on Monday sevennight, in thunder, lightning, and in rain, and was welcomed by an earthquake the Thursday after.

The eldest Miss Meredith is to be married, the 23d instant, to Mr. Banks of Winstanley in Lancashire, her relation, (a second-cousin to the Duke of Somerset) whose estate is 2,300 *l.* per annum: but, far above all, is a man of strict honour, benevolence, and good nature, and hospitable to the greatest degree; and his proposals to her, generous to as great a one. Had it not been for this event, Mr. Meredith would be now here: he is with her in that country; the rest of the family are at London. I had a letter from him upon the occasion, which shews his joy; and I will impart it to you when I see you and the roses appear together in my Shrubbery: for you know they take it ill you have never yet visited them. The humble violet would be still more glad to receive you; but scarcely dares propose it.

I am almost angry at Lord Stamford for visiting your Walks at such an unseasonable time: it was quite wrong-headed; but I hope he and his

his Lady will see them in summer. Do they live near you? I wish I could meet her there. She is a woman of excellent sense, and a great admirer of the beauties of nature; which she will see to the best advantage in your environs.—I agree with you as to the wreath round the French-Horn; and have bespoke it.

You are so far from being censorious, as to Mr. Miller's place, that your description gives me an infinitely more advantageous idea of it, than any I had conceived before from what others had said to me of it. Undoubtedly advantages might be taken from the view he has on the spot where Edgehill battle was fought; but the memorandums raised there must proceed from a genius something more sublime than that which seems merely turned to Gothic architecture. Many a man can sketch out a bow-window or heavy castle, who is unacquainted with the beauties of a genteel urn: but many more people could do the one and the other more easily than dedicate it properly, and impress such ideas as the history and the place might suggest to those of a more refined though less mechanical genius than I conceive him to be of. You could easily assist him, if you thought it worth your while to give your advice;
yet

yet beware of advising him to remove remains of monuments, or even a single stone from the church-yard. The parsons would call it sacrilege, and cut up his woods as they did yours; perhaps pull down his *lofty* tower, and you would trepan him into this.

I have ended four sides before I was aware of it; but you will know it too well: and now I must add, that I do not yet know what to say about the inscription to the urn. Mr. Allen is vastly against its being in English; and I am also inclinable to give that up, unless it might be allowable to let the prose be so, and the motto Latin, as a quotation: but according to your letter, I find it is against rule, if rules there be in *Urnary*.—I liked your first thought; and the motto you pitch upon, viz. *Postquam*, &c. and have no fault to find with it now, but that it gives an idea of Mr. Somervile, merely as a poet. Is it impossible to put the intended English inscription, or at least what is adequate to it, into Latin within the wreath, retaining also the abovementioned motto? I am sure you could do it well; and verily believe you would be glad to do it for the sake of your deceased Friend, and of

Your faithful living one,

H. LUXBOROUGH.

Tell me whether Mr. Aris gets your Paper for you, and if he has good pens.—Last Friday Mr. Hall lay here, and begged his compliments to you. He had been above three weeks together at Harborough.

LETTER XLV.

SIR, February 25th, 1749-50.

BY the inclosed, you will find the Urn is finished; and I am to fix a day for sending my team for it. The inscription being undetermined, stops me: for I think it would be better done at Warwick than it can be by the fools at Henley; and I would order it so, as to give them only one day to write it, and send for it the next.—By my last letter to you, I mentioned the inscription's being in Latin; and hoped you would think of something which might transmit to posterity an idea of Mr. Somervile in his private character, as well as you have shewn his capacity as a poet, by the Latin motto you proposed, and by the emblematical ornament on the pedestal, as Author of the *Chace*, and as a lover of hunting.

I hoped

I hoped to have heard from you laſt Thurſ-day when the farmers returned from Birmingham; but had not that pleaſure. I wiſh you could be here at the erecting this ſaid urn. It will not however be long (at leaſt ſo I hope) ere you pour libations over it to the memory of our deceaſed friend.—The violets are almoſt faded, the ſyringa is ready to blow, the rooks build their neſts, and every thing ſpeaks approaching ſpring, except the more than common winds, which are inſupportable to my ears, and deſtructive to many things of more conſequence.

Sir Peter Soame, Mr Allen, and Mr. Hall, paſſed a few days with me laſt week, and deſired their compliments to you. All of them have left me to ſolitude.

If you write an anſwer to this very ſoon, you will oblige

Your ſincere and faithful ſervant,

H. LUXBOROUGH.

LETTER

LETTER XLVI.

SIR, Barrells, March 14th, 1749-50.

NOT having feen Mr. Allen fince I received yours, I defer an anfwer to the query about the infcription. I am not a proper perfon to decide; but am inclinable to the alteration you mention, as it will take away the objection to the two motto's propofed coming together.—The urn was erected this morning, and now makes a good figure under its canopy of oak. If the weather continues dry, it will be fit to be painted in a fortnight: and the man who fet it up will come at the fame time to infcribe it. The letters are to be carved in the ftone, and then blacked. Collins, who made it, does all Lord Brook's and Mr. Wife's work; and his foreman appears to be a good workman. The French-horn, wreathed with laurel, was done by the beft ftone-carver in Warwick. All this is good.—Now for the bad. Firft of all, the fhaft is not all in one piece. I afked the man the reafon, and he protefts he could not get a ftone of that fize in Warwick: that he tried every quarry, and went purpofely to the principal one; but in vain. So there are two pieces of five inches each, one above, the other below

below the wreath, which hangs on a hoop not fufpended by a riband. The next misfortune is owing to a mercenary, ill-natured rafcal, who is a weekly carrier from Henley to Warwick; by whom I fent a letter laft Saturday to Mr. Hands, to fay that I would fend my team for the vafe and pedeftal on Monday: but, if Mr. Collins did not choofe that day, defired he would name another. Mr. Hands was not at home; but his people fent the fellow to Mr. Collins, who told him by word of mouth, that the team muft not come till Wednefday; for the things could not be fent fafely before: which meffage the rafcal never brought, nor ever mentioned to my fervants, though he faw four of them on Sunday at Henley, and fpoke to two of them. If it had been wrote down, he would have brought it, and demanded Three-pence at leaft for it; but as it was verbal, he did not think it worth delivering. So when the team got to Warwick on Monday, Mr. Hands fwore; Mr. Collins fretted: both faid the urn would be damaged; for they had befpoke cafes of deal for every diftinct part, and but one cafe was made; yet to fend the waggon back empty they did not dare: fo, in fhort, they packed it all up as carefully as they could. But

But the roads being very rough and bad, they with difficulty got home by One in the morning; the mouth of the French-horn ſtruck off, and two ſtones broke off the lower plinth, and a ſmall notch on the urn, and one on the cap of it, but trifling. The foreman and another man came in the morning and mended the two ſtones very well (as I had ſome of the ſame ſtone in the rough); and have put the mouth of the French-horn on again (for luckily it was not loſt); and they ſay it is as ſtrong as ever, and the paint will hide entirely the piecing.

I was very well entertained on Sunday evening, and on Monday till Five in the evening, with Mr. Smith's company. He brought me the Prints I had ſubſcribed to. I alſo ſubſcribed to four, which he intends to put out; and I bought of him four others, and alſo the eight Derbyſhire Views; and he gave me one of Chatſworth; and would have given me a whole ſett, if I would have accepted it. Mr. Hall ſaw him here, and has ſubſcribed to his new ſett. He promiſes me the little book with Virgil's Grove, at the time he delivers the others.—Would but the Green Book come too, I ſhould be completely happy!—We talked much of you. He is charmed with your taste, and with the Leasowes; and would be more charmed with you, if you would have shewn him any of your writings: but he says you used him ill in that point; for he has seen only what is in print. He got up at Seven, and walked all over this place; and again with me, when I arose. He commends it more than I think it deserves. He agrees with you entirely in admiring the amphitheatre of wooded hills that we see from the windows, and the situation of the Hermitage; which he thinks preferable to any in England. He laments my want of water; but thinks I might find springs (as indeed most people do). He liked the shell-urns, and the situation for the new one; as also the aspect of the kitchen-garden, and the pond and oak-tree; and agrees to moving the pales, so as to guide one to the Shrubbery. The gloominess of the night shewed the Long Walk to advantage, with the moon just seen through the trees on Sunday, when he came by my coach-side from Henley; and he was delighted with the Gothic arch they form: but he is against planting the Service-Walk bank with flowers, or doing any thing to it; thinking its roughness is a good contrast to divide the Shrubbery from the Coppice, which is also a kind of shrubbery.

shrubbery. He is also against my painting the niche where Venus is; for he says she is supposed to have been bathing, and to crouch herself in that manner, upon the approach of somebody, by way of hiding herself: and he would have the niche adorned with moss, &c. like some bathing place in a remote corner; and (he says) some bits of looking-glass among it to reflect what is to be seen, and also to give a watery look at a distance, will have a good effect from the Hall-door. He is much for the pediment; to which my only objection is the price. He is much pleased with the place where you have set your urn; but thinks, as you do, that it looks too small from where it is most seen.—I have begun the Ha! Ha! across the Service Walk; and the urn is seen from every place, Shrubbery, Terrace, Bowling-green, Long Walk, and the End of the Kitchen-garden; which is to be taken in.

I send you half the jessamine-water I have left; and will write to ask Mrs. Wymondesold, if it is to be bought at London.'

I inclose Mr. Meredith's two last letters. I hope you will meet him here; and that we shall pour libations together over Mr. Somervile's urn. But will you not come besides, for a day or two, to see the inscription wrote? It would be very satisfactory, as well as pleasing to, Sir,

Your obliged and faithful servant,

H. LUXBOROUGH.

Pray send me Lord Lovat's Trial, and I will send you back Socrates's Life.

Whether you intended it or no, my curiosity is excited, and I must see the Ode to our Duchess; and hope it will not be improper to shew it her ere long.

LETTER XLVII.

SIR, Barrells, April 25th, 1750.

THAT the interruption to our correspondence should happen on my side, I blush at, though I well know it was not my fault. I wish you could know it as well; for you could not then blame me. But if you are inclined to blame me, pray consider that I have been sufficiently punished already, by being deprived of your letters, which I greatly esteem. I must have been my own enemy,

had

had I deprived myself of them willingly. The truth is, that when your last letter came, I had company, who staid a week (Sir Peter Soame, the Consul of Ostend, and Mr. Allen); and you know I have nobody to assist me in doing the honours of my house. At that juncture of time I received the news of Lady Bolingbroke's death; of my Brother's vast affliction for her, and of his own indisposition: All which obliged me to send a servant express to London, and to offer to go myself; which if my brother had accepted, I would have set out immediately: so that I had the journey in some measure to prepare for, and a great many letters to write by the messenger I sent; since whose return an accident happened among my domestics, which shocked me, and caused me a good deal of trouble and thought. Diabolical weather, added to all this, lowered my spirits yet more, and solitude contributed to my dulness. Judge then, Sir, whether I was fit to write to you; I, who in my brightest moments am unequal to the task.

I see with pleasure the advancement of Spring; but though its progress has been quick, there are few flowers, except the lilac: the woodbine begins to shew itself, and the

sweet-briar is fragrant: but I fear there is not quite stability enough in the weather, nor variety enough in the Shrubbery to invite you as yet; but there will be ere long. The Coppice has the advantage at present; for Nature has embroidered it thick with all kinds of wild flowers. The Hermitage looks ruinous, the roof being pulled to pieces, in order to have it thatched; without which I shall never keep the wet out: but it shall be covered speedily. I have not yet had time to fill up the Walk, which you know I had ungravelled; nor to ungravel the middle one, as you advised: but it shall be done. As to the urn, I told you it was erected: if dry weather continues, I will have it painted next week. As the motto Mr. Allen chose, and that you had chose, cannot, in your opinion, be on each side the same plinth; and as neither of them singly take in both the moral and the poetical character of Mr. Somervile, nor my friendship, I searched Francis's Horace, with a view to find *one* only, that should express in some measure the whole; and Mr. John Reynalds happening to come in, looked over it with me, and we both hit upon a short one, which to my thinking answers the intent, and will not oblige me to write any
other

other on the sides. As the forepart of the pedestal only is adorned with carving, I think it is best to have no writing but on the front. The motto is

"Debitâ sparges lacrymâ favillam
Vatis amici."

This upon the plinth; and under it, on the pedestal, over the wreath, Mr. SOMERVILE's name in Latin, and $\genfrac{}{}{0pt}{}{H.\ L.}{P.}$ and at bottom, the date (*not* of this year, but) of the year he died, because of the word *Favillam*.—I do not imagine *Author of the Chace* can be put agreeably into Latin; and I confess it appears to me that the emblematical *horn wreathed with laurel* will suffice to put all who knew him in mind of that poetical performance, which is so well known, without any explanation by words.— I shall be glad if you happen to think as I do.

I am sensible of the merit of the *fallow*-tree; but must not aim at having any in the places where I wish them, for want of water. My stiff soil can never do.—I am sorry your Grove will not be well pictured by Smith: Had I known it, I should have been so angry, that I should have abated of my generosity to him.—

There

There is no keeping the people out of the Service Walk: they come through the neighbouring Coppice into the Lane, and from thence over my hedge that is on the bank, which they have broke down in forty places, and so into the Service Walk, and away for Henley, &c.

Seeing the green leaves does not revive me more than the hopes you give me of seeing the Green Book: but as I am insatiable in my desires of seeing your performances in all the Sister Arts, I shall not without regret give up the illuminated Decorations you shewed me a specimen of.—I do not think the poetical prose (which is the style of Fenelon's Telemachus) is at all the common style of French novels; which is, for the most part, very good; especially *Marivaux*'s, *Crebillon*'s, and others.

A new comedy is acted at Paris, which I send you to read, as it is not in verse, and as it ridicules justly an Ignorant Pedant; which I dare say you think (as I do) deserves the highest ridicule; as indeed every thing does that affects to be what it is not, and hypocritically endeavours to impose upon the world, as *Tartuffe* in Moliere's Plays; and many other characters that are falsely assumed and well satirized by the French Comedy-writers.—I return your Life of Socrates; which I am told

'Squire

'Squire C———r has taken out of the Lives of the Philofophers, *though he detefts a plagiary.*

Pray return good for evil, and write foon.— I will let you know when I know it myfelf, when Mr. Meredith will be here.—Now, Sir, (as the Irifh gentleman wrote word to his fon) pray take care you do not break this feal in opening my letter.

Your moft faithful fervant,

H. Luxborough.

LETTER XLVIII.

SIR, Sunday, 13th, 1750.

IMAGINE you receive this from the Elyfian Shades, where it is next to a miracle but I had been, inftead of writing to you from my parlour; which act is contrary to the rules of chirurgery, and is full as much as I can execute in this fcrawling fafhion. But I was refolved to attempt for the firft time what moft people would have been unable to perform in fix months: whereas it will not be a fortnight till to-morrow morning, fince I had a fall in my chamber, in getting out of bed: which, by the circumftances of it, muft have
proved

proved fatal, had I not been reserved by Fate for some other end, which I am as yet a stranger to. The goodness of my constitution prevented any humour falling to the parts affected, and I had very little fever. Young Mr. Holyoak the Surgeon has proceeded in so skilful, and yet so precipitate a manner, that my plaisters are already reduced from eight or nine to two only: one over my eye, which will perhaps be scarred, and one just above my knee, where *the loss of substance* (as they call it) makes it longer in curing. *New flesh* must grow there, and *new skin* on my face: but he has treated me in the French way, and used no lenitives, nor kept my eye bound up longer than till it could open. I have been tractable and in spirits; and am now allowed to go once in the middle of the day to the Hermitage; where I hope to receive you about *Ascension Week*: for I fear several of the flowering-shrubs will be gone off if you defer it longer, and I long to have you see it in full bloom.

The oaks are quite green here; and the urn is painted, and the motto and whole inscription were carved the day before I received your letter (which did not come till Friday, though it was wrote on Sunday);

day); and I did not know how to detain the stone-carver, who came purposely from Warwick.—I have not seen Mr. Allen or Mr. Hall to shew your motto's to; but will do so the first opportunity. In the mean time, let me beg you to make use of the first (meaning your own English one), which I am charmed with; and think I can answer that our friend Mr. Somervile will be so, if any intelligent spirit is allowed to advise him of it.— Adieu. My eye can no more. You have a friend more than you was like to have a fortnight ago; and whom you will ever find

Faithfully yours,
H. LUXBOROUGH.

Why don't I understand the beauties of Latin? or why have I not somebody to point them to me? I guess at the sense of one of your motto's, which seems to express what I dare say you feel; and is a kind compliment to him, beginning, *Non tam illius famæ*———But I am as impertinent to offer to speak, as a parrot would be that had not been taught.

LETTER

LETTER XLIX.

SIR, Barrells, June 8th, at Night, 1750.

THIS letter goes by some colliers belonging to Halesowen, who pretend to be well acquainted with the Leasowes. I hope it will reach you; which I much fear my last did not, as I wrote it near three weeks ago, to acquaint you of a very terrible fall which I had had; and to desire your company here the *Ascension Week*, lest the blossoms of the Shrubbery should be gone if you deferred your visit: since which time I have daily expected you; and the flowers have hastened more than usual to display their beauties, which are consequently nearer decay: so that I hope you will not postpone the visit you promised to my garden, till it is stripped of its ornaments. As to your visit to me, it is agreeable in every season; and I remember with gratitude, that you have given me your company, when every body less friendly was afraid to peep out of their door.—I would have returned you the inscriptions directly after my letter, had I not supposed you would be here before they could get to you. I never have seen Mr. Allen but once since I received them, and that in a hurry. Mr. Hall I have seen twice, and he explained most of them in English, and seemed to like them well; but was both times in a hurry also: so that I could not possibly form, from their translation, a judgment which of the Latin ones I should prefer; neither am I capable of it otherwise; but am almost sure I shall approve that which you fix upon. This is owing to my vanity I confess, which makes me believe that my judgment will tally with yours: for if it did not, my sincerity would force me to own it, as it obliges me now to assure you, that I am, Sir,

Your most faithful
and obliged humble servant,
H. LUXBOROUGH.

I sent you the impressions of the two seals in my last.

LETTER L.

SIR,   Barrells, June 30th, 1750.

HAD I not expected your servant to come for the geese, I should have wrote by the usual conveyance, to thank you for your last agreeable and kind visit. I am glad you liked the road by which you returned home. It is in part the same as Outing and I went once to the Leasowes: but if a vehicle (that is not for the waggon track) could go all the way you rode, it would bring us much nearer together than we are: however, your kind invitation to me to stay three or four days with you obviates all objections concerning length of way: therefore, since you will be troubled with my company, you may depend upon it in July; and as early as I possibly can in that month. I dare not name a day yet, for fear of disappointment, especially as my hay-making is not begun; but I could wish to go about the 17th.—As you are building and altering, the accommodation may not be in the order you would wish it; but you may depend upon my being exceeding well pleased with it: ceremony is no more my taste than it is yours. I
am

am glad the Duchess and her train behaved without any shew of it, when they visited you and your environs; with which I make no doubt but they were pleased. I love Colonel Lyttelton for wanting to give you their shell-urn, which would have a good effect on many spots of the Leasowes; and is I think very ill placed in their garden. I hope Miss Lyttelton will get you the small statue and the old Abbey-windows; which Abbey (with your permission) I intend to visit; as also Lord Dudley's Green-House.

Mr. Hall came here Yesterday, and is this moment returned to Harborough; but left his compliments to you in charge with me; and says he will not fail to visit you some afternoon: but I believe his visit will scarcely be confined to so short a space of time.—Nanny is highly pleased that she is to go with me to the Leasowes: perhaps Mr. Hall may meet me there; and that will be all my train the first visit. As to the second, Mr. and Mrs. Wymondesold will I hope be here, and Mrs. Davies, who is to spend the summer in the country with them. Colonel Hildesley (a relation of mine) talks also of coming. If you let us go to the Leasowes, I propose lying at Birmingham, that we may stay the later with you.—You see how ready I am to accept of invitations which promise me so much pleasure as that of your company in your beautiful Walks: so that you would do well to be cautious how you lay such temptations in my way, lest I should cause you to repent, by troubling you too often.—I hope the Bishop and the Baronet will treat the Parson as his usage in regard to you deserves.

I thank you sincerely for your advice with respect to my improvements here; and am sensible all the things you mention are wanting. I had already mentioned to a carpenter my intention of having some garden-skreens made; which will be deferred no longer than till the wood is thought to be sufficiently seasoned.— The day after you left me, I finished the apartment of the urn, all but turfing; that shall be done when the sky pleases to pour forth showers to moisten the earth: but for that I must not pray till my hay is in.—I have turned the Path in the Coppice towards the Bank, where a seat is proposed above the Pit; and have filled up the place, where we did turn in before, with trees, and have put the white bench, which did stand on the Bank, into the corner; from whence one has a view of Skiltz; and the urn looks also well from it. I have
also

also made another opening in the Long Walk, and am thinning the branches of the trees that lead to the Old Orchard; so that I now discover three little edifices, besides Oldborough Church, through the trees.

I return thanks for Swift's Works. The fertility of his imagination cannot tire. I send you the Conqueft of Mexico, in French; and think it entertaining. I alſo ſend Voltaire's Tragedies, that you may read his *Alzire* before I ſee you; and I will put Mr. Somervile's Tranſlation of it in my pocket, to read with you at the Leaſowes.—Your ſtile is always pleaſing to me, whether you write at different periods, or otherwiſe. I confeſs, this laſt way, which makes a little journal, is the more agreeable, becauſe it imitates converſation, and makes one fancy one's ſelf upon the place, and in the company deſcribed.—You could not, Sir, have ſaid any thing more flattering to me, than that *there is a reſemblance between my imagination and yours*. It would be too vain in me to own that I think ſo; but I may ſay with truth, that there is a great ſimilitude in our way of life, and our ſolitary amuſements; and *that* may alſo cauſe a reſemblance in our turn of thought. Whenever mine tallies with yours, I ſhall conclude I am right, and be

proud

proud of it. For example, I am as pleafed as you are to have people of tafte fee my improvements here, and take a pleafure in hearing them commended; and am glad when Chance fends fuch perfons here: and my friendfhip for you makes me alfo glad to hear when they go to the Leafowes: but I fhould not like to have it a fhew for the Public in general, as Lord Cobham's; of which every body tires.—Your neighbourhood to Hagley will often caufe you to have good company drop in at the Leafowes; and thofe who have once feen it, will wifh to fee it often: nor do the beauties of Hagley in the leaft obfcure thofe of your place. Proceed, Sir, in your fchemes, which will diffufe pleafure around you, as well as give pleafure to yourfelf. But I would not have you (nor would I myfelf, though we were ever fo rich) execute our fchemes all at once: for I think there is more joy in forming the plan and feeing it grow by degrees towards perfection, than there is in feeing it perfect.

I fend you a Goofe, a Gander, a Mallard, two Ducks, and a rumpled Egg-Shell. This rural tribute Barrells humbly pays to its Lord *the Leafowes*; where by the care of good Mrs. Arnold the fowl cannot fail to profper.—

That

That you may do so in all your undertakings, is the ardent wish of, Sir,

   Your much obliged servant,

      H. LUXBOROUGH.

I don't like the account you give of your health: Pray give me a better next week.

LETTER LI.

SIR,   Barrells, August 2d, 1750.

THE bearer (Mr. Moore of Warwick, Plaisterer) is going to Sir Thomas Lyttelton's, for whom he has done a great deal of stucco-work; and is to do more. He also did the inside of Lord Archer's summer-house, and of mine, when he worked for Mr. Wright: but he is now set up for himself; and has mended my figure of Milton so well, (though it was broke in a thousand pieces, and a hand and arm lost) that I shall employ him further. As you will have stucco-work to do probably, when you finish your two rooms, I thought you might not dislike my recom-

recommending him to you, especially as his working often so near you as Hagley may be a conveniency. He also works for Lord Broke, Mr. Wife, &c. and by that means has an opportunity of seeing variety of tastes. He is desirous of seeing the Leasowes, and of offering you his service: so that I have wrote this letter to oblige him; as also to desire you will let him see your white Bust of Pope; for I have a mind to have Lord Bolingbroke's painted the same. He is to stucco the outside of my Summer-house in March: in the mean time the mason shall white-wash it. One skreen is made and the cistern is taken off the Green-house.

Mr. Outing is still waiting in London for Lord Luxborough, who was to be there as to-day; and I wait here for Outing and a lawyer; as also for Mrs. Wymondesold and Mrs. Davies, with whom I hope to see the Leasowes.—Mr. Meredith has been here, and Mr. Smith, with Price: as also Sir Peter Soame, Parson Allen, and Mr. Hall; so that my house was full. They all enquired after you. I had also Lord Archer one day, and Mr. Chambers and Mrs. Kendall another; and am to have Mr. and Mrs. Chester, and Mr. Bromley,

ley, to-morrow: but the weather is a great draw-back to the pleasure of company.

I am at all seasons, with equal truth, Sir,
Your obliged humble servant,
H. LUXBOROUGH.

Pardon blots, for the man is in haste.

LETTER LII.

SIR, Barrells, Monday, August 13th, 1750.

MR. Williams appears in my parlour very opportunely, as I wanted a conveyance for my answer to the letter you last favoured me with; and he tells me he intends waiting upon you the end of this week. I desired him not to forget to look at your Bust of Pope; hoping he may be able to paint mine of my Brother Bolingbroke after the same manner. I envy him the pleasure he will have at the Leasowes, whilst I am chained down here in (hitherto fruitless) expectation of Mr. Outing and the Lawyer Mr. Woolfe, who is to come with him: and when I shall be releafed God only knows; as Lord Luxborough is the cause of the delay.—I will give you previous notice when I find myself able to go to the Leasowes.

I am sorry, for Mr. Moore's sake, that you was pre-engaged to another operator in stucco; but hope, for yours, that he will do as well as Moore; but do not know Crosbie.

I beg my compliments to my Lord *of* Dudley: and as to your Parson, he cannot expose himself more in his pulpit than he did out of it, when he took advantage of your absence to indulge his ill-natured disposition by preventing you from executing the pleasing scheme your good taste had suggested to you, and which would have heightened the beauties of your place. Had he one of his own that could vye with the scenery of yours, it might have made envy an *excuse* (if it is an allowable one) for what he did, which, without it, is sheer malice as ever any of *hell's own* inhabitants was capable of.

Mr. Williams carries my History of Barbadoes to Aris to bind, and with it the sheet of writing-paper for a sample.

I was sorry to see Mr. Meredith's name used in the strange letter the Clergyman wrote to one Mr. Webb, about the 10th of
June;

June; and for which the latter is taken up: but Mr. Meredith was not at the meeting.

Mr. Williams waits; so I must cease writing when I have desired a favour of you in behalf of Mr. William Holyoak, Apothecary, second son to Parson Holyoak, who with his wife, (whom I believe you have seen here) is at Birmingham in lodgings, with an intention of setting up there. He served his time with Mr. Stephens (his father-in-law) at Worcester; but, upon some disagreement about family affairs, chose to quit that town, though he was set up there, and might have had very good business. Doctor Mackenzie has told me often that he does not know a better apothecary any where than Mr. Holyoak; and Dr. Attwood recommends him greatly:—and his family hope you will be so good as to speak to Dr. Evats in his favour; which would much oblige them, as well as, Sir,

Your faithful humble servant,

H. LUXBOROUGH.

LETTER LIII.

SIR, Barrells, August 31st, 1750, Friday.

AS this letter is intended to set out with a load of my wheat at Twelve o'clock, I hope the diligent Mrs. Scudamore will find it at the Posthouse when she calls for letters To-morrow morning. It will carry you neither agreeable news nor sprightly thoughts from me, as I am an invalid, though upon the recovery. I should at least have imparted my complaints to you before, but that my spirits flagged, and my hand faultered as much as you would have perceived my tongue to do, had you been here; and is not now very steady, though much better since Monday evening; when I insisted upon being let blood in spite of the advice of the Galenical gentlemen, who feared it would deject my spirits yet more: but as their advice was mechanical, I thought *I* could advise better; because *I felt*, and *they* only *suggested*. I proved in the right: bleeding relieved me. The first nine ounces were black as ink; the tenth was good blood; and no sooner had I begun to bleed, but I felt easier, and have been mending ever since;

since; and have been able to go once, my usual tour round my Coppice, &c. Before that operation, my fever never intermitted; and I can scarcely say it remitted. The *immediate* cause of it is supposed to proceed from the anguish I felt by the most uncommon sting of a wasp, which perhaps you ever heard of: it stung a tendon on the outside of my arm near the elbow, on the 17th instant; on the 18th, it was swelled to my fingers ends, and by night had infected the blood so, that the inside, at the bend of the arm (where lies a vein, an artery and a tendon) was inflamed so greatly, that it obliged me to send for my surgeon. He also found the arm no less hard (though much less beautiful) than that of Venus in her Shrine in my Walk; insomuch that he feared it would imposthumate, and has prevented it only by hot fomentations, &c. &c. and cooling physic; and it was kept in a sling above a week. The same day this misfortune happened, I buried my trusty servant James, who had lived with me twenty-two years; and was incorruptible where my interest was concerned. He died the 15th. On the 16th, I received the news of poor Mr. Hall's having broke his arm, just below the shoulder, by a fall from his horse, in riding only two miles from Rugby to Sir Edward Boughton's; where he still lies. And as (thank God) I feel for my friends full as much as for myself, this did not raise my spirits; and ever since all this, I have been, and still am, perplexed with various affairs, and accounts, which I would willingly set to rights; but am plagued with impediments of one kind or other, (especially from London), and cannot do it with the same readiness as if my poor man James was alive, as several things were under his direction. One ought to have a supernatural assistance to keep one's spirits up so as to unravel all these accounts, and manage things properly at such a juncture; and I look upon my uncommon desire of being blooded, as the whisper of some good Genii, since it has succeeded so well. I hope some of the same benevolent beings (if such there are) will waft *you* here, or *me* to the Leasowes, ere long, and let a calm succeed to a storm. At present I am alone; and must be a farmeress too, unknowing as I am; and am entertained (by letter) only with the reproaches of some, who ought to commend me for the money I have laid out here: In spite of which I have pursued your scheme of joining my kitchen-garden to my Coppice, by removing the palisade, fade, and making a drain and caufeway acrofs the Walk; which will be always dry.—I have had the pleafure of feeing Mrs. Dewes three times lately; who is now at Mapleborough-Green for change of air for her children. It only ferves to make me regret her not continuing at that houfe of her hufband's; for Wellfbourn is almoft too far for a vifit. She is very agreeable in converfation, and fhews all that politenefs, delicacy, foftnefs, and grace, which one diftinguifhes in her uncle Lord Lanfdown's Poems; and which I have fo often obferved in him, having been perfonally acquainted with him.—You, Sir, have alfo had an agreeable Lady at your houfe, who has the further advantage of youth and beauty; I mean the Countefs of Aylefbury, whofe charms and whofe conduct have always been equally admired by thofe I have heard fpeak of her. I have been told fhe was a lover of retirement in her old Lord's time: I do not know what fhe may be in her young Colonel's. She is, you know, daughter to General Campbell, and to Mifs Bellandine, who was fo celebrated when Maid of Honour to Queen Caroline. It is no wonder then fhe is pleafing.

I could

Wednesday, September 5th.

I could not sell my wheat the day I intended; so have not sent to Birmingham, and could not convey a letter to you till now.—I am (thank God) perfectly recovered of my fever.—I expect Outing very soon, and, I hope, Mrs. Wymondesold and Mrs. Davies.—Mr. Hall is, I hear, expected home to-morrow. He was advised not to trust to a chaise, lest a jolt should hurt or even break his arm again; so he proposed walking from Sir Edward Boughton's to Warwick to-day, and to-morrow to Henley. I sent him word by Sadler Ward, that if he found himself too much tired to-day to proceed, he might send for my chaise to Warwick, unless he preferred Parson Adams's way of travelling on foot; and hoped in that case he would wear his gown and cassock on the road.

Parson Holyoak begs his compliments, and thanks you for your kind intentions concerning his Son.

Second Letter.

I tore the inclosed antique impression off a letter I received. Alas! I am ashamed to tell that the said seal is spoiled by my fault.

I am

I am assured that the paper carvings are quite as beautiful, and more durable, than either wood or stucco; and for ceilings infinitely preferable, especially as they may be moved, being only fastened up with tacks. They adorn chimnies and indeed whole rooms with them, and make picture-frames of them. The paper is boiled to mash and pounded a vast while, then it is put into moulds of any form;—but farther I know not; only that when it is tacked up, you either paint it white, or gild it, as you would do wood. Several Ladies take the trouble of making this themselves: but it is to be bought in single ornaments, so much a piece, or a dozen. So Lord Foley's Chapel-ceiling was bought.

I want you to invent something for me to make, either within or without doors, of those beautiful Bristol stones of all colours, which Mr. Hall brought me. The second cargo he sent are sunk, with the barge, near Tewkesbury; but it is to be hoped they will be got up.—Lord Hallifax is cutting off part of a gallery with four pillars of these stones, which will cost him 500*l*. each; and fixes branches for candles in them, to reflect the light.

Do not take it unkind that I do not go to the Leasowes

Leasowes immediately: my reason for choosing not to stir as yet, you would approve; for I have information that Lord Lux—— and his Son and Daughter-in-law are coming to Edston; and I shall be curious to know how the two latter will behave by me; and besides, I would keep garrison at Barrells: for I believe they have all three a longing eye towards it. Besides all this, I have hopes of seeing my brother Bolingbroke here: but do not mention it yet.—This being the true state of the case, I hope you will come (in case your Brother is recovered) and make me a visit before I make you one. My bees join with me in inviting you to my little Library, where they rejoice in their labour, and work abundantly. It is a situation that Virgil has not marked out for them; but I dare say, were he to inhabit this earth again, he would not fail to call in an army of these useful creatures to form a colony in his Study, where he would view their works, and fancy himself one of their fellow-citizens. Would it be amiss if every person in power was obliged to have this piece of furniture, not for their amusement only, as I have it, but for their instruction in the art of government? Be that as it will, it is really very entertaining to us Hermits.

LETTER

LETTER LIV.

SIR, Sunday Night.

I IMAGINE some messenger has proved unjust to us; for you seem not to have had the list of disasters I wrote.—On Wednesday the 15th ult°. (said I) poor James, my old trusty servant, died.—On the same day my friend Mr. Hall broke his arm;—on the next, I had the news of it;—on the next, James was buried,—and I was stung by a wasp or hornet on a tendon, in an unaccountable manner: the Surgeon feared it would imposthumate: a fever succeeded, which was continued. Bleeding &c. &c. relieved me: then fell out a million of affairs, some not quite agreeable, others such as I was not used to intermeddle in when James was living.

To change the scene, Mr. and Mrs. Wymondesold came to Stratford last Friday. I dined with them there; and we left Mrs. Davies with Mrs. Bartlet for the present: next day Mr. Hall *walked* home from Sir Edward Boughton's to Henley (thirty miles in two days). He is now here at supper; and though an invalid, is tolerably well. But three weeks is a very fhort time for rejoining a broken arm juft below the fhoulder.—Outing was to have been here yefterday; but is taken ill of St. Anthony's Fire: he hopes to be here next Saturday. I have a return of my fever to-day; and take wormwood-draughts; fo that I muft not venture to appoint a day (but Mr. and Mrs. Wymondefold, who fend their beft compliments, will go with me to the Leafowes); but will fend a fervant to let you know which day we fhall go; which I wait for with impatience, and it fhall be as foon as ever the fever leaves me. We will dine with you, and lie at Birmingham.

After this dull narrative, I can only thank you for your very agreeable letter, which is (as yours always are) very obliging, polite, and entertaining. Pardon me for not attempting to anfwer it elegantly: but believe me truly

Your moft obliged
and faithful fervant,
H. Luxborough.

LETTER LV.

SIR, Thursday Night.

THE first good night I have passed these last three weeks, was last night: and the first use I make of the return of my health is to acquaint you of it, and to appoint Monday next, (if agreeable to you) for Mr. and Mrs. Wymondesold and I to dine with you; as also Outing, if his St. Anthony's Fire allows him to be here on Saturday. We propose going in the morning to the Leasowes, and lying at Birmingham (whither perhaps you will accompany us); and shall be glad if you approve of these schemes. Could we see Lord Dudley's Exoticks besides? but no matter; it is you we want to see, and your charming retreat.

As to my letter, it is not worth your reading; and as I (who still live upon viper-broth) am not *joyous* enough to make it more worth perusing, I accompany it with one I received to-day from the Duchess of Somerset.—Were you at Mr. Miller's Ball in his Gothic Room? He is sending to Birmingham for cannon-balls, and such like military store, to defend his Castle.

Pardon this scrawl of scrawls, and believe me

   Yours faithfully,

      H. LUXBOROUGH.

Mr. and Mrs. Wymondesold's best compliments.—We pray for fair weather to be on Monday.

LETTER LVI.

SIR,   Barrells, November 28th, 1750.

THIS day I have ventured down stairs for the first time, and have no complaints at present but weakness, which wants to be assisted by a more serene sky, a better appetite, and more sound sleep; all which I wait for with tolerable patience. This step from my chamber to my parlour appears to me a step of consequence; and I write to acquaint you of it, as I am vain enough to believe it will give you pleasure; and also, as it is a duty incumbent upon me to return my earlieſt thanks to the friends who moſt intereſted themſelves in my illneſs, and moſt wiſhed for my recovery; which I cannot doubt but you did very ſincerely, as you gave yourſelf the trouble to write, and ſend twice, though from ſo great a diſtance, at this ſeaſon, and notwithſtanding the illneſs of your truſty Tom; who is I hope quite free from his complaints. Dr. Wall of Worceſter was my phyſician; and I think him a very ingenious man: he and Mr. Holyoak were obliged to be ſpeedy, to prevent a mortification in the bowels; but after five or ſix days, I believe the danger of that was over. A ſlow fever has tormented me almoſt ever ſince: but as I am now determined to ſhake off all complaints, I muſt implore your affiſtance: for what can contribute ſo much to the recovery of the body as the entertainment of the mind (particularly where the ſpirits and nerves have been much affected)? And what can entertain mine ſo much as your agreeable converſation? I leave the conſequence of this argument to be drawn by yourſelf; from whom I always expect what is generous and humane, without fear of being diſappointed. I expect you then, as ſoon as your own affairs permit, to viſit one, who is ſo lately returned from the Banks of Styx,

Styx, that she remembers little of any thing that passed before she went there, only the friendship you gave her so many proofs of; and for which she will always retain due gratitude in spite of all the waters Lethe can produce. This is saying that you may depend, Sir, upon more sincerity than one commonly meets with at the end of a letter; therefore I will not adulterate mine with common-place compliments.—Adieu till we meet at Barrells, and let it be soon.

H. Luxborough.

The Doric Pediment is begun; and a little alteration I have made in my hall is completed, which will shew the intended pediment to some advantage within doors.

LETTER LVII.

SIR,   Barrells, Twelfth-day, 1750.

THESE few lines are only to express my uneasiness at not receiving an answer to the letter I wrote you a month ago, to acquaint you of my recovery, and that I hoped to see you here, and to thank you for your kind enquiries when I was ill. The apprehension of your being ill yourself makes me write again; for Aris, whom I enquired of, sent me word he believed you was at the Leasowes.— I have only to add my sincere wishes for your health, happiness, and pleasure, both at this season and all others; and beg you will not cease to think me, as I really am, Sir,

Your sincere friend, and
most obliged humble servant,
H. LUXBOROUGH.

LETTER LVIII.

SIR,   Barrells, Monday, January 28th, 1750.

THE favour of a visit from you, at any season, but more particularly in this rigid one, demands my earliest thanks; and the little disorder you complained of here makes me anxious to hear of your perfect recovery, and of your good journey home; therefore I begin my enquiries this day, though probably it may not be in my power to send my letter before

before Thurfday, when fome honeft butcher or other may poffibly convey it to Birmingham. But I was unwilling to defer even thofe few days writing; for my late illnefs and your journey into Berkfhire have caufed fuch a chafm in our correfpondence, that I am impatient to have it filled up. I could wifh a daily courier was to go between the Leafowes and Barrells: yet it is happy for you that the cafe is otherwife; for my defire to receive letters from you would certainly make me felfifhly troublefome, by forcing mine upon you; which at beft are not much worth reading, and can be no other than ftupid, when want of converfation and of agreeable objects deprive me of every thing amufing, and furnifh me with no ideas: no more ideas than the Pyramids of Egypt afforded to Dr. Perry; which he affured Lord Chefterfield were *none at all.—A propos* to his Lordfhip; he is not the author of the Œconomy of Human Life.

I was agreeably furprized yefterday with a vifit from Dr. Wall, who dined with me, and returned to Worcefter. He talked to me of a Poem that I am impatient to fee: he had it in the manufcript, and has it alfo in print; but it was publifhed for the Public but on Saturday

Saturday laft: the author is Mr. Cambridge, the gentleman who entertained the Prince and Princefs of Wales fo elegantly laft fummer at his Seat on the Severn; as you muft have read in the News-papers. The title of the Poem is, I think, *The Scribleriad, an Heroic Poem.* The fubject is the fuppofed travels and adventures of Scriblerus; of which Dr. Wall named no particulars but one, which was his being enamoured with a Princefs, whom he meets in a Gothic Caftle: and I imagine this Poem is not calculated to pleafe Mr. Miller, and the reft of the Gothic gentlemen; for this Mr. Cambridge expreffes a diflike to the introducing or reviving taftes and fafhions that are inferior to the modern tafte of our country. The Frontifpiece to this Poem Dr. Wall prefented Mr. Cambridge with: and as it is the Doctor's own drawing and inventing, I did not think it civil to afk the defcription of it; fo I wait, till I can get the book, to judge of it; and fhould be glad to have your judgment of it, when you have feen and read it. He fays the Poem is all finifhed: but I do not know whether this, which is publifhed, is more than the firft part.—We talked of the Leafowes: he wifhed to fee it, and feemed to regret that

his

his bufinefs deprived him of the pleafure of going to fee the places he fhould relifh. If he has as great a relifh for money as Dr. M———, the misfortune he complains of will be none to him: but I rather imagine him not to be of that exceffive craving temper.

As one is ftill wifhing for what one has not, I wifh for fine weather, leaves on the trees, flowers in the Shrubbery, and all other the gay products of fpring, and with them your company and Mr. Whiftler's under my Double Oak. Am I not exorbitant in my wifhes? Half thefe pleafures at a time might fuffice, one would think; but I am fo angry at being deprived of them, that I cannot be appeafed without enjoying them all. In the mean time I am freezing by the fire-fide, which fcorches without warming; and my ink is as frozen as my hands and my ideas. Your genius, Sir, does not freeze fo eafily; therefore I hope, in fpite of winter, you will employ it for the benefit of the Public, or at leaft for that of your friends, and not let your pen, ink, and paper remain ufelefs. It is a crime, you know, to bury a talent.

When I receive a letter from the Duchefs of Somerfet, I will impart it to you, to make amends

amends for the barrenness of my own, which has but one merit, and that is the veracity with which it assures you of my being

Your faithful humble servant,

H. LUXBOROUGH.

LETTER LIX.

SIR,   Barrells, February 13th, 1750-51.

AS the frost is gone, (the good effects of which change I feel in my health) I hope your ink is thawed, which I am persuaded has hitherto been froze; for I am sure your genius cannot freeze, and I believe your friendship to be as warm as that: therefore can impute your cold silence to nothing but the stagnation of your ink; but hope now some streams of it will flow this way, in return for those I sent you from my ink-bottle a fortnight ago. I ought perhaps to have waited till I heard from you, before I troubled you a second time; but I was impatient to send you the Draught I promised to send about to Warwick, for your satisfaction as well as my own. I believe you will think (as I do) five guineas

very

very dear: at least I think it too much to give for a glass-frame for such an humble edifice as mine. The larger Daught Mr. Hands sent me, and the small one Mr. Moore the stucco-man sent: whether they employed the same carver, I cannot tell. I find a slighter sort than either of the three will be three guineas. I imagine you could draw something genteeler than either, which might come to less. The proposal for stuccoing my little passage makes it come also to more than I expected. Moore (who has lately been at London) talks to me of a sort of stucco-paper, which I had never heard of; and says Lord Foley has done his Chapel in Worcestershire with it (the ceiling at least). By his description, the paper is stamped so deep as to project considerably, and is very thick and strong; and the ornaments are all detached, and put on separately.—As suppose, for example, it were the pattern of a common stucco-paper, which is generally a mosaic formed by a rose in a kind of octagon: it seems, in this new way one of these roses is to be bought singly; so you have as many in number as the place requires, which are pasted up separately, and then gilt: the ornaments for the cornices are likewise in separate pieces, and, when finished, cannot, I suppose, be known from fretwork. The difficulty, and consequently the expence, muſt be in putting up theſe ornaments, which, as I underſtand, muſt be done by a man whom the Paper-ſeller ſends on purpoſe from London: but perhaps your ingenuity might avoid that, if you could ſee any finiſhed.

The Ducheſs of Somerſet is going on (as ſhe writes me word) with the Chapel ſhe is making, which was a large Drawing-room. She gives 300*l.* for the three windows for it; which are ſtained glaſs, done by one Pries, a moſaic without figures, and of a Gothic form, and all the ſtucco in the ſame taſte, and ornamented. —Her Grace ſays there is an inundation of new books. She commends Mr. Fielding's Enquiry into the Cauſe of the Increaſe of Street-Robberies: and ſhe talks of a copy of Verſes wrote in a Country Church-Yard; but ſuppoſes I have ſeen that, though not printed.— I wrote you word before, that Dr. Wall had dined with me, and recommended the Scribleriad:—and here I muſt end my ſcribble, for want of room.

Yours, &c.
H. Luxborough.

Pray ſend back the Draughts.

LETTER LX.

Barrells, Tuesday Afternoon, Feb. 26th, 1750-51.

SIR,

NOT one single line or word have I received from you since I had the pleasure of seeing you, except your letter of the 20th, which is imperfect to *me*, because it alludes to what you had *wrote* before, and imagined I had *read*. The loss of the shortest sentence of yours would be regretted by me; judge then how much I regret a letter which you tell me was very long. I envy those whose hands it has fallen into; and yet it is perhaps doing an injustice, and envying people who are not capable of relishing what they enjoy: for most probably it is some butcher's or farmer's clownish servant, who is possessed of this treasure, which he would gladly part with for half a pint of ale, and which I should think not too dear to retrieve with a hogshead of champaigne: but fear it is irretrievable, and do not know where to enquire.

Mais voyez un peu la bizarrerie du Sort! voila cette lettre qui arrive précisément dans l'instant que je vous mande qu'elle est perdûe:
cela

cela redouble le plaifir que me donne tout ce qui vient de vous. Mais en vérité, Monfieur, votre lettre eft en elle-même trop bonne pour avoir befoin de cet affaifonnement ; ainfi je vous fupplie de chercher à l'avenir des couriers un peu plus alertes : pour moi j'imagine que cette lettre tant attendue eft venue fur le dos de quelque limaçon ; car il n'y a qu'un meffager de cet efpece qui ait pû mettre treize jours à venir de chez vous ici. Ah que cela fait languir ! et de plus, ces retardemens rompent le fil de la converfation qu'on tâche d'imiter par une correfpondance réguliere ; et puis comme tout change dans ce monde (et encore plus fouvent en Angleterre qu'ailleurs) ce que l'on mande dans une lettre qui marche fi lentement, ne fe trouve plus le fait, lorfqu'on la reçoit : Par exemple, Monfieur, vous me parlez de la gelée, et je reçois cette nouvelle dans un orage de pluie ; ainfi du refte : il n'y a que de notre amitié dont j'ofe répondre de la ftabilité : j'aurois dû répondre feulement de la mienne, mais je veux me flatter que vous ne me dédirez pas, Monfieur, quand j'y joins la vôtre.

Vous avez voulu que je vous écriviffe en François, et je vous obéis d'abord, au dépens de la réputation que j'ai de poffèder cette langue ; car vous direz fûrement, après avoir lû ce que j'écris, qu'il n'y a rien de moins vrai que l'éloge qu'on me donne. Mais pour vous, Monsieur, c'est je crois de l'Arabe que vous m'écrivez ; je ne comprend rien à ces Messieurs et Dames les Glums, les Gawries, &c. car non seulement ce langage, et le livre où vous le prenez, me sont inconnus, mais je n'avois jamais ouï dire qu'on en eût donné un dans ce goût au Public ; et j'eusse encore moins deviné qu'il auroit été dédié à mon amie Madame de Northumberland. L'auteur ne me paroît pas trop délicat dans la comparaison qu'il fait de cette Comtesse à Mademoiselle la Gawry (ailée comme une chauvesouris) : il faut espérer que son esprit a plus d'agrémens que sa figure. Je veux me faire acheter cette piece extraordinaire ; en attendant je m'en vais lire le Scribleraid, qui a été aussi long-tems en voyage que votre lettre. Je lis ce qu'on imprime avec bien plus de plaisir, lorsque vous voulez bien m'en dire votre jugement ; c'est un bon guide pour empêcher le mien de s'égarer.—Voulez vous sçavoir pourquoi vous vous ennuyez plus qu'à l'ordinaire cet hyver ? C'est que vous n'écrivez point ; pas un petit mot de poésie ! donnez nous du moins quelque petit madrigal : ne soyez pas si paresseux, Monsieur, je vous en prie ;

prie; vous verrez que cela vous occupera, et vous aurez de plus le plaifir d'en faire à vos amis et amies, et d'être loué par tous les bons connoiffeurs : n'en voilà-t-il pas affez pour vous faire prendre la plume ? vous, qui en fçavez faire fi bon ufage. A propos, mon petit livre verd où eft-il ? mon Dieu ! comme il fe fait attendre ! et ces jolies miniatures, que ne les puis-je revoir ! je vous promets, Monfieur, que vous aurez beau faire, vous ne les rattraperez pas comme l'autre fois ; dépêchez vous donc de me faire ce joli préfent : Monfieur —— ne fe fait pas tant prier ; il imprime volontiers, et vous ne voulez ni compofer, ni imprimer. Cela s'appelle cacher fes talens : en vérité, quand on en a comme vous, et qu'on ne s'en fert pas pour le profit des autres, cela mérite punition, autant que l'avarice d'un homme qui auroit des millions, et qui ne dépenferoit pas un fou. Si ma belle leçon avoit le bonheur de vous corriger, Monfieur, le Public m'en auroit une obligation fenfible : en tout cas ne prenez pas en mauvais part mes petits confeils.

Votre deffein pour la bordure du miroir eft fort joli ; et tout ce que vous en dites eft fort vrai : mais en vérité le trou pour lequel ces ornemens fe devoient faire ne les vaut pas.

Vous faites des complimens à Monfieur Hall;

vous ne fçavez donc pas qu'il y a un mois qu'il eft à Briftol, avalant à longs traits de grands verres d'eau, parceque fon frere en a befoin, et qu'il n'en a point ; il m'écrit, et je reçois fes lettres le cinquieme jour, et les vôtres le treizieme : L'on vous croiroit aux Antipodes, fi l'on jugeoit par vos couriers tardifs : j'ai envie d'établir une pofte entre vos champs et les miens.— Que ne trainons-nous des pigeons à cet ufage? Mais dans ce pays barbare on les tueroit peut-être, et nous ne nous confolerions pas de nos pauvres colombes et de nos lettres facrifiées.

Ce que vous dites de la *Bienféance* du théatre François eft fort vrai ; les meilleures chofes fe peuvent outrer, et cela empêche fouvent des faillies que les auteurs n'oferoient mettre, et qui rendroient fouvent leurs pieces plus agréables.—Je plains, comme vous, ces pauvres Méxiquains ; et je détefte ces conquérans, autant que les Chinois détestent les miffionnaires.

Je vous félicite d'être délivré du jardinier de Hagley ; vous vous y promenerez plus à votre aife, comme moi, depuis que j'ai chaffé le mien : Qu'ils s'en aillent planter des choux en Acadie, s'ils veulent.

Happily for you, Sir, Mr. Scriblerus enters my

my chamber, and relieves you from more French *nothings:* for such one may call the things I say. I shall soon be like Dr. Perry, and have " no ideas at all;" for what should produce them? My tongue and ears have been useless a great while, and my eyes are employed ever upon the same objects, except when I read; and as I have had no *new* books of late, so have I no *new* ideas. *Je les attends (ces idées) à la première Hirondelle:* and in the mean time beg you will make much use of your pen whilst the weather prevents your making use of your legs; for when once you can range about your delightful walks, adieu Standish.

Present my compliments to your last new cascade, which I *heard*, but never *saw*; and assure her I will pay my respects next time before sun-set, and will make a long visit. The last was only leaving one's name at a door.

If any body finds this letter (which may be the case) at some ale-house between this and Birmingham, I fancy they will hang it up with the ornaments of their kitchen-chimney, and admire it as we do exotics; not for their beauty, but their oddness or irregularity; or, as some Ladies do their dogs, for their ugliness: but if it reaches you, I hope you will value it for its simplicity and sincerity, which speaks the friendship and the real esteem with which I am at all times, and in whatever language I speak it,

Sir,

Your obliged and faithful servant,

H. LUXBOROUGH.

Let me hear from you soon.—Keep the books as long as you please. If you care for French Letters, I can lend you Bussy Rabutin's; which will give you an idea of what is accounted a good style to imitate: for Voiture is stuffed with wit, but is too formal to please.

LETTER LXI.

SIR,   Equinox, past Midnight, 1750-51.

THE faithful Tom did not arrive here till late; and (contrary to custom) I was not alone, having Mr. and Mrs. Holyoak eating a barrel of oysters with me; after which we supped. They are just gone—It is twelve o'clock—I must go to bed *par ordre du médecin*, whether sick or well. Your man must return, as he says, in the morning; so my answer to yours must be deferred till I send my servant to you with it; which shall be in a short time. —I am obliged to you for liking my French letter. As to my *thinking* in French when I wrote it, I certainly did, and ever do when I write in that language; but hope you do not mean that I think with the same insincerity they are accused of, though you accuse me of their *excessive complaisance*; of which I am rather wanting than guilty.

I searched for the Green Book in your packet, and found only the Red Book, which I have not had time to open. The Ode to the Duchess I just read over, and saw enough of it to make me wish it finished and sent. The corrections will, I dare say, take very little time, therefore the task is short, and mine will be pleasing to send it to Her Grace. Percy Lodge should be distinguished, as she has distinguished herself by preferring it to grandeur. Were she to change, (which I dare say will not be the case) it would be no blame to the Poet, nor to the Friend.

The letter of yours, which lay so long, you had not directed, as usual, *To Mr. Williams, at Birmingham*; which caused perhaps the delay: the best way would be to direct to him, without mention of me, and inclose your letter to me in that cover; and if any reason prevents *that*, you might direct to Mr. Williams, &c. to be transmitted to me: for if my name is first, those stupid messengers, who are *our* only Mercuries, read no farther; nor do they know what that means.—I am glad to find you design me a letter in French. Be assured that, in whatever language you write, you will equally oblige your scrawling, but sincere,

Humble and obliged servant,

H. LUXBOROUGH.

LETTER LXII.

SIR, A Barrells, ce Mécredi, 13 Mars, 1750-1.

PUISQUE vous êtes dans le goût de la prose Françoise, je vous promets, Monsieur, que vous en aurez autant qu'il vous plaira de la mienne : mais je vous avertis par avance que vous la trouverez une très mauvaise marchandise ; et que vous la payerez trop cher avec votre bon Anglois, et votre bon sens. Mais enfin il faut vous servir à votre mode, et j'aurois grand tort de m'en plaindre : au contraire, comme le profit sera pour moi, je vous en suis aussi redevable que le seroit un trafiqueur à qui l'on donneroit des lingots d'or, en échange

pour

pour du clinquant.—Continuons donc ce commerce tant que vous voudrez, j'y tope de bon cœur.

Au reſte, Monſieur, je me reproche mon impoliteſſe—En premier lieu, je crois avoir manqué à remercier Monſieur votre Frere de ſon ſouvenir obligeant, en vous priant de vous charger de compliments pour lui de ma part ; mais lorſque minuit a ſonné, l'on ſe croit diſpenſé des regles de la politeſſe. Ah que voila une mauvaiſe excuſe !

Seconde impoliteſſe. Je ne vous ai rien répondu ſur ce que vous m'avez demandé à l'égard du portrait de feu notre ami Monſieur Somervile : mais auſſi vous pouvez répondre pour moi, puiſque vous devez être perſuadé que vous n'avez qu'à ordonner, et le portrait vous ſera confié dans l'inſtant ; car je me fais toujours un grand plaiſir de vous en faire, quelque petit qu'il ſoit. Je compte vous l'envoyer par un de mes gens avec votre petit livre rouge, lorſque je m'en ſerai bien amuſée. Et lorſque j'irai chez vous, j'aurois preſque envie d'y porter mon propre portrait fait le même jour que le ſien, et deſſiné par le même homme. Ce Monſieur, dont vous me parlez, voudroit bien peut-être ſe donner la peine d'en faire la copie. On dit qu'il y a beaucoup de reſſemblance,

semblance, mais l'habillement gâte tout ; c'eſt celui de la Reine d'Ecoſſe où elle porte un chapeau pointu qui lui tombe ſur le front et qui le lui cache. Pour changer cette coiffure, il faudroit que votre homme vit le deſſus de mon propre front pour en faire ſon modelle, quelque mauvais que ſoit ce dit modelle !

Du reſte de votre lettre qu'ai je encore à parler ? Oh ! vous me demandez mon opinion du *Scribleriad* ; en vérité il me plait fort, et le poëme de Monſieur Whitehead auſſi. Mais quand je dis *fort*, ce n'eſt pas que les ſujets me plaiſent ; je ſuis comme vous pour l'allégorie ; c'eſt ce qui me touche le moins en fait de vers. Je vous envoirai, ſi vous voulez, tous les ſix livres du *Scribleriad*, lorſqu'ils feront imprimés, car je les ai fait demander à Dodſley. Vous avez vû ſans doute ces vers écrits dans une cimetiere, dont notre Ducheſſe m'avoit parlé ; ils me plaiſent beaucoup.—A propos de cette Dame, ne la privez pas, je vous en ſupplie, de cette ode que vous lui aviez deſtinée ; ſoyez plus content de vos ouvrages, et vous vous déterminerez d'abord ; vous trouverez même que vous ſerez approuvé d'elle et de tous les bons connoiſſeurs. Je l'ai relû vingt fois, et je ne m'en raſſaſie point : ſi j'y trouvois quelque choſe qui ne me parut pas propre à lui être envoyé, je vous le dirois tout naïve-

naïvement. Vous remarquez très bien qu'il seroit à propos de faire allusion aux environs de sa demeure, et que cela s'introduiroit tout naturellement dans l'endroit où vous avez mis cette marque ‡ : et je trouve que vous feriez bien de changer ou de rayer les deux lignes que vous avez distingué par cette autre marque ● ; mais retenez, je vous prie, les deux lignes que vous avez écrites avec un crayon seulement ; elles sont selon moi, une fin fort juste. Je puis approuver mieux que je ne sçaurois critiquer : j'approuve, ou je désapprouve ordinairement en gros, car je ne me sens pas capable d'expliquer pourquoi un endroit me plait plus qu'un autre, lorsque je lis des vers, non plus que quand j'entends jouer une piece de musique ; et cependant le hazard fait quelquefois que je trouve bon ce qui est bon, et mauvais ce qui est mauvais.

Just at this place of my letter, Captain Robinson comes in from Worcester to stay the rest of the week with me ; so I must defer sending my letter till the next.

LETTER

LETTER LXIII.

SIR,   Wednesday, March 20th, 1750-51.

THIS should go by my servant, accompanied by the Red Book, the Ode, and Mr. Somervile's Picture; but I cannot spare any body to go till the next week is over, as I send my coach, &c. to Warwick with our High Sheriff; upon which occasion plowing and sowing must stand still: but preparations for it go on this week.—Captain Robinson staid with me about four days; and it was a pleasure to me to converse with any body who could tell me what passes in the world; for I live so much out of it, that I am almost as ignorant as a Savage. He liked my urn to Mr. Somervile very well; and talking about motto's, he said that, if he ever erected an urn to a friend, he would use the following, which is in a copy of Verses of the Revd. Mr. Shipley's, and which he had not about him; but will send them me.—All that gentleman writes is Miltonic.

" ——————————Oh worthy longest Days!
" For thee shall flow the solitary Tear,
" And thoughtful Friendship sadden o'er thy Urn."

                                 I think,

I think, if I may pretend to judge, that there are four very moving lines in the Epitaph which follows the Elegy wrote in a Country Churchyard: I mean the following ;

"Large was his Bounty, and his Soul sincere;
"Heav'n did a Recompence as largely send:
"He gave to Mis'ry all he had, a Tear;
"He gain'd from Heav'n ('twas all he wifh'd) a Friend."

I have been to-day all over my Gardens and Coppice, and find the former in very nice order, by the indefatigable care of my Scotch gardener; but the feafon has not favoured his labours: however, I believe you will find a great amendment in the appearance of it. The Coppice is juft ready to produce the fpontaneous gifts of Nature, which will adorn its banks moft beautifully in lefs than a month's time: but you never will honour it with a vifit in Spring, fo that Flora murmurs at you yearly. I wifh you would come about that time; and hope you would find Captain Robinfon here, for he expects a field-officer to releafe him; at prefent he is commanding-officer, and therefore tied by the leg. I fhewed him nothing of yours but your Autumn, which he likes vaftly, both as to the turn of thought, and the verfification; but joins with me in loving the

autumn

autumn feafon, notwithftanding you prefer all the others to it. I have had the greater reafon to admire it, becaufe I have generally vifited the Leafowes about that time: but I propofe my vifit this year to be earlier, and before the borders of your ftreams are deprived of their flowery ornaments.—My Brother Bolingbroke has fent me, it feems, the moft exquifite forts of melon-feeds, and of lettuce.—Mr. Hall has got me feeds of the greateft curiofity of a flower which the world produces, if I can but raife it. The merchant fhewed him one pod only, which is as big as a pine-apple, and perfumes a room even now it is not in flower. He has alfo got me a water-engine, made of Lignumvitæ, which will water my garden with much eafe. We expect him home next Saturday.—The fnow-drop, to which Mr. Whiftler pays fo genteel a compliment, I have alfo had given me, as double as a yellow rofe. My gardener defigns to raife fome Spanifh Broom from feed; and you may command what you pleafe of it. So much for gardening.—This being a moft ftupid letter, here let it end, and free you from the trouble of reading any thing more than the affurances of my efteem and friendfhip, on which you may depend.

H. LUXBOROUGH.

P. S. Outing goes to London next Monday, from Somervile's Afton, with the two Meſſrs. Reynalds and Sir Robert Cocks. Will Reynalds is married to Mr. Durham's daughter, of the Paper-mills; and the Bride is to be left at Wooton.—I never ſaw any thing of Dr. Wall's drawing but his Frontiſpiece to Hervey's Meditations, which I did not like, and now this to the Scribleriad: but Captain Robinſon ſays that the Doctor's Rooms are adorned with his own Works: but he did not ſay a great deal in commendation of them. *Mais le deſſein n'eſt pas ſon métier; il faut donc lui laiſſer ſes ouvrages en ce genre pour ſon propre amuſement.*

LETTER LXIV.

SIR, April 16.

YOUR apology for keeping Tom Jones is needleſs: I do, and ſhall do the ſame by you; and you may command any, or all my books for yourſelf and your friends, *ſans cérémonie.* That upon Gardening I ſhould be glad to ſee; and it may be uſeful to me in laying out the additional Shrubbery, as propoſed;

poſed; though I ſhall not embelliſh it with *Minerva* and *Pallas* *, nor even with the goddeſs Flora, nor my little wood with Pan; nor have I a drop of water to admit of ſo much as one Naïad, though Mr. Jago, in his Paſtoral, formerly beſtowed ſome on me. With you, Sir, they will always dwell; you make their habitation ſo delightful. You are very good in inſtructing me how to amend mine, and to improve the limited and ſcanty beauties of my ſituation. Your miſtake in calling the *Service*-Walk a *Lime*-Walk may prove a lucky hint: for why not make one of my Crooked Walks lead to my new Lime-Walk, which is planted with Hornbeam between, and ſo wind as to go behind it into the Lane which is planted with abeles, and ſo form a Serpentine through them to the Coppice, coming in ſomewhere at the farther end of it, or behind the Great Oak? In the mean time, I will fill the Gravel-Walk with ſhrubs, as you propoſe, and hide or take away the door that leads to the Coppice. Let me know if you comprehend my meaning. It will make the place private, and ſurprize more at the entrance.—I find I can take away the foot-road to Henley. This propoſal would be

---

* Alluding to a blunder of Batty Langley's.

cheaper

cheaper than to make a fence behind the Service-trees.

I sent for a master-workman from Warwick; and we have laid out the ground to receive the Pavilion. Regard is had to what you mention of the distance from the trees. There will be thirty-eight feet of planting behind the Pavilion, within the hedge. The Ha! Ha! will bound the Green from the outside of the two rows of elms; the sloping part to be towards the Green, the perpendicular part towards the Pavilion, and walled. Four feet of turf will range with it before the Pavilion, which is to stand upon two stone steps. The gate, which is now on one hand of it, and the stile on the other, to be taken away.—The mason will alter the coves of the niches by the new Summer-house.

I have made, or rather am making, the court before my house so as to drive in with a coach from the Green, by enlarging it considerably; that is, by setting the palisades back to the Green, where there were posts and rails; and also adding ten feet to the length. The two stone pillars are taken down, and are setting up again at the extremity of the court, viz. even with the end of the Aviary, and the corner of the Upper Garden, close to a tall fir. The palisades will be very low, and range all equal

without

without shewing a gate. I have ordered that none shall be in the middle, for it would obstruct the view of the Pavilion; only on each side two gates will open; one to let in a coach, and the other to let it out when the company is set down; but will be imperceptible when shut. The two ends of walling I have finished building. I propose the court to be entirely gravel; and perhaps the handsome sun-dial, that is in the upper garden, in the middle. There will be low white posts and rails round the court, to prevent drunken coachmen going down the Terrace.—This is my own plan, and I am all over embroidered with dust and mortar daily; but should prefer it to embroidery of another kind, if I thought it would please you; as you are the only touchstone of true taste that I can have recourse to here.—Lord Archer's copper Globe and Cross, gilt, are coming by the carrier from London, for the Obelisk.

My Guinea cocks and hens are all dead, except one of each. The hen has laid a few eggs; but it is impossible to convey them to the Leasowes without being addled. I will endeavour to rear you two or three young ones, and send them. The late Colonel Peers sent me a basketful, very carefully, from Stratford; but all were spoiled.

What

What shall the Pavilion be floored with?
Where shall we enter the Coppice?—Adieu:
the Oxford postman waits to go to Birmingham.—I am at dinner, and going to church.

     Yours sincerely,
      H. LUXBOROUGH.

LETTER LXV.

SIR,   Barrells, Monday, April 29th, 1751.

HAD I been informed, even by a dream, that you and your Brother were suffering such pain of body and mind, (which must be the case when one suffers for one's friend, as well as for one's self) I would have sent immediately to enquire after you both, and should have suffered great anxiety till my messenger had returned: and even without these ills, (unknown to me till the 24th instant) I had sent long before to return the Book, the Ode, &c. and to enquire after you; but not having so pressing a reason as I should have had, could I have heard of your illness, I did delay it, and, I confess, delayed it too long: but it was next to impossible to have done otherwise; the circumstantial reasons for which would make my letter a greater torment to you than my silence could possibly be: so I only say, that my avocations, and those of my servants, have been attended with so many rebuffs from weather and disagreeable accidents, that I have been still obliged to defer from minute to minute, day to day, and week to week, the business I would most willingly have done, and the *devoirs* that I ought to have paid my friends; but my heart has never been influenced by disappointments, nor allured by any pleasures, to swerve one moment from its fixed attachment to the persons it has devoted itself and all its stock of friendship to. Judge then, Sir, whether it can have been as ungrateful to you as it appears. Melancholy your situation must have been, and is therefore now I hope the more joyful by the recovery of your Brother; of which you gave me great reason for hopes.

Wednesday, May 1st.

JUST at the break of my letter, I had a good deal of company come in; and two of them (Mrs. and Miss Chambers) came to stay some time. Their coming obliged me to quit my pen; and indeed prevented my sending Joe: but

but I hope nothing will prevent his going to the Leasowes to-morrow morning.

I beg my best compliments to Mr. Joseph Shenstone, as does Mr. Hall to you both; and he hopes you are both able to enjoy the beauties of your Groves otherwise than through the window. He feels the more for you, as he has reason to fear his Brother is dying (if not dead by this time) at Bristol, where he left him exceeding ill. I am glad you have a neighbour resembling good Mrs. Holyoak, to attend your sick-chamber; as I have lately experienced the comfort she was to mine.—I do not know Dr. Hervey nor Dr. Wilks; but shall be as inclinable to love him who attended your call, and did his best services, as I shall be to dislike the other, unless I hear some very good reasons for his refusing to come at such an extremity.

My correspondence (had it not intermitted) would have afforded you no pleasure: for as the effects of my mind have as strong an influence upon my nerves as yours have, and as I have had *divers and sundry* things to affect my mind; so am I ill company to myself, to my visitants, and to my correspondents. Would you make me otherwise, pray hasten to give me a good account of your health, and of your Brother's,

Brother's, and say that you believe me to be, as I sincerely am, Sir,

Your faithful friend
and humble servant,
H. LUXBOROUGH.

P. S. I fancy *Pompey the Little* may have served to amuse your sick-chamber!

I *send* Mr. Somervile's Picture, and will *carry* my own to the Leasowes, to see what you can get your friend to do about them.

LETTER LXVI.

SIR,   Barrells, Monday, May 6th, 1751.

*J*OE goes to enquire after your Brother's health, which I am willing to hope is better; but cannot shake off my anxiety till I hear it from you. I sincerely pity *you* for your concern, and *him* for what he suffers. It is, I think, fatal to have a friendship for *me:* my ill fortune reaches to my friends; and indeed if it did *not*, I should not feel its stings as strongly as I do.

The

The weather is intolerable, though in the month of *May*; and in short, pleasure and happiness have absented themselves from Barrells; and I expect their return only by good news from the Leasowes. Grant me that, and believe me to be

Your ever faithful servant,
H. L<small>UXBOROUGH</small>.

Mr. Hall had the misfortune to lose his Brother (who had every good quality requisite to his family) on Friday last, at Six in the evening. I have not seen him since; but he wrote me word at Three in the morning on Saturday.

LETTER LXVII.

SIR, Barrells, May 27th, 1751.

YOU have relieved me from anxious fears; for I imputed your silence to your having no good tidings to impart: but I have now the pleasure to read of your Brother's better health, and consequently of your own better spirits; both which I rejoice at sincerely, and hope fine weather will complete what your great care of him has so far effected, as your letter gives an account of; which is having done a great deal, considering the severity of his illness, of which I hope he will have no relapse.

My own spirits are much lowered by my Brother Bolingbroke's misfortune; which thunderbolt fell upon him quite unexpectedly, by the injustice or unskilfulness of French jurisprudence, and the chicane of their lawyers. He has appealed now to their parliament, where if he does not find redress, it will be to *their* disgrace; but so much to *his* detriment, that I dread the thoughts of it. The French judges are partial, even without having the modesty to disguise their partiality; and of the customary law of Paris it is said proverbially, *Que les formes emportent le fond*. This iniquitous and absurd judgment, given against my Brother, is upon a presumption that he was married to his late Lady before the year 1722, which he was *not*; though, out of honour and friendship, he did too much to let it be believed in France: and his delicacy is thus rewarded by her own Daughter and Son-in-law, who owe him great obligations. They take from him 18,500 livres a year in annuities in that country, and condemn him to pay 300,000 livres to the Marquis de Montmorin,

his

his Daughter-in-law's Husband. Every livre is about one shilling; so the sum is very considerable to any body, much more to a person harrassed by attainders, forfeitures, &c.—But why do I harrass you with all this account? it is seemingly not the part of a friend to do so, as your spirits rather want to be cheared: and yet it is a strong proof of friendship; for to whom should one open one's heart and speak of one's sorrows, but to the person whom one thinks capable of feeling for one? and of course that must be one we have a friendship for, and on whose reciprocal friendship we depend.

But now to talk of your favourite season *Spring*: Are you not a little ashamed at the appearance she has made this year? Such an advocate as you she must surely have forfeited; and where will she find such another? *I* triumph at present, and hope Autumn will be so fine as to increase my partiality to what your charming lines had almost made me desert. Before that season arrives, I hope to see the Leasowes: for I have usually gone to it later in the year than was convenient. I am sorry you cannot see my Shrubbery now; for it is in its prime. I am new-laying with sand all my Walks in that and the Coppice. My Kitchen-Garden is much improved by your having directed

directed it to be lengthened: the Melon Ground is also made warmer and more private. I am going to fence-in the Service-Tree Walk from the Sheep; for my new gardener has at last contrived to keep other intruders out of it by a Ha! Ha! and high bank he has made across the Lane. My Hermitage has been perfectly dry all this wet season, by the alteration I made when I thatched it; and more than this I cannot say, though I seem at present in a humour to extol my *environs*: perhaps it is because I have been deprived of the enjoyment of them by the bad weather, and therefore prize them the more, as some sort of tempers are fondest of their friends when absent from them, and grow tired of them when they have their company. However my resemblance to those persons may be as far as relates to my gardens, I do not say; but I will affirm I have no resemblance to them as to what relates to my friends; for, absent or present, they are always dear to me: but their presence is what I most wish for. I must, however, use myself (or rather am used) to love people at a distance; for I see nobody near to bestow my affections upon. Those few who deserve them are, for the most part, snatched from me by one awkward event or other; and I seldom find use for that member the tongue, which

which is fuppofed to be fo effential to women. My ears are *as* ufelefs to me; for the whiftling of the winds is their only entertainment: but my eyes have at prefent an agreeable verdure to admire, and forty-three troop-horfes to obferve fcampering in my meadow, which, with the tent of the grafs-guards, really makes the fcenery pretty from my windows: and, folitary as I am, I neither envy the frequenters of Vauxhall nor Ranelagh; and can read of a Jubilee in the News-paper without once wifhing to fee it. My Brother fays that I am almoft buried civilly before I am fo naturally; and feems to think of following my example; but *that* I am forry for. *My* being cut off from fociety is of no confequence to it; but *his* being fo is.

I would fend you Pompey the Little, if I had it; but the Gentleman who lent it me, borrowed it of another Gentleman, to whom it was to be returned on a day named. It is entertaining enough for fuch a trifle. Fielding, you know, cannot write without humour. Peregrine Pickle I do not admire: it is by the author of Roderick Random, who is a lawyer: but the thing which makes the book fell, is the Hiftory of Lady V——, which is introduced (in the laft volume, I think) much to her Lady-
fhip's

ship's dishonour; but published by her *own* order, from her *own* Memoirs, given to the author for that purpose; and by the approbation of her *own* Lord. What was ever equal to this fact? and how can one account for it?—I never read the letters from the characters in David Simple till the other day, though Mrs. Fielding published them four years ago; and her Brother commends them much. I think the Vision, at the end of them, is the best thing in the two volumes.—I cannot tell who wrote the Verses in a Country Church-Yard, but I like them well; and think all the first part of the Elegy very beautiful. I cannot see why it did not end at the most beautiful line in it.—I send you Mr. West upon Education; as being the only new thing Dodsley has sent me. I would eagerly embrace any opportunity of contributing to your entertainment, and am grieved it is so little in my power: my few correspondents at London are too much taken up with their own amusements to think of regaling their country friends: nay, I believe few of them think at all, being giddy with the whirlwind of diversions of which they are in a continual rotation, and impart none of their pleasures, not even the relation of them, to us *Campagnards*; so that we have nothing to impart

part that is new to each other. The stagnation of the commodity *Scandal*, I am *not* sorry for; but *that* of the currency of wit, humour, or indeed the mere occurrences of the day, we suffer by: for when *they* circulate, *we* give less way to melancholy thoughts, which are too apt to prey upon the minds of us recluse people, and do us as much hurt in one sense, as the people of the world's having no thought at all does them in another.—But I just now perceive that I let my own thoughts ramble without bounds, and that my pen obeys them to your misfortune. I console myself a little in remembering to have heard you say you loved to receive *long* letters from your friends. Happy should I be, were you (*who to my cost are not*) like an Irishman, who being sent with three-pence for a letter directed to his Master, slyly changed it for one he saw at the Post-house, charged sixpence, being double; and though it was directed to another Gentleman, brought it home to his Master, rejoicing at his contrivance, as this letter was twice as big as that he expected: Were this, I say, your case, the letter I am writing would have some merit with you; whereas, intrinsically it has just none at all, except its coming from a sincere Friend, though stupid Correspondent.

But

But to continue this rhapsody (which I advise you to throw into the fire before you read it); I, who never was given to speak much in praise of Kings, cannot but commend the humane conduct of our own, upon occasion of his Son's death, and the tenderness he has shewn to the Princess Dowager and her children. But I need not have excused my commending Kings, since the actions I commend in him are not owing to his Royalty; but when humanity is joined with it, those actions are more conspicuous, and, I fear I might add, more rare.—I am assured (*à propos* to Kings) that the Memoirs of the House of Brandenburgh are wrote by the King of Prussia himself; which makes me wish to read them.

Now (*à propos* to nothing yet said) I must tell you that it is true Mr. Hall felt strongly for his Brother's illness and death, and was assistant to him to the utmost of his power: he has since been fatigued with the consequences of it, which will, I imagine, continue some time, as he voluntarily takes the trouble of settling accounts, &c. with no less than three or four persons his Brother was concerned for, viz. the Bishop of London, Mr. Savage, Mr. Kendal, and perhaps more; but I do not know. He was a great loss to his family; and since his

death,

death, a Sister of his has had a great shock by her Father-in-law being found dead suddenly, and in an odd manner; and by her own only daughter being at the point of death, which she was when I heard from our friend Mr. Hall last; and he seemed to be in great apprehensions at the fear of losing his Niece. He had been sent for to this man's funeral at Birmingham very suddenly: On Friday last he went to the Visitation at Warwick, and from thence to Harborough, to officiate on Whitsunday; and is expected home to-night. As soon as I see him, I will deliver your kind message.

My own servant Ann Harrop goes upon business into Cheshire this week. Price is obliged to go at Midsummer into Hertfordshire, and my absence at the same time might be of ill consequence, as I have this troop of horses here: but I promise you solemnly, that if my health (which is now very good) permits, I will spend a few days at the Leasowes; which will be the greatest pleasure to, Sir,

Your much obliged
and very humble servant,
HENRIETTA LUXBOROUGH.

My best compliments attend your Brother and Mr. and Miss Dolman.—Write soon, and
I will

I will send you word when I can go to your house.

P. S. Shall I write this letter over again? Yes; it is slovenly wrote now.—Well, but I never could copy a letter in my life. So be it then: Mr. Shenstone winks at faults in friends.

Mrs. Wymondesold writes word, she has not forgot your *Eau de Jasmin*; but it is not arrived. She sent me a very little *Eau de Millefleurs*; of which I send you a drop.

LETTER LXVIII.

DEAR SIR, June 14th, 1751.

I AM sending my horses to fetch my coach from Birmingham, and I take that opportunity of enquiring after your Brother's health by letter, though my servant cannot possibly have time to go to the Leasowes and bring the coach home; but he will leave the letter with the trusty Mr. Williams; and I hope it will find you in spirits.—I made your compliments to Mr. Hall, who is sincerely concerned for your Brother's indisposition; and wishes to spend

spend a week with you this fine season; but finds himself fuller of business than he could have expected: for besides serving three churches this Whitsuntide, and attending two of our Hundreds as Commissioner of the Land-Tax at their meetings, he has had, and still has, many accounts of his Brother's to make up. He finished one the other day with Mr. Savage, which was of 500*l.* and looked out all the vouchers, and produced them. He is making up another with the Bishop of London; and there is Mr. Kendal besides; and I believe more people: and though his Brother's Honesty and Punctuality does not leave it a difficult task to do, yet it takes a great deal of time from a person who has other employments: but he will go to the Leasowes as soon as he has more leisure. I long to go there; and will do so as soon as I possibly can. I wish in the mean time you saw my Shrubbery now: it is in more perfection than when you did see it.

I have not seen or heard of any thing new lately. The King's kindness to the Princess and his Grandchildren—the Jubilee Balls—the beauty of the two Irish women, Miss Gunnings (one of whom they say Lord Coventry has married)—and the untimely death of poor Mr. Dalton, who had all the merit a man can have;

and

and is murdered by his friend——Thefe, I fay, are all the topics I hear of, or rather *read* of; for I *hear* nothing: fo adieu. It is the kindeſt thing not to proceed, after telling you that I have nothing entertaining to write. I am, Dear Sir, with the moſt ſincere friendſhip,

   Your obliged humble ſervant,

      H. Luxborough.

'I wrote you word of my Brother Bolingbroke's ill fortune in his law-ſuit in France.

My beſt compliments to Mr. Joſeph Shenſtone, Miſs Dolman, &c.

P. S. I have confidered that it will be more ſatisfactory to me to have Joe go to the Leaſowes; ſo I will fend him out the earlier in the morning, that he may make you my compliments in perſon.

I think I could never forgive myſelf if I had been the cauſe (though the Papers call it innocent) of Mr. Dalton's death; as Miſs G——n was, by her fooliſh action in giving the ſnuff-box *he had given her* to Mr. Paul. Mr. Dalton's Father had but one other child than this which is now killed, and he was drowned laſt year in a ſhip that ſunk in bringing him from abroad.

This

This (whose death is now recent) was a young man of great learning, great, good nature, great honour and sobriety, and a most genteel behaviour. It was he acted so well the top part in the play Miss Patty and Mr. Meredith acted at London.

LETTER LXIX.

SIR, Ascension-Day, 1751.

THE anxiety of doubt one cannot too soon remove; therefore I will not neglect this opportunity of enquiring after your Brother's health, by the state of which your spirits do at present ebb or flow, as I imagine; and by their influence, your friends must feel pain or pleasure. Your last kind letter relieved me from my fears, by some paragraphs; but increased them by others, especially by the latter one. I will however hope that I construed it in a worse sense than there was occasion for; and I should have sent again ere now to be more fully informed, had I had it in my power; but business, company, and weather, all impeded: and even now, Joe carries this to Mr. Williams,

yet

yet does not go on to the Leasowes. This appears inhuman; but so it must be: for with four of my horses he conveys my landau to the said Mr. Williams to paint anew, and to get mended; and must return at night with the same four horses to Barrells, where he will find full forty horses more; being those of Captain Robinson's Troop, which are to graze here till winter, if grass ever appears. Thus harrassed with that incumbrance (which might have been very profitable) and confined to my chimney-corner, without a flower to adorn my chimney-piece, or a gooseberry my board, I languish out this everlasting winter, without so much as prognosticating its end. I did indeed yesterday dine with Mrs. Kendal at Stratford, whom I had not seen since the loss of her only Son, and her favourite Sister: but found the roads, the weather, and every thing so bad, (except her company) that I never was so fatigued in going forty or fifty miles in a day.

If your Brother is better, you will have read Little Pompey: It is Fielding's.

The King's tenderness and humanity shewn so strongly to the Princess Dowager and her Son, seems to please every body.—I hear of *many* weddings; *more* deaths; and the latter has happened to the affliction of several I wish well

well to: fo that if the remaining part of the year does not beſtow upon me a ſcene of more pleaſure, I ſhall begin to give up the ſentiment you and I both agreed in,—Of the equal diſtributions of Fortune's ſmiles or frowns. Let that happen as it will, I think I never had ſo good a chance as now of finding you give up your favourite ſeaſon Spring. It has ill rewarded your zeal; and I do not think Autumn can poſſibly prove equally ungrateful to *mine*: but let ſeaſons vary as they liſt; my affection to my friends varies not; for they will find me (as long as I enjoy life) immutable; as I hope you, Sir, do me the juſtice to believe I am, in my regard for you, and my good wiſhes for your perfect happineſs.—I cannot make a truer ending: ſo be it.

H. LUXBOROUGH.

P. S. My compliments attend Miſs Dolman, and my good wiſhes Mr. Joſeph Shenſtone. Mr. Hall expreſſed his when I ſaw him four days ago: ſince which the Father of a Brother-in-law of his was found dead at Birmingham; which muſt have been a freſh concern to him on his Siſter's account; and his family have had an irreparable loſs in his Brother, who died lately;

lately; which lowering of spirits makes every new event more sore, at least so I feel, and I fancy none are hardened by misfortunes but those who were hardened by nature.

LETTER LXX.

Barrells, Wednesday, July 10th, 1751.

DEAR SIR,

MY not having answered yours, of the 14th ultimo, is owing to the hopes you gave me of surprizing me agreeably with a visit. The season is now favourable for it; and I promise you to return it soon. Why should you not come and celebrate St. Swithin's Day with me? Your company will make me regard the day which gave me birth with much more pleasure than the circumstance of its having first shewn me the light: for what is light, or any other blessing, without social friends?

I return Mr. Somervile's Picture (as I suppose you meant I should). I think it very like Worledge's, and indeed like Mr. Somervile; but methinks it scarcely does him justice, as some of the least agreeable features in his face are

are rather too ftrongly marked; as under the eyes for example; and I think as he was very fair, the pencil might be fainter. But upon the whole, had I not another of him, I would not give this for a great fum. His urn is now beautifully fhaded by its canopy of oak; under which I fat laft night agreeably, though alone, looking at the neighbouring hills; hearing my mowers whet their fcythes, feeing the troop-horfes fcamper about my avenue, and hearing one of the Grafs-Guard Dragoons play on his German Flute; which he does very well: he has alfo a pair of Irifh Bag-pipes, with which he can play in concert; they having fixteen notes, and the Scotch but nine. He has no pipe to put to his mouth, and but very little motion with his arm; his fingers do the chief. You fhall hear him on Monday, if you pleafe; and I hope you will pleafe.

I dare fay your new windows will pleafe others, though they may not pleafe you. You have not indulgence enough for your own tafte; nay, you do it injuftice. Do not talk of *altering old houfes,* or of *maturing and perfecting errors*; that touches me home, and makes me wince: for too true it is, that after a vaft deal of money laid out, one has nothing perfect, nor within many degrees of perfection.

Your town of Birmingham grows very polite. I think the Players, who enjoyed the pleasure of your Grove, should have entertained you there. How delightful would be the Masque of Comus acted on that spot!

I think Mr. Dolman's objection to coming here the day you proposed it can hardly be received as an excuse. Deficiency in point of dress is never observed, where there is no deficiency in sentiment and sense; therefore he might have come safely any-where, and still more so to me, who lay very little stress upon the outward ornaments of my acquaintance.

I am extremely glad Mr. Joseph Shenstone continues pretty well; and beg my compliments to him.—Lord St. John is still at Battersea, but is going to Caen, in Normandy, to the Academy.—My servant Price is at London upon business. I expect him home on Saturday; when I hope to hear more of my friends in those parts. In the mean time I can inform you of nothing new; for I hope it is not so to say that I am, with great truth,

Your obliged and faithful servant,

H. LUXBOROUGH.

N. B. St. Swithin's Day is on Monday, July 15th.

If you cannot come, write me word.

To WILLIAM SHENSTONE, Esq.

WROTE AT THE LEASOWES, AUGUST 7, 1749.

"TIS Nature here makes pleasing scenes arise,
  And wisely gives them SHENSTONE to revise;
To veil each flaw, to brighten ev'ry grace;
Yet still to let them wear their parent's face.

How well our Bard obeys, each object tells;
These lucid streams, gay meads, and lonely cells:
Where blended Art so craftily's conceal'd,
And Nature's charms so gracefully reveal'd;
That pleas'd *She* claims the glory of the plan,
As proud for once t'adopt the work of man.

      H. L————.

Thus altered afterwards.

"TIS Nature here bids pleasing scenes arise,
  And wisely gives them SHENSTONE to revise;

To veil each blemish, brighten ev'ry grace;
Yet still preserve the lovely parent's face.

How well the Bard obeys, each object tells;
These lucid meads, gay lawns, and mossy cells;
Where modest *Art* in silence lurks conceal'd,
While Nature shines so gracefully reveal'd;
That *She* triumphant claims the total plan;
And, with fresh pride, adopts the work of man.

H. L.

LETTER LXXI.

Sunday Night, St. Swithin, my Birth-day.

SIR,

YOUR servant came just as Lord Archer and Mr. Justice Chambers came in to dinner, and found me so suffocated with heat, and so hurried with company that was here, and company that is to be here to-morrow, that I could but just read your letter; by which, I find *your* hay-making tallies with unexpected business of *mine*; and both agree to prevent our meeting so soon as intended, and wished for. *My* business is the expectation of a Lawyer
from

from London, and Mr. Outing, who are to come at my expence in a post-chaise, as Commissioners, to see me execute a fine, in consequence of my parting with my house in London to Mr. Wymondesold. I dare not be from home till this affair is over, as you may imagine; since I have had notice given me of it: and Lord Luxborough, who must join for form's sake, is equally confined in Surry, till they have been to see him execute his part. As soon as this is over, I will let you know, and embrace the agreeable opportunity you offer of enjoying your conversation in your cool retreat, (if any cool there be) and in seeing the beauties of other Seats within your reach. —I will shew Mr. Hall the obliging part of your letter which concerns him, if I see him to-morrow; which I suppose I shall, as my birth-day being to be celebrated may bring him to this side of Warwickshire.

I congratulate Lord Dudley upon gaining his law-suit; for I believe he would be glad of any good that befel me or any body else; or his looks belie him.

I am glad *Don Pedro*'s solemn demeanor does not appear unworthy of your solemn woods; and that *Donna Elvira*'s tenderness for her absent children has ingratiated her to Mrs. Arnold,

who

who will recompenfe the fully for whatever
fhe has left behind, and be as tender of *her*, as
as fhe of her feathered babes.—If the *Antiquarian
Dean* lays no ftrefs upon the old Abbey, I
think you may venture to pillage it without
fear of a holy war. I wifh it was Loretta for
your fake, and that it might make you as *happy*
as *rich*: but if treafure and happinefs muft
(as generally they are) be parted, may you
enjoy the *latter* undifturbed, till I ceafe to be

   Your very faithful
    and obliged fervant,
      H. LUXBOROUGH.

LETTER LXXII.

DEAR SIR,   Barrells, Monday, July 22d, 1751.

THIS is only to enquire whether you
received my letter, by which I invited
you to come to Barrells on St. Swithin's Day,
(it being my Birth-day) which was on Monday
the 15th. As I did not hear from you, I concluded every minute that you was juft coming.
I hope no illnefs, either of yours or your Brother's, prevented you; and that I fhall fee you
           very

very foon.—Lord Dudley fent to me yefterday from Henley; but did not call.

I am ever your moft obliged
and faithful fervant,
H. LUXBOROUGH.

LETTER LXXIII.

DEAR SIR, Barrells, Auguft 1ft, 1751.

AT twelve o'clock at noon, and in bed, (to my fhame be it fpoken) I received your packet: the only thing fortune has favoured me in this laft fortnight. I hope her next gift will be your company here or at the Leafowes, if I have fpirits enough left to go that far. You never knew mine at fo low an ebb as they are at prefent; and confequently I never had fo much occafion for your company and your letters; which I find a relifh in, though in few other things in life. You fhould have beftowed upon me the fight of the Verfes that went to Hagley. I envy the company there the pleafure they have in perufing them; which their good tafte and good judgments make them

worthy

worthy of: but if the sentiments of hearts alone were to be consulted, I feel myself as worthy as they can be of seeing your Works, by the sincere regard and friendship I have for the author.

I find the Leasowes is become the resort of the *beau monde*; nor do I wonder at it; but I think the Masters of the Vauxhalls, Ranelaghs, and the Playhouses in the neighbourhood ought to file a bill against you, for decoying their company from them.—If Sir Harry Gough has no better taste for the environs of a place than he shews in his choice of liquor, he does not deserve to see your Grove; for whey is, I think, what one would not go so far to drink.

A Mr. Gough of Perry-Hall was here, about three weeks ago, to ask leave to see my Hermitage, and said he liked it. I do not enjoy it much myself: the cold weather and incessant rain, would hinder me, were I even in better spirits. Indeed, you will say, it is just a proper place for indulging melancholy thoughts; which is true; but therefore I ought to shun it.—I am to dine to-morrow at Umberslade, as little as I like going out.—I dare answer that Lord and Lady Archer would have been glad to meet you here. I have not been to see Lord and Lady Plymouth yet, nor Mrs. Chester; but when

when they return from Warwick Races, I muſt make them two viſits; and I ought to go to Mr. Weſt's, whom you mention, if I did any thing that ceremony requires; and after theſe viſits, I propoſe to pack up my night-cap, and make a more agreeable viſit at the Leaſowes; which pleaſure, I hope, the ingratitude and malice that perſecutes me, cannot deprive me of. In the mean time, I flatter myſelf that your workmen will ſpare you to have a peep at the Bees in my Library, and at my venerable Oak: The ſoldier that played on the German Flute ſo well, whilſt I ſat under it, is returned to Worceſter, which I am ſorry for; it ſounded ſo well amongſt the trees as I walked in my little wood; and even his bagpipes were not diſagreeable. He played on both on my birth-day, whilſt we bowled, and had our ſyllabub out of doors; for I had no entertainment to offer but *des amuſemens champêtres.*

My Brother Bolingbroke is every day in ex-pectation to hear ſome account from France of his troubleſome law-ſuit: after that, he will determine what to do. He ſeems moſt inclin-able to end his days with me: if ſo, here will be a Hermit and Hermiteſs in reality; to which the wooden one muſt give place.

My

My friend Tom is (they tell me) in haste to return, as his having got here so early availed him nothing, because of my laziness: to make up for that, and reconcile me to his favour, I must now be diligent and hasten to assure you that I am, Sir,

   Your most faithful

    and obliged servant,

     H. LUXBOROUGH.

LETTER LXXIV.

DEAR SIR, Barrells, August 21st, 1751.

THE depression of spirits my letter discovered to you, turned into a dangerous bilious fever; and the bile which has by proper medicines been discharged, proved to be as black as in my late illness (when you sent to enquire so kindly after me, and when it was supposed I could not live). I need say no more: this is a full sufficient reason for not

      having

having anfwered your laſt obliging letter, nor having returned your delightful Ode; which has run in my head, and been the only pleaſing thought during my confinement to my bed; but the pleaſure was generally eclipſed by pain before I could have ſpoke (much leſs have wrote) my approbation of it; and now I do it with a weak hand and head, the fever never having left me for a week; but my heart thanks you for *my ſhare* of the compliments you pay to your viſitors at the Leaſowes, and which every party deſerves more than myſelf, by their merit; but can never deſerve it more by their ſentiments in regard to you. Sincerely, I think it fine poetry, and am perſuaded better judges will think the ſame.

I cannot write much more; yet muſt tell you one ſecret which nobody in this neighbourhood knows, viz. that my Brother Bolingbroke is to ſend a ſet of horſes from Batterſea on Saturday next, to fetch me to him. He would have had me come ſooner (as being his only comfort) if I had been able. I am now by my bed-ſide expecting Mr. Holyoak, to know if he thinks I ſhall be able to ſet out on Tueſday morning: I muſt be dying if I do not; and I repeat my medicines every two hours, hoping to advance my cure. My Brother

ther has a cancer on his cheek-bone, which is already an inch and half diameter, and three quarters of an inch thick. He is not under so much apprehenſion as I am for him.—I hope (if I do not hear before) that I ſhall hear from you when I am with him. Direct to me at Batterſea Houſe, Surry, by London.—I hope your Brother is well, and that you are perſuaded of my ſincere attachment. Adieu.

H. LUXBOROUGH.

P. S. Outing propoſes to be here next week. He little thinks that he will be diſappointed.

Pray do me the favour when you have an opportunity, to aſk Aris for a Bill of Paper, &c. that I have had of him, and incloſe it in one of your letters to me.

LETTER LXXV.

DEAR SIR,   Barrells, Auguſt 25th, 1751.

AMONG the many diſagreeable things I ſuffer from the *iniquity of Chance*, (as you expreſs it) it is none of the leaſt, that I am deprived

prived of seeing you and your improvements at the Leasowes. I sometimes form an idea of them; but they amuse me in that shape only as a fairy-tale. You do me justice, when you believe that I would willingly (I may add joyfully) have gone and spent some days with you: but, as the vulgar French proverb says, *l'homme propose, et Dieu dispose.*

You are extremely kind in sending to enquire after my health; as also in advising me to be less precipitate, than I generally am, in my journies. My Brother Bolingbroke desires the same of me; and adds, that he is hopeful I shall find his cancer near, if not quite, extirpated; which revives me a little. If it be so, it will do honour to the person who undertook the cure, and whom Mr. Chiselden, in a letter to me, treated with some scorn, as a *Cancer-curer, Operator*, &c. But before my Brother employed him, he had sufficient assurances that the remedy had succeeded in a multitude of cases; which he took care to have examined and verified: therefore he says, he should *even* be more unfortunate than it belongs to *him* to be, if it failed in his case alone. Perhaps I may bring him back with me; and who knows but we three may meet here? as to the Leasowes, I cannot answer; for I believe he will not make many peregrinations the reſt of his life.

I will undoubtedly write to you from Batterſea; and have ſent this day covers to Lord Archer to frank, with that intent. You muſt not expect much news, or any thing jovial from thence; but ſincerity of heart you may always expect from me; nor need you doubt my remembering you wherever I am. The affection of my real friends, and the civilities they ſhew me, make a much ſtronger impreſſion upon me than the injuries of my enemies, or even than the treachery and ingratitude of ſuppoſed friends.

The ſituation of the Prince's Pillar at Hagley, as I remember, did not much pleaſe me: the effect it will have in the other place I cannot judge of at this diſtance. If Sir Thomas dies, I ſuppoſe his Son and Mr. Pitt will extend their genius and taſte ſome miles: but they cannot obtain for money what Nature has preſented you with at the Leafowes; I mean, a command of water.

That I approve your Ode is no merit in me; unleſs you account it one to know that a good thing is good.

As to Peregrine Pickle, I hired it, and that merely for the ſake of reading one of the volumes,

volumes, wherein are inserted the Memoirs of Lady V——; which, as I was well acquainted with her, gave me curiosity. The rest of the book is, I think, ill wrote, and not interesting. Pompey the Little is pretty and humorous, and the language good; but it was only lent me; and I have had nothing of late from Dodsley: but you may depend upon it, if I pick up any thing worth reading at London, I will send it you. I am glad your Brother has had no return lately of his asthma; and beg my compliments to him, as also to Mr. and Miss Dolman.

I have laid your letter to Mr. Outing upon my chimney-piece, where he will find it if he comes to Barrells: when that will be, it is not in my power to say, any more than it is in his, I suppose, to be more ambulant.

I cannot give your message to Mr. Hall, not having seen him this month. He is, I believe, at Harborough; and would undoubtedly accept of your invitation.

I beg you will favour me with your commands to London; which I can execute with ease, and will do it with punctuality.

I must now ask pardon for keeping your servant-maid all night against her inclination and duty: for she said she had promised to come home,

home. I sent her word, I was apprized of the length of way, and that the fatigue would be too much, and moreover that I would take the fault upon me, if it was one; so, dear Sir, you are to punish me and not her, if this proves amiss. I have sent her to see my Gardens and Coppice; but fear she will despise them, being used to your's.

What more can I say from this solitude, but that in all places I am equally, Dear Sir,

Your faithful friend
and obliged servant,
H. LUXBOROUGH?

LETTER LXXVI.

SIR,   Sunday, December 27th, Two o'clock.

AS I was stepping into my post-chaise this morning, your servant delivered me your obliging letter; which nothing should have prevented my answering immediately, but going to church; from whence I am this moment returned, so pinched with cold, and my fingers

fingers so numb'd, that I can scarcely hold my pen; and your servant sends me word he cannot well stay, having so far to ride. These reasons will I hope excuse my not answering your letter in the manner I ought. To which I may add another reason, Sir Peter Soame being just come in to dinner: but I must find time, in justice to myself, to tell you that I am greatly pleased with the hopes of seeing you at Barrells next week; and I esteem myself *no small Heroine*, since I have removed such a bar to my pleasure as was your *indolence*, which prevented my seeing you here; but since that is removed, I glory in my exploit, and am, Sir,

Your most obliged
humble servant,
H. Luxborough.

LETTER LXXVII.

SIR,

MY paralytic fingers will not obey the dictates of my heart, which thanks Mr. Shenstone for his kind letter; and begs for more such epistles. I believe the Green Book would cure me, and save a journey to Bath.

Mr. Mallet begs, for the sake of himself and the world, that your Muse would not be silent.

Adieu. Je n'en puis dire davantage sans l'usage des doigts, qui me paroissent avoir reçûs l'impression de tous mes autres maux; car, Dieu merci, je me porte passablement bien d'ailleurs.

H. L.

LETTER LXXVIII.

DEAR SIR,   Bath, January 20th, 1752.

MY fingers *shall* make an effort to write to you: you *must* make a great one to read what they write. Such is my present situation.—The Doctors give me hopes, that bathing and pumping will soon restore me to the use of my hands. But as yet, I have only drank the waters at home, the week I have been here.—I spent three weeks at London

after

after my Brother's death, at Mr. Wymondefold's. They enquired much after you.

Your grief for your Brother I feel in its full force, and am perfuaded you feel the like as to mine: but as our loffes are irrecoverable, we ought, I believe, not only to fubmit, but to endeavour to fhake off the melancholy ideas they fuggeft.—I preach what I do not well practife; and will prefcribe what I do not well execute—Come into company; Bath is your place—and I am in all places, and at all times,

Your faithful fervant,
H. L.

LETTER LXXIX.

Orange Grove, February 29th, 1752.

DEAR SIR,

LEST my fingers fhould refufe me their affiftance for more than two minutes, I begin my letter by telling you that your recommendation leaves me no room to hefitate; and I readily accept the houfe-maid from your hands (who knows, I prefume, that fhe is alfo to do the dairy, as her predecessors in my service did) and I would have her go to Barrells immediately, if possible; for I have been obliged to send for my laundry-maid hither, to assist for the present (my own servant, who is also my housekeeper, being married); so that there is not one female now at Barrells. Joe and she will settle the day of her going.

For once bid business avaunt, and ask us how we do at Bath, and at your friend Graves's. We can offer you friendly conversation, friendly springs, friendly rides and walks, friendly pastimes to dissipate gloomy thoughts; friendly booksellers, who for five shillings for the season will furnish you with all the new books; friendly chairmen, who will carry you through storms and tempests for sixpence, and seldom else, for Duchesses trudge the streets here unattended: we have also friendly Othellos, Falstaffs, Richards the Third, and Harlequins, who entertain one daily for half the price of your Garricks, Barrys, and Rich's—And (what you will scarcely believe) we can also offer you friendly solitude; for one may be an Anchoret here without being disturbed by the question *Why?*—Would you see the fortunate and benevolent Mr. Allen, his fine house, and his stone-quarries? Would you see our law-giver Mr. Nash, whose white hat

hat commands more respect and non-resistance than the Crowns of some Kings, though now worn on a head that is in the 80th year of its age? To promote society, good manners, and a coalition of parties and ranks; to suppress scandal and late hours, are his views; and he succeeds rather better than his brother-monarchs generally do: hasten then your steps; for he may be soon carried off the stage of life, as the greatest must fall to the worms repast: yet, he is new-hanging his Collection of Beauties, so as to have space to hang up as many more future Belles. His Apelles is Howard (in crayons); his Praxiteles is Howard's Brother, who, though a statuary, deigns also to exercise his art in sculpture on humble paper-ceilings, which are very handsome.

You ridicule the trifles I sent you, by calling them *elegant presents:* in revenge, I send you nothing this time in Joe's pocket but a bit of dirty rock, and a snail petrified by the waters hereabouts. If you please, I can buy you, for four shillings, a quart of durable cement, to make urns, &c. in rock-work with these sort of materials, and Bristol stones, or even of shells.

How infinitely I scrawl! I who can scarcely hold a pen, and could not write to my

Nephew

Nephew Bolingbroke, till laſt week, ſince his Uncle's death.

Adieu, Monſieur: je n'en puis plus; ma *main* ſe revolte, mais jamais mon *cœur*.

H. L.

I am told your Friend Mr. Graves does not leave his Wife an inch.

P. S. I will make your compliments to any body you pleaſe, let them live in what latitude ſoever, when you name them to me.—Mrs. Maynard ſends her reſpects to you.—My letter is ſo ſcribbled, interlined, and blotted, that I hope you will copy the part relating to the Houſe-keeper, inſtead of ſhewing her friends my whole prepoſterous letter.

Pray, How does Eolus's harp perform?

Mr. Bradley's family are well recovered from inoculation, and not marked. There were ſeven or eight at once inoculated at home by Mr. Holyoak.

LETTER

LETTER LXXX.

DEAR SIR,   Barrells, Thursday, June 4th, 1752.

HAD I had a servant to send to the Leasowes, I should not have omitted thanking you for your kind (though short) visit, long
before this time: but Price and Joe were both
at London; the rest of my domesticks all new
servants, that are as unknown to me as the
road to your house is to them. Price came
home in my post-chaise last Saturday, but returns to London on Friday next. He brought
me a letter from Mrs. Wymondesold, in which
was the inclosed Postscript, as also a very di-
minutive bottle of Sweets, which I send with
this letter to the care of Mr. Williams. She goes
to Tunbridge the first week in July, and to
Bath the first week in October; between which
seasons she will endeavour to prevail with her
Father-in-law to dispense with her company
three weeks, in order to spend them here
with me.

I must now beg the favour of you to instruct
me about the ceiling of my bed-room, which I
would have adorned a little with *papier maché*

and the ground painted of a colour; but do not know where to get the paper ornaments, nor how to have them fixed up: for no person hereabouts has the smallest idea of it. Should not the ceiling and cove, which are at present plain stucco much cracked, be mended by the Warwick plaisterer, before the rest is attempted? Be so good, dear Sir, as to send me an answer to these queries as soon as possible.

When you write to Mr. Greaves, pray do not forget my compliments to him and to Mrs. Greaves; whom I am sorry I did not see at Barrells.

Let me know how your new apartment goes on; to which this rainy weather will have caused you to give fresh attention, as your environs cannot have drawn you far from it; and yet we are in the month of June—so says the Almanack—but I cannot believe it. I am at all seasons (however mutable *they* may be) ever immutable in my friendship to you, and very much

Your obliged humble servant,
H. LUXBOROUGH.

LETTER LXXXI.

Barrells, Saturday, June 6th, 1752.

DEAR SIR,

YOUR quick return to my troublesome letter gave me much pleasure, but no surprize, as you have long accustomed me to all friendly attentions on your part: but your taking down your whole *ceiling* to send me, merely to satisfy my impertinent curiosity, is a gallantry that quite confounds me; and your maid's charging herself with it, and bringing it safe, though unaccompanied, and riding single, shews her a Heroine. Had you seen me open the parcel, you would have found me a contrast to her. Fear and trembling seized me ere I read that it was extremely tender and apt to break. It increased so much upon viewing the truth of that, that as I received the pieces I returned them in five minutes time to your servant, lest any thing should happen to them here: but however, in that short time, I perceived that your advice to me was proper in regard to *my* ceiling, and that your ornaments must look very pretty in *yours*. I will write to Bromwich to send me some in that taste, and will get the accidental cracks I mentioned to you repaired; after which, if the Gentleman your neighbour favours me with a visit and with his directions, it will infinitely oblige me.

You please me in telling me you have had company, and more so, in telling me you are not at present the least averse to such dissipation; for your averseness to it prevented the effect which you seemed to want from such a remedy. I am myself too averse to that remedy to wonder you are so: but it is common to preach better than one practises.

I know Mrs. Stanley; for I suppose you mean the Daughter of Sir Hans Sloane, Sister of Lady Cadogan: Admiral Smith I do not know: but who is there but must wish to know him, when *you* say he is the *delight of mankind?*—I am glad Lord Dudley is restored to you, and beg my compliments to him and Miss Lea.—Mr. Outing is still at Henley at Mr. Holyoak's: he comes here sometimes as a day-visiter; sometimes stays a night, which he did yesterday with Jack Reynalds'; and they left me this morning. He knows he is welcome for longer.—I am glad Sir George Lyttelton has a view to modern plans for his house;
which

which certainly ought to be more modern (or more antique) than it is.

Mrs. Wymondefold in my opinion deserves no thanks for such an ideal present: for my part, I saw nothing in the little bottle (which I durst not open) but a green small shadow: if any thing was ever in it (as undoubtedly there was) it must have evaporated, as well it might, being covered with *nothing*, and stopt with a common glafs-stopper.—You do Price too much honour:—he is at London; how *well* or *ill*, I do not know at present.

Talking of illness, I mention with real concern that of your maid's sister; and the more so, as she is a servant you recommended to me, and whom I much wished to have found capable of the work her post here obliged her to; which is in itself such as only a strong and healthy person used to work can go through; I mean when I have my whole dairy; but since she has been here, I have had but one cow, and no labour; yet the poor girl was seized with pains in all her limbs about four days ago, which grew worse, and are more fixed in one arm now. I no sooner knew it, but I sent for Mr. Holyoak, who is the person with whom I intrust my own health: after he had talked with her, he told me she said any cold was

apt

apt to give her such pains (which he called rheumatic); and that wetting her feet would do it immediately. This is a great misfortune to a servant, and makes it impossible to a mistress to keep one so tender; and would be great imprudence in the servant, however willing, (as I dare say this is) to attempt it. Therefore hope dear Mr. Shenstone will not take it amiss that I part with her. I offer her and your own maid-servant my post-chaise to carry them together, as it would be more easy for Hannah on Monday; and hope your own maid will accept the offer, that she may accompany her sister, and also see Barrells tomorrow (Sunday) with less interruption.

I am, dear Sir, with constant truth,

Your faithful humble servant,

H. LUXBOROUGH.

I enquired of your man after Mrs. Arnold. If he does not tell her, pray let this letter say, I am her hearty well-wisher.

LETTER LXXXII.

DEAR SIR,   Barrells, July 19th, 1752.

AS I have eight people at table, and as you requeſt me to diſpatch the truſty and valuable Tom to-night, you muſt not expect an anſwer ſuitable to your agreeable letter, either in length or ſtile: ſo I haſten to return thanks for your punctuality about the label, and for your kind invitation to the Leaſowes. I muſt next tell you the reaſons you have been ſo long without hearing from me; which are, Firſt, A journey to Oxford I was obliged to take upon buſineſs; and ſince that, Company I have had in my houſe. At preſent, here are Sir Peter Soame and his Son, Mrs. Davies, and Mr. Outing, who will write his own excuſe.—My hanging-paper is arrived, and the cracks of the ceiling have been filled. The papier maché is not yet come, but is be-ſpoke.—You may depend upon my inclination's guiding me to the Leaſowes as ſoon as it is in my power: but I am as buſy in hay as you can poſſibly be, and having loſt half my ſett of horſes, and not yet being able to ſupply their places, the three remaining ones are fully employed, and cannot be spared for me to use; and moreover my post-chaise is gone to have new wheels put to it. These distresses removed, I shall wait upon you, and Lord Dudley; to whom, and to Miss Lea, I beg my best compliments.—I shewed the *Débris* of my Bathrock-work to your man Tom, who will carry a small basketful.

I am most inviolably

Your obliged humble servant,

H. LUXBOROUGH.

Sir Peter and Mr. Soame's compliments attend you.

LETTER LXXXIII.

DEAR SIR,   Barrells, August 15th, 1752.

YOU are always obliging, but doubly so now, in sending to enquire again after me, though I have not yet been at the Leasowes to thank you for all favours: but my company has but just left me; and whilst they were

were here, I could neither find time to go any where, nor even to write.—Sir Peter Soame and his Son are gone back to Heydon. I carried Mrs. Davies home to Stratford yesterday-was-sevennight; and this day sevennight Mr. Outing went to Gloucestershire, in order to embark last Monday for Monmouth: so he may probably be afraid with reason, and become a prey to the fish, having so young a guide as his pupil: and, as I told him, if such an accident happened, nobody would pity him; but all would say (as in Moliere's play)

"Qu' alloit il faire dans cette galere?"

This *juvenile* party consists of Lord Somervile's two Sons, Outing's Pupil, himself, and Jack Reynalds; who go this voyage by water they know not why nor where. Landrinden they talked of taking in their way, when the Somerviles, &c. lay here and formed this party: but they were no sooner gone than I perceived Outing's heart failed him, but he was ashamed to own it to them; however, he said he would go no farther than to Monmouth, and told Lane he intended to be back at Barrells in a fortnight's time. If he is so, he will undoubtedly go with me to the Leasowes. If I can also get Mrs. Davies to go, she will contribute to our mirth, and will sing all day: Sir Peter taught her two or three new songs. She can lay with my servant; so that she will not take up a bed the more. I have thoughts of going in my landau, and of sending back four of the horses the same night, and keeping two at your house, which will I suppose be sufficient to carry me to the Grange. If convenient to you, I propose going to the Leasowes on Friday the 28th instant: if not convenient to you, pray write me word. Price begs he may attend my coach.—I rejoice at your jollity, and will join in chorus, when you sing

   " Banissons la melancolie:"

but your *writing nothing* I do not approve of, no more than of your not finishing my Green Book.—Your inscription upon the Label should be *Vin de Païsan*, without the *s* at last.

Joe translated the French receipt for cauliflowers, and has dictated it to Lane, whilst I have been writing this letter.

My best compliments wait on Lord Dudley and Miss Lea; and I am ever

   Most sincerely yours, &c.

     H. LUXBOROUGH.

LETTER LXXXIV.

*NOtwithstanding my partiality to Autumn, I long for Spring, as it will I hope bring you to Barrells, and as it ushers in Summer, which will carry me to the Leasowes; where I will, as long as it is in my power, pay my devoirs to you, and make libations to our departed Friend over his urn, which I am glad you have erected to his memory; as I think it is pity that so worthy a man should meet with so few people to pay to his memory the honours it deserves; and so many, that, on the contrary, vilify his character: And though I am far from laying a stress upon funeral pomp, no one (Jacky Reynalds excepted) shed a tear over his corse, or has laid a stone over his grave,—notwithstanding Lord Somervile is so a great gainer by his dying, and the Vicar was so great a one by his living: but ingratitude is now as fashionable as bribery and corruption.

Here I end, left you should be quite tired out, and not return me an answer soon, for fear of drawing upon yourself a troublesome reply,

---
* The beginning of this Letter is wanting.

reply. It is late; but I can, with the worst pen, and the sincerest heart assure you, that I am, Sir,

Your obliged and faithful servant,

H. LUXBOROUGH.

LETTER LXXXV.

DEAR SIR,   *Barrells, September 28th, 1752.*

MR. Pixall has just been saying he intends to go home to-morrow: You would otherwise have heard from me by another conveyance; for I could not longer have forborne returning my sincere thanks for the very obliging, hospitable, and pleasing reception I met with at the Leasowes, and for your agreeable, though too short, visit at Barrells.

My cough continues; but I am otherwise well, and inhabit my lower apartment and my Summer-house, where I hope to receive you and Lord Dudley before the days grow much shorter, and the elms quite bare. My compliments attend his Lordship, Miss Lea, and all your neighbours.

My Dressing-Room looks just as *I* would, and

and as I believe *you* would have it (fo well has Mr. Pixall performed his part); and the feftoons over the windows are not the leaft elegant ornaments of the room: the doors feem to envy the windows, and are in as plain a drefs as that of the Quakers; but are very ready to fubmit to any ornament *you* will be pleafed to beftow.

I defire the bearer may lead my coach-horfe home; and I beg the favour of you to pay the farrier, and to let me know what his bill comes to, which will be better than letting him make it to me, who am a ftranger.

I have juft been writing to the Earl and Countefs of Ferrers, from whom I received compliments this day, and information of their marriage; fo that my hand is *tired*, but my heart is *indefatigably true* to my friends, and would be equally ferviceable, if power was given to

  Your faithful and obliged
   humble fervant,
    H. LUXBOROUGH.

LETTER LXXXVI.

Barrells, Sunday, October 15th, 1752.

DEAR SIR,

ANY messenger that comes from the Leasowes is sure to be welcome at Barrells (as Hannah would have been, if you had permitted her to come).—You are very kind in being solicitous about my health, which is good now, my Birmingham cough has left me; but it continued a considerable time after you went from hence.

I congratulate you upon having had so much agreeable company, who will undoubtedly visit you often; as, by your account of them, they seem to be people of taste.—My pride cannot be heightened by Sir George Lyttelton's approbation of my Lines, because Mr. Shenstone had commended them before, and has thought them worthy of being retouched by himself.

Lord Dudley is slow in fixing a day for giving me the pleasure of his and your company; but I hope the resolution will come upon

upon him suddenly, and will as suddenly be executed; though I cannot promise his Lordship any pleasure in the journey, except that of *obliging*; which I know is a great one to him.

Mr. Outing and I have lived like two Hermits since you left us. The few fine days we have had I have employed in making small improvements (alterations at least) in my Coppice, and in the way to it: but much more planting is required; and I want greatly a hedge that will grow as quick as yours did, and I shall prize it as much (but with far more reason) as the *venerable* Dean does his newly-found Druid-Idol.

I return your small Red Book, after having copied the Ode on Indolence, which pleases me much.—I also send you by trusty Tom three Roses for your Gothic windows, which you may fix up without censure, for they are all *red*.

I observe your aversion to Autumn continues, and that, when you find your spirits depressed, you are ready to lay the fault on the season; but I take it that solitude is the chief cause, and the nurse of *painful ideas*.

I hope Mrs. Arnold is well, and shall be obliged to her for a Guinea cock, when convenient.

Pray

Pray remember me kindly to Mr. Pixall, and ask if he bespoke my long stools and fire-grate at Birmingham? and whether he spoke to Mr. Williams?

Adieu. I am interrupted by Mr. John Reynalds, and Mr. Bradley, and Lady Plymouth's servant, from writing more; but never can be interrupted in my sentiments of friendship and gratitude towards you, which are immutable.

H. LUXBOROUGH.

LETTER LXXXVII.

Barrells, Tuesday, October 24th, 1752.

DEAR SIR,

LONG have I expected the pleasure of your company and Lord Dudley's, but have expected in vain; and my impatience at the delay will sufficiently show the greater impatience and the concern I now feel at finding myself obliged to prolong that delay, which I wished to shorten.—The truth is, that my old

old servant Price is struck with a palsy, and one half of his body is dead; so that he is entirely helpless: and as his weight and size do not agree with the narrowness of my garret-stairs, there was not a possibility of carrying him, last Saturday, higher than the first story; where he has continued ever since in the bed Mr. Outing lay in till then; and another person lays in the other bed, in the same room, to be ready at hand to assist him, and turn him as he lays. This accident, and the consequences of it, perplex me a good deal; but it was unavoidable: for so faithful an old servant could not be sent out of the house, unless inhumanity had guided me; which I hope will never be the case, though I forfeit my own pleasure; for I cannot ask to see you and Lord Dudley, where I could not lodge you. I have literally but one spare bed at present, and that is used by Dr. Wall when he comes to the sick man.—I never till now wished for a spacious habitation: my small one was sufficient for my use, and fully satisfied my ambition; but now that it banishes my friends, it is insupportable to me: it is, however, but for a time, and *that*, I hope, a *short one*. As soon as these difficulties are removed, I will acquaint
you

you of it for my own sake. In the mean time, be pleased to present my compliments to Lord Dudley and Miss Lea, and acquaint his Lordship of my disappointment.—Mr. Outing presents his compliments to you, and asks your commands to London, where he is obliged to go soon.—I am most sincerely, dear Sir,

Your obliged humble servant,

H. LUXBOROUGH.

LETTER LXXXVIII.

DEAR SIR, Barrells, November 6th, 1752.

IT is both kind and polite of you to send so far to enquire after my honest old servant Price: but the answer is such as I believe you guess:—He is no more. It pleased God to release him from his misery, but not till yesterday morning, at two or three o'clock. He had his senses to the last, and made his will. We propose to bury him on Wednesday. I have sent into Herefordshire for Mr. Smith, the
Clergyman

Clergyman you saw here. My hurry, and the confusion of my house, has been very great, and is not yet at an end: The having almost all new servants makes it lay harder upon me. —Mr. Outing was to have gone for London to-day; but does not go till next Monday, and desires his best compliments to you.

If you see Mr. Pixall, pray say that I do not mean to give two guineas for a fender; and I even think I need not have any bought: but would be glad of a small grate; and I am obliged to him for the trouble of getting the things made which I bespoke.—My great Parlour looks very handsome now it is painted with flake-white.

Thanks for your Stanza to Admiral Smith, which is genteel and elegant. You are happy in having neighbours deserving of your panegyrics.—Mrs. Dillon's beauty claims a considerable place among them.—I can scarcely form an idea of Lady Lyttelton presiding over a Dairy, any more than I should of the venerable Dean, if you told me he preferred a modern Guinea to a copper Otho.

My best compliments pray, at the Grange; and hope the visit intended me, though postponed, will be made ere long.

I send you Mrs. Wymondesold's compliments

ments to you, and her reasons for not coming to me at present, in her own hand-writing, to the perusal of which I leave you, after assuring you that I am, dear Sir,

Your ever obliged and faithful
H. LUXBOROUGH.

Sir Peter Soame wrote me his compliments for you.

LETTER LXXXIX.

DEAR SIR,   Barrells, November 27th, 1753.

I THINK it long since I heard from you; and write this only to enquire after you, and to say that I hope it will not be long before I have the pleasure of seeing you and Lord Dudley here.

It seems the Pediment for Venus's Temple has been finished and brought hither these nine months, I have desired Mr. Hands to defer erecting it till you come, since it has not been done before, by my being ignorant of its being here.

Lord

Lord and Lady Plymouth dined here last week, and Mrs. Kendal made me a visit two days before; except which, solitude has reigned triumphant here: but, whether with or without company, I feel myself equally attached to my friends; and, in consequence, must ever be, dear Sir,

Your faithful humble servant,
H. LUXBOROUGH.

P. S. I write in a hurry, by my waggon which goes for coals.

I have not heard from Mr. Outing since he went to London.

LETTER XC.

DEAR SIR, Barrells, December 4th, 1752.

THAT you are two letters in my debt I do not reproach you; for the last which I inclosed to Mr. Williams, I imagine neither *you* nor *he* ever received. It was to ask if I should not now be favoured with your company and Lord Dudley's at Barrells? to whom I desired, and

and do desire, my best compliments: and to prevent farther *mistakes*, or even *delays*, I send Joseph to enquire after your health, and when I may depend upon the pleasure of seeing you?—My Parterre and Shrubbery are frozen, and will yield you no pleasure: but my hearth and my heart are warm to receive my friends; which I hope you will believe, though you are only told it by fingers so 'num'd with cold, that they can scarcely say this truth, which is that I am

Your obliged and sincere friend, &c.

H. LUXBOROUGH.

When you write to Mr. Greaves, pray make my best compliments to him and to Mrs. Greaves. I owe him more civilities than I can pay, for his obliging expressions of me in the letter you shewed me, and for his remembrance of the cornel-tree, which I hope he will be able to procure, and that Mrs. Greaves has not forgot the polyanthus-root.

LETTER XCI.

Barrells, January 11th, 1753.

DEAR SIR, From my Bed.

THIS is, upon my honour, the first moment I have been able to hold a pen since I received your obliging letter; and I was unwilling to send without writing, or dictating at least; but I could do neither. Lane would have wrote of her own accord; and I would have permitted her, had I consulted merely good manners; but friendship would have remained unsatisfied, and the delicacy of yours might have made you suggest that I was more dangerously ill than I really was.

My disorder proceeded I believe from a cold I got the day we went to see the Monument: and after you left Barrells, it turned to a fever of a slow kind, chiefly nervous, attended with pains in my bowels, which, added to want of rest, have weakened me so much, that I have not yet crossed my room; nor have I seen a mortal except Doctor Wall

Wall and Mr. Francis Holyoak, and once Mrs. Bradley and good Mrs. Holyoak of Oldbarrow, who was so kind to sit up with me. As to Mrs. Davies, she has not enquired after me, nor have I heard from her, or of her, since you was here; nor indeed of a considerable time before: Why, I cannot tell. Whenever I do hear, I will make her your suppliant compliment, and make no doubt but you will soon be forgiven.

I rejoice that you and Lord Dudley were not the worse for your disagreeable journey. I shall, for the future, hold the Saracen's Head in great esteem for having shewn you the hospitality it once denied me.—I beg of you to make my best compliments to his Lordship, with many thanks for his kind visit, which gave me great pleasure.—Do this by letter, if he is out of the country.

Mr. and Mrs. Bradley are pleased and honoured with your kind remembrance; and it was as welcome in your Postscript as if it had been in a higher place. They, and Mr. and Mrs. Holyoak, desire their best respects and thanks for your kind invitation to the Leasowes. Miss Molly went to Worcester the day after I received your letter, and had just time to receive your commands, which she

seems

seems prone to obey in every particular. Her Mamma defires you will keep your brains fteady, and not think it neceffary they fhould be affected, becaufe fhe in mirth called them fo: and as you prefcribe rules of behaviour to her daughter, fhe, in return, prefcribes to you to fhake off the depreffion of fpirits you complain of; and, if folitude and reflection caufe it, to quit your fhades for a time, and vifit your friends, without admitting one reflection, till the days are long, and the fun has cheared the heart and eyes, and has brightened all gloomy ideas; for you are her favourite pupil; and fhe would not give a *dading* for a fplenetic one. I add to this my humble requeft that you will con over Mr. Green's Poem called SPLEEN, or elfe compofe one yourfelf, to keep you out of idlenefs.—*A propos*, finifh the Ode you muft, fince I have named it to the Dutchefs of Somerfet, whofe anfwer I inclofe in this letter. As to the Green-Book, how fhould I truft you with it a fecond time? but it fhall be copied.

No enemy to you fhall ever find fanctuary in my houfe; therefore I fent the Abyffinian Hero, whom you conquered, to remain your captive, and affift at your triumph, or receive death from your hands, when they are not better employed: and his faithful harmless companion accompanies him, hoping with his musical inſtrument to lull your anger to ſleep.—I hope they marched to the Leaſowes time enough to wiſh you a happy new year; which I do moſt ſincerely; and am, dear Sir,

   Your ever obliged
    and faithful ſervant,
      H. LUXBOROUGH.

Lane deſires her beſt reſpects.

LETTER XCII.

DEAR SIR,   Barrells, February 2, 1754.

IT is true the time has appeared long ſince I heard from you; but moſt of it has been a ſeries of ſuch very bad weather, that I would not have bought even the pleaſure of a letter from you at the expence of the hazards my friend Thomas muſt have run in bringing it. Were I to tell him ſo, he would not conceive how great a compliment I paid him;

nor

nor can you, Sir, unless you guess at the degree of joy you afford me each time you write. Yours, at hearing from me, would perhaps be reciprocal, if I could entertain you as well: but alas! how far short am I of being able to entertain you at all! particularly at this time, that my spirits are not only depressed with what affects yours, as solitude, winter storms, and more heavy winter evenings, but also by the storm my Daughter's imprudence (to call it by no worse a name) has raised not only in her family, but in the world. This melancholy scene to her friends is I suppose an amusement to the public, and will shortly be a still greater one, who will divert themselves at her and her favourite's expence, whilst her Husband and Friends lament her folly.—I had a letter of condolence to-day upon this subject, which is no secret one, from the Duchess of Somerset; but, as it is a kind of sermon, I will spare you so serious an epistle, which will be more useful when your spirits are too much enlivened, (if they ever are so) than at this languid season.—I desire you will not fail to write to Mr. Greaves for the Ode, that I may keep my word with Her Grace: and when you write, assure him of my esteem, and make my compliments to his agreeable Wife.—I return

turn the enamelled Label for a bottle, which I suppose is meant for him. The design of it is exceedingly pretty; and I should not so long have deprived him of the pleasure of seeing it, had I not waited for your servant to carry it safe, who, by the way, was so kind to bring me a pretty large book from Aris, who bound it for me: it is called "Memoirs of "several learned Ladies of Great Britain." I have not read it; and should not have subscribed to it, but to oblige a Lady who desired me, having no idea of its merit; therefore I do not send it you: besides, how should trusty Tom be able to carry that, and with it thirteen more things I load him with, to leave at Birmingham? viz. 1st, a jack for boots; 2dly, a reading-desk; 3dly, a cribbage-board; 4thy, a pair of snuffers; 5thly, a ruler; 6thly, an eighteen-inch rule; three pair of nutcrackers make nine things; a lemon-squeezer, ten; two candlesticks make twelve; a piquet-board, thirteen:—but lest you should think the burthen too great for your man or your horse, be it known that these thirteen useful things go all into one coat-pocket, and are made out of one piece of mahogany, eighteen inches long, when open, nine when shut, and barely five broad. Mr. John Reynalds brought this Proteus

teus yesterday to shew me, and I send it to have one made by it, first, for the curiosity of this maggotty invention; secondly, for the use of it, when it is in the shape of a reading-desk. I saw him take his boots off with it with ease; and I believe it is equally good as a lemon-squeezer. I think a place might be contrived to let in a small ink-bottle and a pen: but as it was invented by a *General*, that utensil gave place to others more immediately necessary to his profession.

But now for Egotism (for you ask after me, and must be obeyed): I have never been below stairs since I wrote to you last, and never but once since I saw you, and that was so long ago as New-year's-day, when I went down, for a very few dull hours, and have been ill since; but am now pretty well; and my lower rooms have had fires made in them some days, by way of preparing them for the reception of my person, which moves but slowly towards them; though I believe I shall go down the ladder, if any charitable person comes to receive me at the bottom. I expected it would have been Mrs. Davies with her Mother-in-law, Mrs. Bartlet, for whom I offered to send my chaise to-morrow; but they choose to defer their visit one or two days. As to Mrs. Holy-oak,

oak, who *was* a very chearful neighbour, she has never been here since the death of her second son (whose death, by the way, is rather good than ill fortune to his family); and Mr. Holyoak has been here but once, though it is above six weeks ago; and Miss Molly lives at Worcester.—Mr. Allen is dead.—Mr. Bradley has been at London, but called on me yesterday; as did Dr. Wall on Sunday, who tells me a turnpike-road is to be made (by an Act of Parliament promoted by Sir George Lyttelton) from Stourbridge to Bromsgrove; and, by Lord Plymouth's desire, on to *Hewell*, and to Crabbs Cross; which last place is but six miles off; and from it one enters upon the Ridgeway. You see how I study the topography of the country, and all in order to facilitate the agreeable visits I propose annually to make to the Leasowes. You, who do not travel with four-wheeled vehicles, want not such helps: Why then come you not? Pray answer, *I come*, and be as good as your word. It is true the invitation is mercenary, and nothing as yet makes Bartells a desirable residence: the Aviary is unpeopled, the Garden produces only snowdrops, crocuses, &c. and all the melody of the Grove is the voice of rooks; but seeing them build (which they have begun to do) introduces
Spring,

Spring, or at least the hopes of its quick appearance, as it is approaching so near—Next week Mrs. Davies will be here, who, when she is in spirits herself, enlivens others: come then and partake of her gaiety, as I shall have nothing else so good to offer you; for at present I am acquainted only with smoaky chimnies, and various kinds of bad weather, which, for want of company, makes me lead directly the life of a dormouse.—I shall certainly grow to my chair, or become lethargic, if my friends do not take compassion on me. As to my only near neighbours, I give up the thoughts of expecting it; for I neither see nor hear any thing from them, but by their servant-boy, who comes regularly three times a week to desire the News-paper.

Au reste, (according to the French phrase) I send you to read Mademoiselle de Maintenon's Letters in the original: you shall see the English translation, if you please; but the stile in French is as good as the sense, which is a double profit to the reader. I also send (but with some reluctance, because I have scrawled family things in the margin; which I do not intend any should see, but such a friend as you) the Life of Lord Bolingbroke, which

interests

interests me, as he was my Brother: perhaps it may not interest you; in which case you need not read it.—Neither Poetry nor Plays have approached me of a long season, and news I learn only from the worst hands, viz. the news-paper writers. My correspondents are few: the Duchess of Somerset is too much retired to hear of what passes, and is too much wrapt up in religious and moral reflections to admit of other subjects, in her letters.—Sir William Meredith and his Sisters are not yet arrived at London. Sir Peter Soame lives almost always in the country; and Outing is too lazy to write a line more than he is obliged to. Happy would you be if I were so too, who have wrote so much, that there is room for no more, but that I am, with unfashionable sincerity,

Your obliged humble servant,

H. LUXBOROUGH.

LETTER

LETTER XCIII.

From my Smoaky Room, on this First Day of April, 1753.

BE it known that I am angry: I would even say *very* angry, but *that* you would not believe, since I *write* and *send* to the person who has offended me; meaning, dear Sir, your identical self, who have neither answered my last letter, nor come to visit my Hermitage, though pressingly invited. I offered you Mrs. Davies's company, as being more chearful than my own; but she is gone (after a month's stay): so now it is incumbent upon you to do penance here on this spot to atone for your past fault; and penance it will be, as I am quite alone in this dull habitation. But remember it is Lent, and the visit will be a meritorious action. As to my own merit, (if any there be in retirement) it will all be lost; for such agreeable company and conversation will turn Lent into a festival; but let it do so, I will run the risk of the punishment, if you, Sir, will make the pilgrimage. At this season methinks my Shrubbery ought to invite you; but to *myself* it is unknown; and all the intelligence I have from it is by a few snowdrops and polyanthuses, which are daily sent as ambassadors into my chamber, tied up in a nosegay, but in no ways inviting, though joined with the *kind* laureſtinus, who is indeed a *friend in diſtreſs*, (as you called him) and is moſt welcome in winter: but I could almoſt wiſh to have him out of ſight, and even the *Robin*'s ſweet note out of hearing, as they remind me of the melancholy winter that is ſcarcely paſt; and nothing agreeable as yet denotes approaching Spring. I ſet Mrs. Davies to tranſcribe the Green Book, and began it myſelf: it was not quite finiſhed, ſo ſhe carried it to Stratford; but it is ſafe, and almoſt done, and you ſhall have the copy. But where are the pretty paintings I was to have? You ſee how covetous I am, and how a little received makes me graſp at more: but as covetouſneſs is inſatiable, ſo is your fund of ſupplying it inexhauſtible.

I expect Sir William Meredith ſoon, who will I hope tell me news, or bring me new things to read; all which is uncertain: in the mean time, I have read the *Gameſter* and the *Brothers*, and a book called *Manners*. As to the *Gameſter*, you have undoubtedly read it;

it

it is true it draws tears, and seems adapted to do good, which I heartily wish it may; but it is much upon a footing with *George Barnwell*; and in my mind, the heroine's generosity and good nature is rather overstrained: but those who paint for the stage must draw larger than life. The *Brothers* I have also read, and believe it to be a well-wrote piece; but as it is poetry, you are the best judge. I find it is liked, and, I think, with reason. The Bricklayer's performance is a surprizing one in him, and has to be sure infinitely more spirit than the other tragedy called also *The Earl of Essex*; but I never was fond of the subject. As these plays will fill but a corner of my servant's pockets, I send them, though well persuaded you must have read them; but he can easily bring them back. With them goes Voltaire's Defence of my Brother Bolingbroke's Letters, &c.

Did your man shew you the little jack for boots, and all the apparatus? If it is at Birmingham to be copied for me, Joseph may ask after it; for I order him to return that way with a compliment to my relation Captain Somervile, who is quartered there, and who lay here with Mr. John Reynalds a week ago: it is Lord Somervile's *eldest* Son I mean; he
whom

whom you may perchance have feen at Edftone; he longs to fee the Leafowes, and has almoft as many good qualities as that place has beauties. I find *your* Beauty Lady Diana Egerton is married, but not to the lover I faw her with the laft feafon that I was at Bath.—Mr. Outing is, I believe, at London, in Charles Court; but not an echo fpeaks his name to me, nor does a poftboy bring a line from him. I would leave him to his contemplations or his nonoccupations, had not fome particular bufinefs, urged by Lord Luxborough, obliged me to write, to convey a letter from the latter to him; fo there are hopes that we fhall hear once more of him, and even from him; but I will not anfwer for it. Jack Reynalds fays, " to be " fure he is going to be married to his friend " Captain Swete's rich widow."

How does Mr. Greaves and his agreeable Wife? My query is not interefted; though I confefs I wifh for the pretty polyanthus root I faw there, which Mrs. Greaves politely offered me.

Alas! will no Chriftian be fo charitable as to beftow one fingle pen capable of writing, upon a deftitute fcribe? No! then farewell
in

in the moſt laconic ſtile, for I can write no more than

    Yours, &c. &c.

        H. Luxborough.

LETTER XCIV.

DEAR SIR,   Barrells, May 12th, 1753.

YOU may be certain that I have been ill, ſince you have not had a letter from me of ſo long a time; for, next to converſing with you, nothing pleaſes me ſo much as correſponding with you by letter. When Mr. Pixell was laſt here, I was ſo little able to anſwer the obliging letter you wrote by him, that I could not ſo much as ſee him; for I was in bed all day. I ſhould have rejoiced to have contributed towards his Son's ſucceſs, in what he deſired to obtain at Stratford; but unfortunately I have no intereſt there: Mrs. Kendall gone to Lord Exeter's, and Mrs. Davies gone to London,—to whom could I apply? (for Mr. Payton he was ſure of before, as well as of Mr. Kendrick) yet I did venture to write

to

to Mr. Brigham and Mrs. Bartlet: the former was from home, but has since sent me the inclosed answer; and Mrs. Davies has also wrote me a line about it, which I inclose. I advised with Mr. John Reynalds about the affair, who said there was no way he knew of, but for Mr. Pixell, the Father, to go and canvass, and get nine or ten Aldermen together and make them drunk, and consequently they would be friends to his Son.—It is too true that this kind of proceeding prevails in England much sooner than merit.

I find your neighbours and mine echo each other, *Air and exercise! air and exercise!* and we no sooner obey but we get cold, and become incapable of even taking the air and exercise which the house and gardens afford. I am sure I find it so; for though I am better in health, I have such a violent pain in my face and teeth, that I can get no sleep, nor apply myself to any thing. This, added to my lowness of spirits, will certainly inspire me with very *bright thoughts* to adorn my letter! but if dulness is my lot, I cannot help it, and you are too candid not to pardon me, though I 'numb you with it.

I sent my horses to London last Wednesday to fetch Mrs. Davies and my new post-chariot. I expect

I expect to see them on Monday at fartheft, and then will take from her the copies fhe has wrote out of your Green Book, which fhe locked up at Stratford before fhe went her journey. Your *other Green Book* is a curiofity more worthy Dean Lyttelton; but is far from diminifhing my real value for the unadorned, unembellifhed, un-illuminated Green Book, which you allow me to call my own.—But to return to the laft Green Book: I muft fay it is beautifully illuminated, and the gilding is, in my mind, furprizingly well laid on; and as to the price, you muft have paid the man with indulgences; for the money you gave is in no ways adequate to the value. I never faw but one like it, and it is the property of Sir William Meredith, whofe merit you extol in fix as elegant lines as I ever read. I want to fee the whole copy of verfes complete; and I much want to fee you two here together. If I have not that fatisfaction, the fault will be yours.—I expect him foon. He is at Wigan in Lancafhire, making intereft to be chofen Member of Parliament: his Sifters are at London in a new houfe he has taken, except the Countefs Ferrers, who is already gone out of town, and I believe was there but a few weeks.

I con-

I congratulate you upon Mr. Hylton's becoming your neighbour: he seemed to me of a gentle difpofition, and capable of being a good friend, as well as defirous of becoming one by his obliging behaviour.—Your correfpondence with Lord Dudley cannot be otherwife than amufing and inftructive; for you fay you *feldom write to him, and never hear from him*. I imagine the cafe is much the fame between you and Outing; from whom I hear occafionally, but feldom; and fcarcely ever but upon bufinefs. Mr. Reynalds tells me he ftill complains of his pupil, who is not yet gone to fea.—The two Captains Somervile are at Litchfield on account of the Review.

P. S. The *Moralities* and *Crito* I fend back: the former is certainly *trite*-iffimo; the latter is the reverfe. I have read with pleafure the new Tranflation from *Solez* of the Conqueft of Mexico, corrected by Mr. Hook, Author of the Roman Hiftory; and find it fets that event in a new light by the old author, and in much newer and better language than we have ever feen it before, by means of the new tranflation. —What you fay of Mademoifelle Maintenon's Letters is perfectly true; but I could not have known how to fay it, though I felt it; fo little

of

of a critic am I; and yet I think I could criticize upon her sentiments, which, when compared with her actions, seem not a little hypocritical. We shall see her Life in print shortly, and then we may judge better, if it is wrote fairly.

I just now have sent for the *learned Mr. Hume*, my Gardener, to consult about your hot-bed for melons. He assures me it is too late to aim at having any *this* year; but will direct your man how to proceed against the next. Had you wrote about it in your last letter, I could not only have assisted you with advice, but also with seeds and plants.—I have exceeding fine anemonies, but the Gardener says they will die long before they get to you; otherwise you should have had a *posie to wear in your breast.*—I am promised a cornel tree; but must wait till September.

I could laugh (if you would forgive it) at *you* and your *apothecary*; the one fears the steeple will fall on his head, and therefore dreads the sound of the bells: the other lives a mile or two off, and gives money to have those bells made harmonious, though he cannot hear them: the latter has to be sure a more public spirit, and the other a more prudential one, according to the self-interested scheme of things.

things. Upon the whole, I vote for no bells ringing when Lord Dudley comes into the country, but those pretty ones I was so fond of hearing in your hall; and methinks I would go and join chorus,

"*Down with your Caps to the Ground, Boys:*"

but first, Sir, be pleased to come here, and see the spontaneous beauties of my Coppice; for you never come till they have run their race, and are no more. In short, if you will not come soon, I will not go to the Leasowes at all. By the way in which you take this threat, I shall know if you choose my company.—Be so good as to let my Gardener see Lord Dudley's Green-House and Hot-Houses: he begged leave to see the Leasowes; and as you had asked him, I could not well refuse.

Your idea of the ink-stand's preventing the new machine from being useful as a pair of breeches, made me laugh (though alone) so loud, that Lane heard me. She presents her respects, and I my affectionate compliments.

H. LUXBOROUGH.

LETTER XCV.

DEAR SIR,   Barrells, June 23-4, 1753.

YOUR two letters arriving almost in the same minute, roused me in some measure out of the lethargic disposition, or rather the heavy stupefaction I have been oppressed with some time, notwithstanding what I have suffered, and do suffer, by a violent pain in my face and teeth, enough to have given spirits, though not by an agreeable method; whereas mine are as dejected as you can possibly imagine; and I see no immediate reason to hope their speedy amendment.

I very seldom have visited my Shrubbery; and have then been obliged to be often supported, or to sit down: and as to my new chaise, (which is a chariot, or rather a landaulet, only drawn as a post-chaise) I have been in it but twice, and then forced in. The last time was only to Oldbarrow, about four days ago, and have not recovered the fatigue yet, nor been down stairs but once. This grim description of myself will not recommend me as a companion or a correspondent; but I am equally a friend; for my sentiments, thank God, are not infected, though my spirits and body suffer. I am sorry you are inclinable to such dejection, which I know so well how to pity: but hope you will shake it off with more ease, and that I shall see you brisk and bonny at this place ere long, with your good and agreeable Friend.

I will not fail to send your packet to the Duchess of Somerset, and to obey all your commands; but it is too big for the post.—I have read the Ode, and think it can receive no amendment.

I understand that Mr. Hylton and Miss Rock both come down with Lord Dudley, and that Miss L—— is jealous of Miss R——, who it seems is very pretty; and that they are to stop in Buckinghamshire, in their way.

The plural number concerning letters, in the first line of mine, may puzzle you; but means the letter you sent me to-day by trusty Thomas, as also that you wrote (in part to me) to Mrs. Davies, dated the 9th, which she sent for my perusal just before your servant came in; and it rejoiced me to find you had remembered, when I feared the contrary. I have never seen her

her since her return from London, but for about six days. She pleads much company and occupation at Stratford. In short, I am as desolate as Robinson Crusoe, even when he had not his man Friday.

Being really too weak to finish copying the Green Book, I send as far as Mrs. Davies wrote, and the titles of the remainder.

The notion of a turnpike pleases me much, hoping it facilitates the way to the Leasowes: but you should have gone to Hagley. I preach, you find; but how do I practise? Helas!— Lady Plymouth, Lady Archer, &c. are in the neighbourhood, and I in my chimney-corner.

I wish I could see Mrs. Donolly's Accusation, and Mr. Outing's Vindication, in a Magazine.

Adieu. So bad a pen, so bad a head, so bad spirits, ought not to trouble you longer: yet, under all these distresses, you will ever find me

Your most faithful

and obliged friend

and humble servant,

H. LUXBOROUGH.

Upon second thoughts, I have desired your man to carry the little machine to the Lea-sowes, as you may be curious to see it; from whence he can convey it to Mr. Cotterell at Birmingham, desiring him to make me one as soon as possible, and to make the joint go quite easy, which, by false workmanship, this model does not. If an ink-horn and pen could be introduced, it would do well, and the whole should be lighter.

LETTER XCVI.

DEAR SIR,   Barrells, September 12th, 1753.

AS you kindly express a desire to hear from me, I imagine one or two lines from my own hand will be more satisfactory than more lines by the hand of any other person. I therefore tell you myself, that I am *tolerably* well; I might say *very* well, if I had more strength; but that nervous disorder, which has long affected my spirits, and which affected my limbs (particularly my hands) when at Bath, is descended to my legs, which have been much

much swelled about the ancles, and made me and my friends apprehend the consequence, as they pitted a good deal; but they are now fallen, and I can walk pretty well alone in a room; but must still be lifted off my chair, and into my landaulet, in which I go three or four miles in a day for the air, and back again, without going into any house; and I lay still below stairs. The worst effect of all these complaints is my being deprived of the pleasure of ranging over the charming Leasowes all day, and of enjoying your conversation there; but, lest you should think me worse than I am, I must tell you that I am just come into the house from the Summer-house, where I drank tea with Mrs. Bartlet, Mrs. Davies, Mr. Holyoak, and Mr. John Reynalds: the two latter we have left at bowls by moon-light. I was led up the slopes, but walk on plain ground; so that it is plain I mend; and next time I write to you, I think to do it with my foot; for that cannot perform worse than my hand and pen do at present.

I think the inundation of fine company you have had at the Leasowes must have been an additional ornament to that charming place; and the place must have given them real pleasure, as they are people of taste.—All the beauty

beauty Miss Banks may boast of, cannot have effaced the other beauties which your Grove presented to your company, and which winter has spared as yet; but beware of what impression her charms may have made upon your heart, if they gained admittance there, as is feared: but pray who is the said Lady, and where does the enchantress dwell?

Adieu. The supper-bell calls; the company waits. I resolve to endeavour to follow your good advice whilst the weather is tolerable; and am in all seasons

Your most obliged
and faithful servant,
H. LUXBOROUGH.

I wait impatiently for the letter you promise me from Mr. Hylton.—My compliments, pray, to Lord Dudley, &c. &c.

LETTER XCVII.

DEAR SIR, *September 18th at Night, 1753.*

EVERY inftance of your partial friendfhip gives me a pleafure, which would be perfect, was it not attended by the confcioufnefs of not meriting that partiality which I am proud of. This reflection humbles me; and I muft own that what you call *brightnefs* in me, is only borrowed, as that of the moon; and is owing to your neighbourhood, and even to your correfpondence; which when I am deprived of, I remain a dull inanimate lump.— Your concern for my health fhews your good nature; which I ought to repay by following your advice: but the weather often obftructs my performances in my poft-chaife, which I think were to be very frequent, according to your prefcription and Sir Peter Soame's; but I go frequently as far as my neighbour Mrs. Bradley's, who is not able to come to me at prefent, being near lying-in. As to my vifit to the Leafowes, I want neither your perfuafions, nor Dr. Wall's advice, to induce me to it; my own inclination biaffing me that way

more

more than any bribe could biafs a mercenary voter at an election; fo that a fun-fhiny week, a continuance of my prefent degree of health, and a little better ufe of my legs, would certainly fuffer me to be attracted by the charms of the *renowned Leafowes*, whofe power draws Beaux, Belles, Poets, Senators, &c. to pay homage to them. Glad I am that fo much good tafte is left in our nation; and proud I am that I had juft enough to difcover its beauties before it had received the benefit of the polifhing you have fince beftowed upon it. Nature and you went hand in hand to perfect it. Nature will perfift in her work.—Pray do not you be idle, but let the applaufe of the polite encourage you. Nay, let Mifs Peggy B——ks's 100,000 *l.* caft in a mite to embellifh what you have fo well begun, and fo near accomplifhed. Where do you fifh for thefe *Golden Ladies*, whofe merit outweighs their purfe? I wifh you fuch a partner for life, unlefs celibacy be your choice. The Lady (who is a ftranger to me) little thinks how much fhe is obliged to me.

Though you have not anfwered Mrs. Davies's letter, fhe, to fhew that fhe bears no gall, fends you her beft compliments; and is 'numbing her fingers to tranfcribe a few lines more

of

of your Green Book, to send you by trusty
Tom, with a melon, which my Gardener does
not boast of, but we hope it may prove eat-
able. Had he any better, they should be laid
at your feet by his good will, as well as mine.

I wish my pen could keep pace with my
thoughts; your letter would be answered more
fully; but you know my hands and legs have
not been of late famous for agility: yet you
encourage me greatly as to one of my inabi-
lities, by telling me that most of your visitants
are *miserable walkers*; and I shall plume myself
with the remembrance of having been a better
one not long since, which enabled me to partake of the distant as well as of the near prospects of your farm, and will again restore me,
as I hope, to that of visiting every corner of
your Grove at least: the other wood might be
too aspiring; so I dare not mention it, but
shall admire it with uplifted eyes.

Now for the Election. As to the particular
answer to every point which I could have
wished to send you, I must be deficient to-
night. You sent late. I am ignorant so much
as of Mr. Coventry's friends or his enemies. I
will speak to the Oldbarrow people to sound
them to-morrow, and will write and send to you
about Thursday, with all the intelligence I can

get;

get: but alas! the intelligence you may expect from an Hermitess, you could not fell for half a nut-shell.

I am greatly obliged to Sir George Lyttelton for his enquiry after my health; and the more so, as I always had the greatest respect for him.

As for you, Sir, you want not, I hope, fresh assurances of my friendship; and for proofs of it, let but fortune put it in my power, and do you command as hastily as you please, you shall be obeyed by

Your faithful humble servant,

H. LUXBOROUGH.

LETTER XCVIII.

DEAR SIR, Barrells, September 27th, 1753.

WHEN your servant was last here, I could not send you a positive answer, nor indeed any answer about the Oldbarrow Voters for the county of Worcester; for indeed I live so much retired, that I am seldom informed

formed of what paffes but by the news-papers, which I think have not mentioned that election. Ever fince I received yours, I have been anxious to enquire who were the voters in my neighbourhood, that I might have an opportunity of obliging you; as alfo Lord Dudley and Sir George Lyttelton; for both which I have the greateft regard and efteem. By means of Mr. Holyoak I got fome names of freeholders, with whom both he and I will ufe our intereft in favour of Mr. Coventry. If you know of any befides thofe named in this lift, be pleafed to fend me their names. Lord Archer made me a vifit to-day: I fpoke to him upon this affair, and found that he and Lord Plymouth were in the intereft of Mr. Coventry as ftrongly as we could wifh; however, I gave him, by his own defire, the inclofed little lift which I got from Mr. Holyoak. As to Mr. Packwood, Lord Archer and we fuppofe him to be engaged on the other fide. There are voters who live at Tanworth: I make no doubt but Lord Archer fecures them, as he appears to be zealous in the caufe.

Mr. Holyoak defires his compliments to you, and fays he is wholly at your fervice for whatever intereft he can make: and you give me pleafure by affording me an occafion of
proving

proving to you the sincerity with which I always profess myself, Dear Sir,

   Your obliged and most
    humble servant and friend,
      H. LUXBOROUGH.

N. B. Lord Luxborough has an estate at Oldbarrow, which he bought of Mr. Thomas Holyoak, deceased.

LETTER XCIX.

DEAR SIR, Barrells, November 12th, 1753.

I CANNOT forbear reflecting upon your kindness to your friends in general, and to me in particular. Your obliging letter came just *à propos* to rouze me from an unpleasing, inactive, and worse than lethargic state of body; for as to my mind, it is ever waking and intent upon my friends; nor do they lose one scruple of the regard I owe them, by my not expressing it with my pen; nor do they lose an instant of pleasure by my silence; for what can *I* say to please, who hear nothing to please myself? But no more of this.—Be assured my friendship
retains

retains its full weight, and is neither *estranged* from you, nor in the least diminished. Your merit and my esteem secure it yours.

I am ashamed of myself when I name your Ode. I am guilty, I confess, of having deprived Her Grace of it long; but I am also innocent of any artifice in my seeming neglect; only I did not meet with any body I could trust with it that was going towards Her Grace's habitation; and the little book was too big and heavy for a frank; but at last I have sent it, and hope to give you her answer about Dodsley's printing it ere long; and in the mean time flatter myself no false edition by piracy, &c. can happen to be published: be that as it will, I shall take the blame upon myself for my delay, and shall excuse you to my Friend the Duchess of Somerset; who is too benign to accuse us, as she must know we mean her well; and I do not doubt but she will permit Dodsley to print it, and that with pleasure. You was kind in contributing something of Mr. Whistler's and Mr. Graves's to his Miscellanies: Would I were capable of adding a line to them worth reading! but I am no Poetess; if I was, the Leasowes and its Owner should still be my theme.

Mrs. Davies has left me to horrid solitude;

but has left the reft of your Poems, which I inclose. You will, methinks, ftare at the epithet *horrid* which I have annexed to *folitude*; as that used to pleafe me, and be called *fweet* at leaft: but changes of one kind bring on changes of another, even without being owing to ficklenefs, as my life has proved to me; yet my taftes are the fame; and I had rather now deck a rural bower than glitter on a birthnight at court: but as we are all made for fociety, the lofs of neighbours and of limbs, make thefe bowers more irkfome than inviting. I am, however, much better in health and limbs than when you faw me, and do not defpair of meafuring your walks once more at leaft with my fteps: provided you come in the mean time to do thefame to mine; why not? Winter is your feafon of appearing: the Leafowes has too many charms; and attracts too good company to be left in Summer: but our country hearts and hearths may be as honeft, pert, and jovial, as any your parifhioners can afford you; and at *more* we fhall not afpire—Come elfe and fee. Outing will be here foon, I fuppofe; for the roads of the Vale of Evefham frighten him from the thoughts of coming from Somervile's Afton hither, when they are at the worft. Parfon Holyoak went

with

with him thither, and ſtaid a few days; and alſo went to Hewell with him, where (according to the news-paper's phraſe) they were *moſt graciouſly received.*—The *great* Mr. Weſt of the Treaſury ſent his gardener to-day to view my ſmall Garden and my Walks; which I wonder at, as himſelf had ſeen them before, and muſt know they would not teach or ſerve as examples to his ſervant.

I did not think of making *more laſt words*; but I cannot go to bed without congratulating you upon the polite company you have received at the Leaſowes. I am vain methinks that what I ſo much approved when in its cradle, ſhould become the reſort and envy of the *beau monde*, in ſpite of the roads and weather.

I am glad you do Lord Pl——'s good nature and politeneſs the juſtice it deſerves. I had a few lines from him and his Lady to-day; ſhe is a deſerving and amiable woman. I am glad you will adviſe as to their improvements without doors; for they intend right as to the inſide. *Mais les pauvres environs reſteront en defaut.* The approach of the waters to the houſe will, I fear, produce more agues than good fiſh, or pleaſant views to the place. I am much obliged to Sir George Lyttelton; had I

power,

power, he might command it, or you for him.

I hear the opposition as to the Election is stopped, and hear it with pleasure. I envy you some of your company more than that of your antediluvian, though Reverend, *Beed*, and that of your Gothic, though modern, Miller.—I am glad Hagley is to stand in a rational place, as it has a rational master, and has lost its unrational controller, the late gardener of it.

I cannot be sorry Mr. Hylton has *hauled* his thousand pounds back, or is so to do. It is far better to *haul* his money, than a *pertuisane*, or whatever else is the name of the tall thing they haul. As to *the bottle*, and what was *over the bottle*, you may assure him I never ventured to let Mr. Ou—g see it; for what might have ensued? No, Sir, I would not offend any *officer* in the King's troops.

I am sorry Lord Dudley's toe has been so offended by his *bed's foot*, of which he should be cautious for the future, as I fear the damages would rather upon trial fall on his Lordship than on *that* offender. I beg my best respects to his Lordship.

Parson Holyoak, &c. are your obedient servants. Mrs Bradley is recovering from a dangerous lying-in; and Mrs. Davies is at present

present with her. Farther than this my intelligence goeth not. I wonder you choose a correspondent of so small a share of intelligence, so barren a genius, and such confined ideas as belong to her, who is with a more expanded heart, Dear Sir,

  Your most faithful
  and most grateful humble servant,
    H. LUXBOROUGH.

Compliments, pray, to all your neighbours who remember me. You would have the like from hence, if neighbours I had.

LETTER C.

Barrells, Monday Night, November 26th, 1753.

DEAR SIR,

AN hour ago I received the inclosed from our Duchess, and thought it incumbent upon me to let you see it as soon as possible; and hastened to send it the rather lest the direction Her Grace had fished for twelve miles off, might not be the true one, and so we all might become the paftime of poftmen and poftwomen: for what has been may be; which the Lord avert!

You obferve the Duchefs forbids her name, or that of Percy-Lodge, to be made public: I dare fay you will obey her orders. I am glad, for Dodfley's fake, and for many more reafons, that fhe has not forbid printing the Poem.

Your Governefs Mrs. Holyoak is here, and defires, firft, her humbleft compliments, and, fecondly, enjoins her ftricteft commands that you leave your chimney-corner, fince all your fine company has left you. I join with her; and though my merit is fmall, yet I am proud enough to defire the preference before your parifhioners, who are the perfons you feem to have chofen to be your winter companions. Mr. Holyoak is alfo here, who defires his beft compliments. *Outing* is at the *Hofpitable Houfe*, Somervile's Afton; and they are deferted by Sir Robert Cocks, who is gone to Bath. I would accompany this with fome entertaining ballad, elegy, or epithalamium; but where muft I find them? Not in my own head, I am fure; fo you muft expect no poetry from me till the Henley bellman has gone his Chriftmas round; and ere then I hope you will hear him utter his *elbowicks* here.

Lord

Lord Plymouth's workmen have left them *one* habitable room till after Chriftmas, (no longer) as his Lady writes me word.—I have not had the pleafure of receiving Mr. Hylton's intended epiftle; but am of opinion that his ftile does not require fo long a delay to make his correfpondence appear the more valuable. Let him write as he fpeaks, and his letters will be agreeable to me.

What more have I to fay? I *think*, and *think in vain.*—Yes; I muft tell you, that I am fo much better than when you faw me, that you would be furprifed.—My heart is always the fame; that is, affectionate towards my friends : judge then whether I can ceafe to be

    Your faithful friend
    and humble fervant,
     H. LUXBOROUGH.

Send back the Duchefs's letter, pray.—Mrs. Davies is ftill at Mrs. Bradley's, as I hear.— My compliments to all your good neighbours.— Perhaps Lord Dudley is gone to Parliament.

I am glad my favourite room is honoured by your books; and think the bed (as you have contrived it) no detriment to the elegance of it, though a confiderable convenience to the place. A a 4 H. L.

Mr. Hylton need not be aſhamed to write to me: late or early, I ſhall be glad to hear from him.

LETTER CI.

Barrells, Wedneſday Night, December 12th, 1753.

DEAR SIR,

THOUGH I undertake to write to you to-night, I do not know how my letter is to be wafted to Birmingham, unleſs ſome kind Sylph offers her ſervice; the terreſtrial meſſengers not being able to travel, at leaſt not in this country, where it ſnows, rains, and freezes, not alternately, but at the ſame time. Is that your caſe in Shropſhire? If ſo, I pity you; but I think you and I, who have not much elſe to do, ſhould utter our lamentations to each other from the corners of the ſame chimney. Sharing the burthen of winter would be leſſening it to each of us. I cannot go to the Leaſowes; *ergo* you muſt come to Barrells, or we cannot meet. Is not this true reaſoning? You will ſay (and perhaps with truth) that it

is

is like an invitation to a funeral; which, I am persuaded, is a compliment moſt people would be glad not to receive; but though it could not entertain you to accept of ſuch an invitation, it would illuſtrate your friendly qualities, by affording you an opportunity of giving, rather than of receiving, pleaſure. The word *pleaſure* reminds me that I have received a very agreeable epiſtle from your Friend Mr. Hylton, whoſe loſs of a place at Court does not ſeem to ſit heavy upon him. It is no more than I expected from the good ſenſe I obſerved in him.

I return you the Ducheſs of Somerſet's letter; and have methinks too long forborne ſcolding you for imagining Her Grace's meaning to be that you ſhould not print your Poem upon Rural Taſte. On the contrary, ſhe is, I am ſure, proud of its being inſcribed to her, though too baſhful, in her retirement, to chooſe her name to be at the head of it; yet well knowing with inward ſatisfaction, that every body will know ſhe is the Heroine of the piece, as much as one knows who was Waller's Sacchariſſa, without reading her real name at the top. Had our Ducheſs not intended you ſhould publiſh it, what need had ſhe to enjoin *ſtars* or *daſhes* inſtead of her and of her habitation's names?

Do not deprive the public of the pleasure they would have in reading it, and do not deprive Her Grace of the compliment you intended her, and which so much seems to please her, both by the letters she writes to me as well as to yourself about it. In answer to your question, I can sincerely assure you, that I never once thought of the Duchess's refusal, nor do I call it one now; and am certain she means no more than what she expresses to you about suppressing her name; so that your *vanity*, were it ever so great, would not be really hurt by this, which your *imagination* only deems a disappointment.

Your Verses to Lady Plymouth (whose name is Catherine) please me greatly, and she as greatly merits your praise. Your expression in the last line ought to be far from displeasing Lord Plymouth, and is, in my mind, more proper and more elegant than any feigned name you could give him. I cannot but say I should rather wish the inscription, being to a Lady, had been in English. Could not that have been, and yet Horace's Latin motto have been preserved? but I am no critic, having neither capacity nor inclination to be one; so that what I say upon such subjects should be wrote in sand.

I con-

I congratulate Lord Dudley upon his good luck; and wish his good neighbour as profitable a *foundless* to warm himself by: Be it known that *foundless* is a Warwickshire word, as I am told: in honour to the county I use it, or should else have stolen a word from the French, and have said, *une trouvaille*, for such is a coal-mine at any time; and I speak of it the more feelingly now that I sit freezing, and can scarcely get a little coal for a great deal of money. Pray, since your county carries such profitable things in the bowels of the earth, ransack them well, and let me hear that you have found some mines or other: It is a selfish wish; for I am sure if you had those of Peru, your friends would share with you; and were it only by viewing the use you would put them to, in making them subservient to your good taste, they would afford pleasure to all who knew how to relish the works of taste; and as to the misers, let them avaunt.—Your *Governess* and I are parted by floods: and *Deadings* are no more, for this season at least; but they will still live in verse, if *you* employ your pen in their praise.

Since you are so favoured by Apollo and the Muses, that you can dream in verse, you ought not to be niggardly of them. I want to
see

see what alterations Somnus or Morpheus have made in the pretty lines you wrote here in the year 1747: They would not easily find what to mend.

Adieu. The wind blows; I shiver; my ink freezes; my pen wants mending: so again adieu,

Sincerely yours,

H. LUXBOROUGH.

LETTER CII.

Barrells, Saturday, December 15th, 1753.

DEAR SIR,

SOME malicious fiend or other has surely, by way of Christmas gambol, entertained himself by resolving to marr our correspondence, and to thwart whatever you or I have innocently projected for our amusement: and what I less forgive is, that when I mean to show my gratitude for your friendly attention upon all occasions, my letter is carried to London instead of Birmingham. I wrote it on Tuesday

day or Wednesday last, and inclosed the Duchess of Somerset's, which you had sent me to see. The frost came, the floods succeeded, and nobody could go; nor did I dare trust my servant and horse to the weather, and still less dared trust my letter to the curious Post-Office at Birmingham: so even changed the cover, put it in a frank, and sent it to-day to go through London to you; and it was no sooner gone past recall, but trusty Thomas brought your last obliging and entertaining letter: but, far from answering it, as I designed, I only must (and that with difficulty) return you more and more thanks for the entertainment you afford me, both by your epistle, and by Mr. Graves's lively Fable, which I return now. —As to your Stanzas to Asteria, I am too proud of them, and too well pleased with your addition and emendations, not to value and preserve them with care both in my memory and in my best pocket-book. If I had preserved Mr. Somervile's little Poems and Impromptu's in as orderly a manner, I would have sent you a parcel to-night to pick out any you liked for Dodsley; but they are in a drawer intermixed so with other papers, that to undertake to look them out now is impossible:

besides,

besides, I have a fever fit upon me, and have not slept these two nights, and live upon wormwood draughts; which, though wholesome, do not immediately restore one to strength, or to one's usual stile or conversation. This is also the reason I must defer for a post or two answering Mr. Hylton's polite letter; which I hope he will forgive; whilst I implore my fever to leave my mind capable of deserving, by my punctual answers, the letters I am favoured with.—You will have mine I hope from London on Thursday next.—Our servants had better be a little fatigued with journies between the Leasowes and Barrells; than we molested with impertinent Post-people, indolent or careless chance-messengers, or idle drunken farmers, who undertake to carry letters they never think of after.—Your own intended Miscellany will be higher in my esteem than Dodsley's, if his are to be deprived of your Works.—I told you my thoughts about your mistaking the Duchess of Somerset's meaning, as you will find in my travelling letter.—I shall be glad to see the *Agriculture* of Dodsley; and as to *Sir Charles Grandison*, only wait its being complete, to send for it. Mr. Hylton recommends it also.

You had better harrass yourself than your

servants, and let me see you this Christmas at Barrells: I asked you before; I ask you now the third time. I will send the flea you intended for Mr. Hylton, to fetch you. I can see no longer; every letter seems double; so adieu. Excuse an invalid, who is

Your faithful servant,

H. LUXBOROUGH.

LETTER CIII.

Barrells, Friday, December 21st, 1753.

AN opportunity offering itself, dear Sir, of sending this letter to-morrow to Birmingham, I resolved without hesitation to write it; being vain enough to believe my last gave you pain; for I wrote it with a trembling hand and confused head, and with a fever-fit upon me. I hope you have burnt it, and will think no more of it, but to the fever's praise; which (causing me to sweat) has raised my spirits and suppled my limbs; so that I am born anew: and, if I continue in my present state, make no question but I shall see the Leasowes in Spring.

In the mean time, it is your tafk, as a Friend, to perfect this cure by giving me your company at the deferted Barrells; which place droops now, but will revive at your approach. You have ufed it to that fenfibility in winter; fo that no other company will reftore it to its gaiety.—Let me know if you received yefterday my travelling letter from London. What fay you to my reproaches about your manner of conftruing the Duchefs's letter of thanks to you about your Poem?

As to the little fcriptions I have of Mr. Somervile's, they are for the moft part too trivial or too local for the prefs. Perhaps you or Jack Reynalds may have others: however, thofe I have you may perufe here, and ufe them *à difcretion*, as the French Recipes term it.

Lord and Lady Plymouth are at Umberflade, where Lady Archer has again been dying. Some inward impofthume has broke; and fhe goes foon to Bath, hoping perhaps to prevent its gathering again.—Mrs. Davies came here a week ago to make a formal vifit, with Mrs. Kendall; whofe vifit was an adieu before fhe quits the country, which will be this Chriftmas, *for ever*.—Some places and things have the quality of attraction: poor Warwickfhire is endowed with the reverfe, or I would defire it to draw you from Shropshire: it *ought* to have pride enough to attempt it; but I fear it has not merit enough to succeed, unless your humanity brings you to my cell.—I think I must read *Sir C. Grandison* in my own defence; for I hear of him till I am tired. Let us read him here together. I remember I heard so much in *Tom Jones*'s praise, that when I read him, I hated him. I want to see Hogarth's Analysis of Beauty: Mr. Outing's usual dilatoriness prevented my being a subscriber.—I see nothing new.— I hope, now the Jews' Act is repealed, the writers, who tormented us about it, will employ their pens on some more agreeable subject:— No, alas! it will be Elections: for the thick air and ale of England inspire such heavy subjects of conversation and debate; to furnish which, Gentlemen ruin their estates, instead of enjoying them gayly and hospitably (yet politely); which they do not do, though they talk of *taste* for ever; but never feel it.

I just now perceive that I am spinning out nonsense and dulness to a great length; so hasten to break the thread, by ending my tedious letter with the sincerest assurance of my being,

Dear Sir, Your most faithful
(though not most sprightly)
friend and servant,
H. LUXBOROUGH.

P. S. May your Christmas be jovial, and your days long and happy!

Remark. This Letter is a volunteer.

Quere. When does trusty Thomas come?

LETTER CIV.

DEAR SIR,   Barrells, January 20th, 1754.

WHETHER you are well or ill, alive or dead? and whether you remember that you have a sincere Friend here, who is impatient for the pleasure of your company, and that you promised to come here before this time? are the queries I desire you to answer by the bearer, who goes to the Leasowes on purpose to receive those answers; which I hope will solve my doubts, and set my mind at ease. You are two letters in my debt.

The *close of Christmas* is surely come; for the rooks are building, and confirm the *new style*; yet *you* remain by your own fire-side, regardless of *us* absent mortals, who regret the want of your company, and which you bestow perhaps upon your parishioners; for I imagine your neighbours

bours of higher rank have abandoned *you*, as *you* do us: I say *us*, but it is improperly that I write in the plural number; for God knows I am as much alone as an Hermit; but however I shall see Mr. Outing, and, I believe, Mr. J. Reynalds here this week; which will rather I imagine hasten than retard your journey hither. Neither roads nor waters, nor wind nor frost, must be mentioned by you, since the *cautious* Mr. Outing resolves to encounter those enemies; for, though you do not wear a cockade in your hat, I believe you as courageous as he.

Adieu: I say no more; for you will come and hear whatever I have to say, if you are a man of your word; and you will take mine, I dare say, when I assure you that I am unfeignedly

   Your faithful and obliged servant,
      H. LUXBOROUGH.

The compliments of the Oldbarrow family attend you.—I have had no reply as yet from Mr. Hylton.

LETTER CV.

Barrells, Friday, February 8th, 1754.

DEAR SIR,

WHEN I sent my servant to the Leasowes, I was very well: when he returned, I had got a bad cold, cough, and fever. When *your* servant came here, I had lost the two latter complaints; but was still too much out of order with my cold and sore throat, to be able to hold a pen, or even to dictate; and have kept my bed several days since that; but am resolved to write now, though my eyes smart for it. Far better it is to smart than to have even the appearance of ingratitude, or of neglecting those one professes a friendship for. This is *no* florid excuse, but is the real opinion of me your culprit, who cannot so well excuse myself for the impoliteness of letting your servant go back without the Duchess of Somerset's letter, and Mr. Hylton's, which you had sent me to peruse; but the forgetfulness proceeded from having company at cards, and talking round me.—Though I congratulated Mr. Hylton upon his disappointment

ment in the affair he had engaged in, and thought he had no great loss in being deprived of the *pleasure* of carrying a *battle-ax*; yet I as sincerely regret your having missed the opportunity, which seemed to throw itself in your way, of executing a more agreeable office without toil, and one both honourable, and attended with great conveniencies to a country gentleman, who chooses to be exempted from some *stupid* or *turbulent* offices in his county. Such would have been your case, had you been Sir R. Lyttelton's Esquire, whose Brother I think should have proposed it to you. It would have been friendly, neighbourly, and in no ways doing you a pleasure at their own expence.—As to the account of your ill health, I am not disposed to believe it (pardon me, Sir, for it was *you* complained); for I think *your solitude, your want of air to breathe, objects to converse with, inclemency of weather, privation from the amusements your own taste has procured you in your own environs*; are all poisons imbibed in winter, and it is not *blisters*, &c. &c. that will expel them. Try the company of your distant friends; perhaps change of air and the exercise of travelling may perform miracles: if one place does not do, go to another; but pray begin by *this*, where I expect you daily. Mr.

Outing and I will nurse you, and the busy rooks will tell you each morning that it is time to prepare for the festivals of Spring, and to bury your complaints in old Winter's grave.

My kindest service to Mrs. Rock, whom I shall always be ready to oblige when in my power; and wish I could serve her essentially, by contributing my interest with Lady Northumberland, in conjunction with the endeavours of her other friends, to place her Daughter about Lady Betty Percy: but unfortunately I cannot be deemed a proper negociator in this affair, having some time ago resented her Ladyship's spending a considerable time in my neighbourhood both at Lord Brook's and Lord Hertford's, and passing through Henley without calling or even *sending* to me. This appeared to me unkind; and I could not forbear expressing my opinion of it to the Duchess of Somerset, who probably might speak of it to her Daughter; from whom, however, I have not heard, and to whom I have not wrote, nor would I *begin* by asking a favour: all therefore I can do is to mention Mrs. Rocks's request to the Duchess; which I will do in a few days.

Is Boadicea a good play or a bad one? I have

have not feen nor read it.—You frighten me
with the prolix ftile of the Author of Sir
Charles Grandifon's Memoirs: fo I defer reading that.—I thank you for the news articles of
your letter; as alfo for acquainting me that
Lord Dudley is well; to whom I beg my
refpects, and hope and fincerely wifh the
fuccefs of his coal-mine.

May you, Sir, gain the mines of Potofi, and
yet retain your generous fpirit! which will
oblige others to be, as I am, (and as I was
prior to *them*)

Your fincere friend

and humble fervant,

H. LUXBOROUGH.

LETTER CVI.

Barrells, February 27th, 1754.
DEAR SIR, Afh-Wednefday.

EVERY day have I been in expectation
of an anfwer from the Duchefs of Somerfet to the letter I wrote Her Grace to recommend Mrs. Rock's Daughter; which I did in

the strongest manner I was capable of. No answer is come as yet; which may be owing to Her Grace's not having had a proper opportunity of talking with the Countess of Northumberland about it. Be that as it will, I am determined not to defer longer than to-morrow sending a servant to the Leasowes to enquire after your health; but have ordered him not to set out till the post is come in, because if it should bring an answer from the Duchess in the morning, it shall go to you inclosed in this; in the mean time wishing it may be an agreeable one to Mrs. Rock, and consequently to you and myself.

The inclosed letter of request to me causes me to make one to you; which is, dear Sir, that you will mention the affair to Lord Dudley from me, in behalf of the young clergyman who writes the letter. He was once at Barrells some days with Sir Peter Soame, to whom he is a neighbour. He appeared to me to be a very sober, modest man. Want of preferment, and at last getting a trifling one, too little to live upon, (especially for a married man) he ran in debt, and has been severely treated by his creditors, who would, if they could, have confined him, and taken from him the honest means by which he proposed to extricate himself,

self, and to do justice to them. Fortune, however, and good friends have hitherto prevented their designs, and have favoured him with some preferment at Sheerness (as you will read in his letter); but yet he fears his person is not safe without some sort of protection. Perhaps Lord Dudley may be able to give him a chaplainship; which would greatly oblige me. Speak of it, pray, to his Lordship, and let me know his answer. I have declined writing to Mademoiselle de Montandre for an Ambassador's protection, for particular reasons regarding only her and myself; and I am the more solicitous to endeavour to serve him another way, which makes me, I fear, too troublesome to Lord Dudley.

I have had a second letter from Mr. Hylton, but have not answered it, because you say you expect him in the country; where I hope to see him with you at my house.

My tedious cold, which torments me in all shapes, stupifies my brain, and makes me incapable of writing more than to give Mr. Outing's compliments, and to assure you of the friendship of

Your obliged servant,

H. LUXBOROUGH.

I forgot, last time I wrote, to make you Sir Peter Soame's compliments.

LETTER

LETTER CVII.

DEAR SIR,   Barrells, March 3d, 1754.

ONE would think there was a *real* or a *paper* war between the Leasowes and Barrells, or at least a negociation of peace not concluded, as so many couriers pass; but I hope there is no *real* war. As to the *paper* war, I am not ashamed of it, however ill I may support my opinion by my weak arguments.—Did I not say you misconstrued the Duchess's meaning, when she desired stars and dashes might supply *names*? and did not that prove she was desirous your Poem to her should be printed? for (as I said to you before) there would be no occasion for asterisks if your Poem was not to be printed. You see that she esteems it, and speaks gratitude as well as applause to you *the author of it*; and she is too sincere to speak what she does not mean; and I should be too impertinent in interfering, if I had not been the person who (by your desire) presented it to Her Grace.—The copy of the request I made her in favour of Mrs. Rock's Daughter, I inclose. The answer I could have wished more favourable: but one can do no more than endeavour to oblige one's friends:—that I have often done in vain; and have ferved myfelf worfe upon many occafions. I have an *unlucky hand*, as the Gamefters fay; but I can brag of a fincere heart, with which I am, Dear Sir,

Your obliged and faithful fervant,

H. LUXBOROUGH.

Mr. Outing prefents his compliments.—I fhall be glad to fee the Analyfis of Beauty, however defcribed; and am forry I have not *now* an *S* in my name to claim any fhare in it.

P. S. Be pleafed to return me the Duchefs's letter.—Pray prefent my refpects to Lord Dudley, and fervice to Mrs. Rock.

Mrs. Holyoak, &c. are obliged by your remembrance; but had rather fee *you* than your written compliments,

LETTER

LETTER CVIII.

DEAR SIR, Barrells, March 16th, 1754.

NOBODY is so unfit as I to answer your agreeable letters; for were I ever so capable of it, my fingers would not obey: the frost having made them almost as useless as when I went to Bath, and more painful; and my head has been stupified eight weeks with a cold that is not only obstinate, but has taken as many different shapes as Proteus, to torment me in various ways.—I am sorry for my friend Tom, who has, I suppose, suffered as well as I, by the inclemency of the weather.

I have no new books, alas! to amuse myself or you; so can only return yours of Hogarth's with thanks. It surprized me agreeably; for I had conceived the performance to be a set of prints only, whereas I found a book which I did not imagine Hogarth capable of writing; for in his pencil I always confided, but never imagined his pen would have afforded me so much pleasure. As to his not fixing *the precise degree of obliquity*, which constitutes beauty, I forgive him, because I think the task too hard to be performed literally; but yet he conveys an idea between his pencil and his pen, which makes one conceive his meaning pretty well.

When I write to the Duchess of Somerset, I will do it in the manner you desire, as to your Poem; and will also name Mrs. Rock's Daughter again; but fear the Duchess (like myself) sees so few of the inhabitants of this terrestrial globe, that she will not readily find a proper person to recommend her to as a Lady's woman, though I make no doubt but the young woman deserves it. I should think Lady Elizabeth might with much propriety desire her Mamma to recommend her to some Lady; nor do I think Lady Northumberland would take it at all amiss that Miss Rock asked the child that favour.—The inclosed will be teazing to you, as it is to me; for it vexes me not to be able to serve the distressed, who address themselves to me. You would however be kind to me, and charitable to the poor man, if you could contrive a way how Lord Dudley might serve him; and his Lordship would add to the favours he has always shewn to me upon all occasions.

I will not positively say one word in behalf of *indolence*, since it keeps you by your fire-
side,

fide, though by promife you ought to be by mine.

Had I not been extremely out of order, I would have feen Mr. Cotterell; but hope at leaft that my fervants have been civil to him. When he has finifhed your Eolian harp, I believe I fhall defire you to befpeak one of him for me. Sure I am, *that* inftrument will fare well at Barrells, fince the Winds are its food.

Mr. Holyoak's family would, I am certain, fend compliments to you; but they are fhivering at Oldbarrow, as I am here.—Mr. Bradley is freezing near Stowe in the Wold, with a fick uncle; and his wife is tormenting herfelf with fears for her four eldeft children, who are to be inoculated on Monday next.—Such anxieties we mortals are doomed to: yet who would be void of feeling?

Mrs. Davies fends you fome more Poems, tranfcribed by her in hafte out of the Green Book with a bad pen, and in a great hurry; fo defires you will excufe her defects; and promifes to fend the remainder of the book foon. If fhe does, I defire fhe will write better, or make her excufes herfelf: but fhe pleads that you owe her a letter.

Lord Ar— fays Mifs Banks's fortune is 10,000 *l.* which wants one cypher of the account

count you had of it; but her merit and charms will I dare say fill up that chasm.

Mrs. Bartlet is here, and presents her compliments. We all three wish you happiness and success in all your undertakings.

LETTER CIX.

Barrells, April 27th, 1754.
DEAR SIR, Saturday.

WHEN your servant brought me your letter, I was ill in bed with a fever fit, which made it impossible for me to sit up, or to put my hands out of bed to write. It went off next day; but then I received the news of the death of an own Aunt (and of her Husband, who survived her but six days) at Geneva. Lord Luxborough sent me word of it, because my surviving relations there did not well know where to direct to me: but I was equally obliged to write to them upon the occasion, and deferred writing to you merely upon that account; and at the same time resolved doing it by my servant Joseph, as tomorrow; but this day Mrs. Holyoak of Henley

ley has sent to me to desire my chaise may fetch her to stay at Barrells some days; so that my epistle cannot reach the Leasowes before Monday. This will, I hope, be a sufficient excuse for not answering yours sooner; which I ought to have done, upon account of the Gentlewoman you recommend to me as an housekeeper. Her character I would take from you, Sir, as soon as from any friend or acquaintance living; but must confess I have had such ill success with servants in that post, that I intend to do without one; and have given the same answer to a friend of mine, who recommended one of Birmingham also.

I never was more surprized nor concerned than at the death of Miss Dolman. I ever esteemed her, and wished her welfare. I condole with her Brother, as I do with you sincerely.

I rejoice that Fortune visits the Grange, and hope she will call at the Leasowes next. Poor Mr. Belchier is frowned upon by her; and though he is much obliged to Lord Dudley and you and myself, for our endeavours to serve him, he thinks Lord Dudley's lawyer a little too scrupulous in his objections: for my part, I am no judge of that; but he says a few months would have been sufficient to

extricate

extricate him; and that the same favour is granted to other clergymen: and Sir Peter Soame writes him word he must not let it be known where he is; for people are ready enough to enquire and to threaten to get writs out against him, which his friend Sir Peter Soame has hitherto prevented. In the mean time, the poor man is tormented with the ague, which Kent has given him, added to the vexation of his mind. If he dares get out, he will come with Sir Peter here, and thank me for my endeavours to serve him.—You will I hope find out that he thinks there are many precedents for Gentlemen in orders receiving, the favour he asks.—Sorry I am to be troublesome to my friends; but more so, that I see the distress of others, without being capable of removing it, when they implore my assistance.

Talk to me no more, I desire, of your *winterly state of health*; for Boreas has at length given place to the Zephyrs, who will shortly blow out the buds in my Shrubbery; which will take it amiss if you should not be here to receive its vernal offerings.

Mr. Hylton is very obliging in remembering me. I beg you will make him my compliments, and assure him I would have answered his laft, but imagined he would have quitted London for the Leafowes long before now. His cabinets and boxes I efteem as his harbingers; and as for his wine, I hope at leaft that you drank his health in it.

I am not forry you have done nothing new of late at the Leafowes: it wants nothing to make its beauties more admired; and your *finances* will be the better for your indolence in that point; as would mine, if I had been always as indolent as I am at prefent.

Sir William Meredith is chofe Member of Parliament for Wigan. One of his Sifters is under inoculation. Sir Peter Soame waits the event of his friend Mr. Gardner's Election for Hertfordfhire, to come to Barrells.

I have not left myfelf room to fay a truth, which is that I am

Your faithful fervant,

H. LUXBOROUGH.

One in the Morning.

You write me four fides of paper—True: but pray count the lines and fyllables of my letter, and then let us reckon who is debtor: but I defire the *contents* may be left out of the account. Should the difference of our letters be mentioned

tioned that way, I should be cast in a moment, and my resource then would be no better than a Lord Lainsborough, who having maintained, some years ago at St. James's Coffee-house, that England was bigger than France, had no way to prove it, but to cut each kingdom out of two maps, of different scales, and to weigh them. If this be my case, I must make my packet as thick as I can: so you will excuse the awkwardness of it.

My respects to Lord Dudley when you write; and compliments to Mr. Hylton.

LETTER CX.

Barrells, Sunday, May 12th, 1754.

I CAN with great truth assure you, dear Sir, that I am in the highest degree sensible of your kindness in exerting yourself in favour of a person recommended by me; whose distresses are his chief recommendations to me: and I am highly obliged to my Lord Dudley for his readiness to consider of a proper method of complying with the request I took the liberty to make in behalf of the diftreffed perfon, to whom I fhall without fail fend his Lordfhip's kind protection by to-morrow's poft; defiring him to acquaint me whether he finds by people belonging to thofe offices where he is to be entered, whether any forms are wanting in the inftrument his Lordfhip has fent? not doubting but if that fhould be the cafe, my Lord will extend his goodnefs by fupplying in a frefh form what may prove wanting in this.

The inclofed I received from the fame Mr. (John) Belchier whom we are endeavouring to ferve; with a fermon he preached upon the Election of Mr. Charles Frederick, &c. for Queenborough.

My refpects and beft thanks attend Lord Dudley; and I defire my compliments to Mifs Lea, and all your good neighbours.

My fervice, pray, to Mrs. Rock, from

Yours fincerely,

H. Luxborough.

I find with pleafure, that Mr. Hylton is with you; and hope he will not forfake you when you come to Barrells. Mr. Outing, my faithful Boftangy, affures me the Shrubbery will be ready to receive you in its fpring-clothing

clothing before next week is out: by which time (if not already) I hope you will have forgot you ever had any diforder in your health, which will be rather eftablifhed than impaired by riding a fhort day's journey.

I have been out in my poft-chaife half a dozen times lately, and walked my ufual round of Gardens and Coppice, &c. on Friday laft; and have fhredded my avenue, I hope, to fome advantage to the eye, as it is undoubtedly to the grounds it fhaded. I would have fent you fome cucumbers; of which I have cut feveral; but it feems all that were fit to fend are devoured already; and a nofegay of the fineft double hyacinths I ever faw, and which I meant to prefent to you, are too mature to bear the fhaking of the horfe without fhedding. They would have gone fafe laft week; but I am now reduced to the cafe of Bonniface in the *Beaux Stratagem*, who had had a fine loin of veal on the Wednefday before it was wanted.

Poor Mifs Carrington's death grieves this neighbourhood. Would fhe and Mifs Dolman had been inoculated, as it has fucceeded miraculoufly hereabouts!—Mr. Outing defires his compliments to you and Mr. Hylton; to whom I defire mine very fincerely, though I did not write them, as I fhould have done, in return of his laft letter; but really then thought him on the road to the Leafowes.—My neighbours are much your friends, or fhould not be mine; I being fo with unalterable friendfhip and gratitude.

H. Luxborough.

I obferve you have a new Seal, with a pretty device.

LETTER CXI.

Barrells, Auguft the laft, or September the firft, 1754.

DEAR SIR,

YOUR letter of the 17th of July is before me; but the date makes me blufh; fo I fet it afide, not to be reproached: my confcience, however, clears me, and I hope you will do the fame, when you are apprized that I have been too ill to write a line, much lefs to undertake a journey of pleafure; for fadnefs would have accompanied me, and I fhould have fcattered it about your pleafing dwelling. You are then obliged to me for my abfence more, I fear, than you will be for my prefence;

which

which (unless you forbid it) I propose to torment you with next week. Say if I *shall*, without regard to compliment. I pay nobody, not even Lady Plymouth, the common compliment of a visit, though I respect her greatly; but really the conjunction of bad roads, bad health, and bad spirits, make me like an owl in the desart.

What attractions must the Leasowes have, which draws the lame, the splenetic, the indolent, from every point of the compass to that one, in order to admire the mixed beauties of nature and art, and to give their tribute of applause to the master of the place, who invents and completes more for the pleasure of his friends or his visitants of taste, than for his own!

As I propose seeing you so soon, I wave any answer to the articles of your letter which do not relate to the present purpose, though I could echo your sounds, and lament the poor Duchess of Somerset for ever. As to Sir Peter Soame, he has been here a week, and I shewed him the paragraph in yours about *July*. He fixed upon a day to go with me; but behold, it rained to a degree, that no comparison can reach. More or less it continued during his stay. Adieu.

Mrs. Davies says she *must* send her compliments to you, as she intends seeing you so soon; she being to go in the chaise with me. I will ask Parson Holyoak; but fear church-duty will interfere, as it will be late in the week.—I would have you expect me on Friday evening,—not before: your supper will be our regale. But above all, let Joseph, my coachman, be instructed to return with your answer by the new and good turnpike you tell me is made by your house; for fears and terrors might be too strong for my weak limbs and nerves. Such is the decrepit company you ask for, and such you shall have, if the journey can be performed by

Your faithful humble servant,

H. Luxborough.

Mrs. Davies's best compliments.

Sunday Night.

Finding an opportunity of sending this to Birmingham to-morrow morning by Mr. Jackson, I do not send Joseph, as I intended; having employment for him concerning fishing, &c. so hope, dear Sir, you will excuse my not sparing him to go to the Leasowes this time; and that you will remember to come to Barrells soon. Adieu. H. L.

LETTER CXII.

DEAR SIR,   Barrells, September 29th, 1754.

YOUR thanking me for my visit at the Leasowes, before I had sent my thanks to you for your very kind and agreeable reception of me there, is very obliging; but being so, it comes the severest reproach you could have made me; by making me sensible of the rudeness I have been guilty of, in not sending to you since I left you. The truth is, that I had nobody to send, having parted with the idle boy I had with me at your house; and every day Joseph has been employed in driving me out: so great a gadder has the fine weather made me, and so much better health and spirits has my journey to the Leasowes given me. Ten physicians, with an equal number of surgeons and apothecaries, could not have effected such an *amendment*; I believe I might say *cure*; for I have never been sick once. I imagine your air is good; and I see that your improvements in your Walks and Cascades make your place a Paradise in miniature: yet, though I am its professed admirer, it must permit me to say

that

that the converfation of the mafter and contriver of the *beauties* I faw there, was to me preferable far to them; fo that I regretted lefs than I fhould otherwife have done the weaknefs of my limbs, which prevented my *trampouzing* fo much as I ufed.

I have been to fee every neighbour I have, but the one I moft wifh to fee, Lady Plymouth.—A crofs tenant of Mr. Sheldon's has cut off all connection between Hewell and Barrells; yet I perfevere in trying for a road, as eagerly as thofe who bore for a mine. If my endeavours are not fruitlefs, I propofe going on Wednefday. Would I could meet you there! Since I am wifhing, I wifh alfo that your new artift was to make a Bufto of you for my Library, to accompany Pope and Shakefpear.—I fend you a frame for the Fruit-piece you mention. It is the leaft fize I have, but muft be cut lefs. I took it from Queen Caroline (for robbing crowned heads is no more than a fair reprifal). My other frames of that fize were not gilt, but lacquered, which I thought not good enough, though Mr. Thomas would have taken one, as it was out of ufe; but I judged it to be lefs genteel than that which I fend, and I remembered this fuited to the frame over your parlour-chimney, which might

might be an advantage if they should ever happen to hang in the same room.

I am obliged to the ingenious Mr. Baskerville for wishing my time had allowed me to call there.—I do not know any Mr. Bingley, nor a Mr. Dingley, except a jeweller at London, who has some place at Court.

Mrs. Davies receives your compliment with the utmost sensibility and gratitude. If in return of your politeness to her, you should ask her a favour, *she can but deny you, you know:* but I think she *cannot.* Pray then let it be that she should not leave me to myself, which is the worst company, and to my thoughts, which are as little pleasing as the sound of the west wind that haunts my little habitation, and which may be soon expected to take up its winter residence here. Oh woeful thought! Oh woeful sound! None but the friendly Robin Red-breast sooths my ear after those rough sounds: but *in the melancholy month of November, in which the English hang themselves,* I expect more pleasure than from the Robin; since you and Mr. Hylton will join in his harmony, and favour me with your company: then (and not now) genius, taste, &c. will reside in my Hermitage.—Adieu then for the present,

present; and let November draw near, as it will bring you nearer to

Your faithful servant,
H. LUXBOROUGH.

I will deliver your kind and polite compliments to Mr. Holyoak and his Wife, who enquired much after you. Mine, pray, to Mrs. Mary and Mrs. Davies. We gave her more trouble than we can give her thanks.—Mrs. Maynard's respects to you.

LETTER CXIII.

DEAR SIR,   Barrells, November 18th, 1754.

IT is an age since I heard from you, and two ages since I had the pleasure of your company.—Sir William Meredith has been here, and wished you had come then. The shortness of the days, the downfall of the leaves, the badness of the roads, and every other mark of decay in the progress of the year, should drive you from home; as the charms of your place

place will be loft for a time, even to yourself; and as coal is to supply the place of fun, you may as well warm yourself at my fire.

I reluctantly send the inclofed, which I received laft night by the bearer. I am perfecuted by his Mafter, whofe letter I fend you; before which I had one to fay he was at his duty on board the Norwich; but was arrefted at Portfmouth, and was fearful left the man of war fhould fail without him; and defired I would write to Lord, or Mr. Barrington, Admiral Smith, &c. I put that off by letter; but now is come this meffenger: and as he fends a letter directed to Lord Dudley, do not think myfelf entitled to keep it. I therefore forward it, though it is giving you trouble; but you will forgive what you know proceeds from mere compaffion to any perfon in diftrefs.—Mr. Outing is your fervant, as I am Lord Dudley's, and ever

Yours moft fincerely,
H. Luxborough.

LETTER CXIV.

DEAR SIR,   Barrells, December 4th, 1754.

THOUGH the sterility of subjects to write upon from this place, might be a sufficient excuse for my not troubling you with a letter at this time; yet my not seeing you here according to promise, in the month of November, urges me to remind you that that month is passed; and to ask you when I may expect you? as also, what prevents my having the pleasure of hearing from you as usual? a pleasure I can ill spare in my situation, which affords so little joy; and which I should prefer to most others, even in a land abounding in gaiety. Besides, Sir, be it known to you, (if it is not already) that I wrote to you above a fortnight ago, by a messenger who was dispatched to me from Portsmouth, by the little unfortunate and troublesome Parson you was so kind to interest yourself for, with Lord Dudley, at my request; since which, I have never seen or heard of the said messenger; neither has Mr. Outing, who sent a letter by him to Mrs. Rock. Pray unravel this mystery to me if you can; but let it be in perſon rather than by letter.

I think I informed you that Sir William Meredith had been here in his way to Parliament, and aſked after you; adding, that he had a little preſent for you of Kennel-Coal, and wiſhing to have met you here. He is ſo kind as to write me what paſſes in the Houſe of Commons in general; and in particular, mentions a ſpeech of old Horace Walpole's, as humourous as good-natured, in anſwer to one of young Beckford's, who ſpoke much of the flouriſhing ſtate of all our colonies, except that which he belonged to. Horace anſwered, "*That* was in the moſt flouriſhing condition "of all; for there was a new growth there, "and a freſh importation from thence: an "importation of political geniuſes, which bid "fair to fill both the City and the Parlia- "ment."

Mr. John Reynalds and his Wife are gone to Bath with Sir Robert Cocks.—Bradley of Edſton is dead rich, from having been poor; and was growing richer ſtill; but it is the common rude practice of death to interrupt fortune in her career.—I have been obliged to take a diſtreſs upon a tenant, and to employ a lawyer. Should you have known me in that occupation?

occupation?—Is Lord Dudley at the Grange, or at the House of Peers? and is Mr. Hylton with you? My compliments attend them and your other neighbours; to whom, as well as to you, Mr. Outing joins his: and I am, (in spite of your laziness in regard to me)
  Dear Sir,
    Your faithful humble servant,
      H. LUXBOROUGH.

LETTER CXV.

DEAR SIR,   December 8th, 1754.

IT is late; your servant is but just come; my fingers are not so alert as in warm weather; my imagination is as contracted as they are: judge then how unfit I am to give an answer to your letter; and far less so to give my judgment of the beautiful pieces of poetry it inclosed. I shall therefore take the liberty to keep them till you send again, which you say will be before the close of this week; and in the mean time will read them with pleasure and impartiality; and will write you my
         opinion,

opinion, since you do me the unmerited honour of desiring it; but am sensible of my unworthiness to be employed as a Critic. I have had only time to read the Ode to Memory; which I had not seen, and which pleases me much. As to the two trifling Songs, which dropt from my pen some time past, and which you propose to let Dodsley have, I give you free liberty so to do, if you really think them deserving of a place in his Miscellanies; being assured that, if you thought otherwise, you would not expose your Friend, nor disgrace Dodsley's Collection.

Your promise of letting me see you soon at Barrells, I build upon; as that foundation will support me in a season when high winds, bad roads, and solitude, depress me so, as to make me sometimes ready to sink under their weight.—As to your past misdemeanours, (such as long silence in particular) I withdraw my charge, and will implicitly believe you could not help it; for if I was inclinable to do otherwise, what should I gain by tormenting myself with the apprehension of having lost a friend, who may be as sincere as he professes himself, and as I am persuaded you are? and if he should not be so, is not an object worthy regretting the loss of: so, in short, write

when

when you can, without reftraint to yourfelf, and I will do the fame; but my indulgence does not extend to allowing you to be abfent from hence fo very long, and to ftay here fo very fhort a time when you do come.

I will tranfmit to Sir William Meredith the kind things you fay of him; and think it poffible, and even probable, you may fee him here, when the Parliament breaks up for the holidays.

Gladly I tell you, that you miftake the Mr. Bradley that is living and well, at Wooton, for the Mr. Bradley who died at Edfton.

I hope Lord Dudley's new equipage will convey him fafe to the Grange; though I fuppofe he muft quit that again after Chriftmas for the Parliament.

I cannot excufe my friend Mr. Hylton for letting his panics deprive his friends of his pleafing company. Tell him I can by no means excufe it.—I fay nothing of Mr. Outing; he writes for himfelf, and of his own accord; but adds by my defire a paragraph about the unlucky affair I embarked in when I troubled you and Lord Dudley about the Parfon, who proves himfelf to have been fo undeferving of the regard we have fhewn him.

Mr. Outing interrupts me to drink your health

health—Here it is done, with a wish of long life and happiness; and I sign my name to it, as it is the dictate of my heart.

H. LUXBOROUGH.

P. S. Observe that I write with a crow-quill, which behaves tolerably at first; intolerably at last; and will make you think me incapable of the use of my fingers. I promise you, however, never to write with it again.

LETTER CXVI.

Barrells, Thursday, December 12th, 1754.

DEAR SIR,

AS soon as my friend Tom had left Barrells on Monday last, my intention was to have sat down to the arduous task you had set me; but I was seized with a disorder which confined me to my bed on Tuesday, and to my chamber yesterday; and though it was a disorder which may prove rather conducive than prejudicial to my health, it totally incapacitated me from performing what I promised

mised you, and even from consulting with Mr. Outing, who was in a distant apartment. Finding myself better to-day, I only waited the absence of company, who dined with me, to begin; and had gone through but two or three stanzas, when Tom came with your last packet. The poor creature was almost drowned last time; and what chance he will stand to-morrow is uncertain; but the present moment is shockingly stormy, and must retard every project, though Mr. Dodsley's requesting dispatch is reasonable; so that I send you the result of our evening proceedings, and write this whilst Mr. Outing writes our desired criticisms.

When you shewed my little Pieces to Mr. Dodsley, you did me more honour than I should have done myself; because I should have feared to have disgraced his Miscellany. I forgot in my last to mention what Mr. Dodsley I find does mention to you, viz. in the Title of the two trifles of mine, to say, *Wrote by a Lady*—which is, I think, unexceptionable.

You was altogether right in assuring Mr. Crawley I would acquiesce in his conduct for Lord Dudley towards Mr. Belchier, whose impositions upon me were reasons sufficient to deprive him of my patronage, and leave

me

me much ashamed of having implored Lord Dudley's protection for such an unworthy person, as time and circumstances shew him now to be.

I wait with impatience the day of your arrival with Mr. Hylton at Barrells; and am ever

Your most faithful humble servant,

· H. LUXBOROUGH.

What is become of your Autumn? I hope Dodsley has it, as the poor Duchess desired.

Mr. Outing is your humble servant; and I am ever, dear Sir, as I profess myself,

Your sincere friend
and faithful servant,

H. LUXBOROUGH.

P. S. If Tom cannot come, I think you might venture to inclose Mr. Belchier's letter in one to me, to Mr. Williams at Birmingham.

LETTER CXVII.

DEAR SIR,   Barrells, December 18th, 1754.

THIS goes upon a different errand than my laſt. It is to tell you, that hearing Mr. and Mrs. Holyoake ſpeak of a mare of Miſs Molly's, which ſhe intended to part with, becauſe ſhe had a little Welch one beſides, which would ſerve her, I thought of Mr. Hylton immediately; eſpecially upon finding by all accounts that ſhe is perfectly ſound, gentle, and free from vices, and comes but four years old; has been rode by Mr. Holyoake's younger ſons a good while, and is tall enough and ſtrong enough for Mr. Hylton's weight, and does not want faſhion; came of ſome very good horſe at Worceſter, and a mare that had been given Miſs Molly. Now in caſe Mr. Hylton is not already provided, why ſhould he not come in the Birmingham coach to Henley? when here, he may ſee this mare, and may hear of others; and if he ſhould not purchaſe, the coach will be a certain vehicle at his return. This propoſal puts a ſtop to your future delays, upon his account, and shows my *empressement* to see you both.

I have no time to write more; for Mrs. *Maydew* must have my letter to-night, and will carry it safe to-morrow early to the post.

Mr. Outing is at Oldbarrow: I am alone and stupid; so adieu.—Believe me unalterably
    Yours, &c.
      H. Luxborough.

The coach sets out from Henley, I think, Mondays and Thursdays, and is at Henley by breakfast (eight or nine). Mr. Hylton might lie over night at Birmingham.

This letter is shorter than ordinary, and perhaps you will complain; I will therefore subjoin a trifling *impromptu* I once wrote in a hurry, and which I am doubtful if I ever shewed you; but think I never shewed any body. It will serve to read, and then kindle your candle, or *soften your flute*, if you use paper, as usual, on that occasion.

Mr. Outing is much your servant, though absent: I am Mr. Hylton's.

LETTER CXVIII.

DEAR SIR,   Barrells, January 7th, 1755.

THIS goes not only to make you the compliments of the season, (which I do very sincerely, and not merely because it is customary) but it also goes to ask how you do, and what can occasion your silence? It is an age since I wrote to you about a horse Miss Molly Holyoake has to sell, which I thought might suit Mr. Hylton; and proposed, that if he was not already provided with one, he might come to Barrells in the Birmingham coach when you should come here: and in that letter I inclosed a few bad Lines of my own, wrote some years ago: since all which, I received the inclosed from our troublesome little Parson, who is, thank God, sailing towards America. I send it, because Lord Dudley's protection is in it; which I desire you will take out and deliver to his Lordship from me, with many thanks and many excuses for having troubled him about this affair.—I inclose, besides the other, a letter I received from Sir William Meredith, as you are mentioned in it.— Mr. Outing is gone to sup at Henley, and does not know of my writing, or you would have compliments from him.

I have

I have not seen the new Tragedy *Barbaroſſa:* perhaps you can lend it me.—Mr. Outing has talked several times of making a visit at the Grange; but does not know whether Lord Dudley is there, or at the Parliament.

Pray thaw your ink and your fingers, and write glibly away till you come. Remember that Twelfth-Day is over, and do not forget your promise:—Remember likewise that I am very truly and unalterably

Your faithful humble servant,

H. LUXBOROUGH.

Compliments to Mr. Hylton.

LETTER CXIX.

DEAR SIR, Barrells, Valentine's Day, 1755.

YOUR silence excites me to break mine; for upon the present footing one of us might be murdered (like the Dey of Algiers), and the other die of an apoplexy, and the longest liver of the two know nothing of the fate of the other. Did you not say in your last, that you would come soon to Barrells? Upon those hopes we have lived: but hopes are meagre food: in punishment for which,

if

if I could command, you should be obliged to do penance here this Lent. It is true I did not answer your last; but Mr. Outing wrote you the reason, which ought to have been excuse sufficient; for I was really ill, and incapable of guiding a pen. I am much better: but as the Warwickshire roads do not invite one abroad at this season, one doubly wishes for the company of one's friends round our deserted hearths.

Mr. Outing sends compliments: mine, pray, to Mr. Hylton, and believe me

Yours, &c.

H. L.

LETTER CXX.

Barrells, Sunday, April 27th, 1755.

DEAR SIR,

I CANNOT well condescend to thank you for your letter of the 17th, considering that it was scarcely the shadow of what I long expected, which was your company and Mr. Hylton's in my Shrubbery, my Hermitage, my Library, and, in the evenings, at my fireside. No less than three weeks are past since the last promise came, the others having been
buried

buried in oblivion: but of this laft I held myfelf fo fure, that, being obliged to go on Wednefday laft to Warwick, I left my butler at home with orders to fetch Mrs. Holyoake to entertain you till my return; but behold! you do not fo much as make mention of your having had thoughts, much lefs of having given promifes to vifit this place and me! The elms are green in vain: in vain the cucumbers are large, and as vainly the Shrubbery fhoots out, and the Coppice has a carpet of primrofes, cowflips, &c. Let them reproach you; and let your Governefs, Mrs. Holyoake, correct you: and may fhe boaft

" ———— Unruly Brats with Birch to tame."

The prettieft thing I ever faw of the kind, is the fhell-room at Guy's Clift: Mr. Greethead and Lady Mary have executed it all with their own hands: *bed-hangings, chimneyboards, pictures* over the doors, &c. If you was not lazy, you would fee it. I came from it through Warwick, Snitterfield, Bufhes, Bearly, and Wooton; but on horfeback you would not have had that trouble.

Mr. Nugent vifits me again. Mr. Soame is under inoculation, very full, and in good fpirits.—I go to-morrow to Kinwarton to dine with a clergyman, who feems to have fome tafte.

taste.—Mr. Outing is immersed in cares about letting his house, and I do not know what; but goes to a Friend's in Essex this week from London.—If we are to have no war, I have done with politics.—I wish Mr. Arne may acquiesce in your request.—I should greatly like the four Roman Ruins you mention, provided I could get them coloured.

I am sorry the weather permits the beauties of the Leasowes to be exhibited; for then no hopes remain for your humble friends in Warwickshire, who have nothing to exhibit but hearts and friendships sincere; such are possessed by

H. LUXBOROUGH.

LETTER CXXI.

Barrells, Wednesday, May 28th, 1755.

DEAR SIR,

I WAS most agreeably surprized yesterday, and at the same time as disagreeably disappointed. You will easily guess that I mean Mr. and Mrs. Greaves's visit; without you, whom I had so long expected. They left Barrells this morning, and gave me the satisfaction to hear they left you well yesterday. May you continue so, is my wish! do not therefore torment

ment yourself more than is necessary about the embroilments of worldly affairs; but avoid if possible, the devouring monster called *Law*; it often swallows Justice itself. I remember once to have heard Lord Chancellor Cowper say, "If every body knew as much of the law "as I do, they would, were their cause ever "so good, give up half, rather than embark "in our courts." This I take to be a good caution. Those lawyers, who are not arrived to the summit of their wishes, and who taste the sweet of large fees, will not speak so sincerely. I hope very very soon to hear you and Mr. Dolman disengage yourselves from them, though both may be obliged to yield a little.

I return Mr. Dodsley's Letters; than which, none can be more polite. Pray keep me in his good favour.

I should like to see Hagley chancel-window; sure it must be bigger than the whole chancel I saw!

My best compliments wait upon Lord Dudley and Miss Lea, and thanks for his Lordship's sending here. I am also Mr. Hylton's most humble servant; as Mrs. Davies is yours, and I am ever

Your faithful and affectionate servant,

H. LUXBOROUGH.

LETTER CXXII.

Barrells, Wednesday Night, June 18th, 1755.

LADY Luxborough sends her compliments to Mr. Shenstone, and if it is agreeable to him in all respects, she would go on Saturday morning to the Leasowes, to lie one night only.—Sir Peter Soame and his Son are at Barrells, and are very desirous of waiting on Mr. Shenstone. Mr. Outing and Mrs. Davies are also at Barrells, and would accompany her, if not troublesome. Mr. Outing is persuaded he has interest enough to get a bed at Lord Dudley's for himself and Mr. Soame, to avoid crowding Mr. Shenstone too much. Lady Luxborough proposes carrying no woman-servant with her; and hopes that Mr. Shenstone will let her know if this project be in any sort inconvenient to him, and that without compliment.

LETTER *from* Mr. HOLYOAKE *to* WILLIAM SHENSTONE, *Esq.*

DEAR SIR, Oldbarrow, March 29, 1756.

I HAVE the favour of yours by your servant; and as you say you have had intelligence, the moment you wrote, of the melancholy news from Barrells,

Barrells, give me leave to assure you I expected Mrs. Davies or Mr. Outing would have acquainted you with it as soon as the poor Lady's breath was gone, as they did the same to Sir Peter Soame, Sir William Meredith, and some others of my Lady's relations. I depended upon this, as my Wife mentioned it to them before me; which if I had imagined they had neglected, I would certainly have wrote to you myself.—We have been, and indeed still are, in hurry and confusion, though at the same time it gives me great satisfaction to say truly, that nothing hath been wanting, either to prolong her life, or to prepare her for the other world, as far as opportunities and intervals would give leave. The beginning of her illness was occasioned by a cold and hoarseness, about a month since, in setting out for Wootton about five o'clock on Friday: the Sunday following she sent for my Wife and Daughter to drink tea, and a message to me, that she expected I would call as I returned from Ullenhall Chapel; which accordingly I did, and observed the above-mentioned symptoms upon her, and told her, that as I had the care of Ullenhall, she would give me leave to say to her, as I thought it incumbent to do, that as she had not attended Church nor the Sacrament very lately, I would advise her to receive the Sacrament. She answered,

answered, I was very good, and that she would send to me very soon; and accordingly received it with great devotion. The night before she died I read the Recommendatory Prayer to her; and I hope she is perfectly happy, though she had so great troubles and afflictions in this life. —My Wife would gladly have wrote to you; but the truth of it is, she returned from Barrells but yesterday, and is very ill; and for this reason, she hopes you will not take it unkind.— Mrs. Davies and Outing have been with Lady Luxborough all her illness, which I am very glad of.—Lord Luxborough is expected at Barrells to-morrow, to give orders about the funeral.—I have nothing more material to add, but my Wife and Daughter's best compliments, and to ask your pardon for this incoherent letter from, Dear Sir,

Your most obliged humble servant,

W. HOLYOAKE.

FINIS.

Lightning Source UK Ltd.
Milton Keynes UK
UKHW010804131218
333948UK00014B/891/P